Trac

6 beginner's guide in 1.

Learn the bases with proven strategies: options, day, swing, forex, stock, and trading psychology to start investing. Learn how to overcome the market for a living

[Henry Hill]

TABLE OF CONTENTS:

Legal & Disclaimer

The information contained in this book and its contents is not designed to replace or take the place of any form of professional advice; and is not meant to replace the need for independent financial, legal or other professional advice or services, as may be required. The content and information in this book has been provided for educational and entertainment purposes only.

The content and information contained in this book has been compiled from sources deemed reliable, and it is accurate to the best of the Author's knowledge, information and belief. However, the Author cannot guarantee its accuracy and validity and cannot be held liable for any errors and/or omissions. Further, changes are periodically made to this book as and when needed. Where appropriate and/or necessary, you must consult a professional (including but not limited to your financial advisor or such other professional advisor) before using any of the suggested techniques, or information in this book.

Upon using the contents and information contained in this book, you agree to hold harmless the Author from and against any costs, and expenses, including any legal fees potentially resulting from the application of any of the information provided by this book..

You agree to accept all risks of using the information presented inside this book.

You agree that by continuing to read this book, where appropriate and/or necessary, you shall consult a professional (including but not limited to your financial advisor or such other advisor as needed) before using any of the suggested techniques, or information in this book.

Options Trading

Crash course for Beginners – profitable and secret options strategies simplified on how to make big money in 2019 with options trading, start investing in the stock market in 10 days!

[Henry Hill]

TABLE OF CONTENTS:

Introduction

An option is defined as a contract between two parties, which gives the holder (buyer) the right, but not the obligation, to buy or sell the underlying asset at an agreed fixed price at an agreed time in the future – or in some cases at any time before the contract's expiry date.

Options, as we saw earlier, were designed to allow institutional investors to mitigate risk and act as tools for ensuring against market unpredictability. Thus the Options contract was originally used to buy insurance against potentially catastrophic price movements that would have led to huge losses. But their inherent characteristics soon made Options attractive to traders as speculation tools in their own right. To see how Option became fashionable with traders, we need to take a deeper dive into what makes up an Option contract.

Options in Common Law

Options can be best explained, and easiest understood using examples from everyday contract law as Option contracts have been in place since trade began. For example, suppose you want to buy a house or a new car, but you don't have a mortgage or finance at hand. In this case, you would perhaps agree with a price with the seller and a date for completion of the sale. However, the seller is going to want a deposit in return for this sales contingency, which gives you the right to buy at the agreed price at a future date or walk away from the sale if you change your mind. The deposit is compensation to the seller for providing you with the right, but not the obligation, to buy the car or house at the agreed price and date. If you renege on the deal and walk away, you will lose the deposit as that is the price of that option.

This is the basis of financial options, and if we consider the transaction through the lens of a financial trade, we can substitute many of the technical terms to make the metaphor more transparent. So for example when you go to buy a house, you agree to a price (strike price) and a date (expiry date) and a suitable deposit (premium) as part of the contingency of the sale (the Option contract). Then on the expiry date, you will exercise your right to buy the house (stock) at the strike price or walk away (let the option expire) losing your deposit (premium).

Don't worry too much about some of the terms, such as strike price and premium all the trading jargon will be explained soon enough. What is important just now is that you understand that with Options trading you are dealing with a contract, the right to buy rather than the asset itself. But because that contract has inherent value, as it derives its value from the relationship between the strike prices, which is fixed in the contract, relative to the current market stock price. And if the contract is deemed attractive to others in the market, then it also becomes a tradable asset in its own right.

Why Options Exist

An Option is considered in finance to be a derivative as it derives its value from an underlying asset. A stock option is similar to a contingency on the sale of a house or a deposit on a car, but it involves the stock market rather than a private agreement.

For example, an Option - MSFT 2019 Mar 39 call - gives you the right to buy Microsoft at $39 per share at any time before the expiration date in mid-March 2019. If Microsoft is trading above $39 per share, you can exercise the option to buy and make a quick profit. The term, Exercising the option, is when you – the option holder - take up your contractual right to buy the shares at the agreed price – typically then to sell the stock on the market at the higher price for a tidy profit.

However, should the stock not perform as expected over the lifetime of the Option contract and the stock is selling below $39, then you would just let the contract expire as it makes no sense to buy a stock at a higher price than market value as you could buy the stock cheaper in the open market.

When an Option contract expires, it means the value of the option is worthless and thus the loss to the buyer is 100% of the cost of the Option – the (deposit) Premium.

To get a better understanding of why they came about, it is best to look at how they are used by taking a closer look at their use in practice.

Options as Insurance

As we touched on earlier Institutional and fund managers, use stock options as a form of insurance. They want to protect themselves against any market turn-around and potentially damaging losses by having in-place a hedge bet, which is a counter-balance position. In effect, they will be placing a bet that works in the opposite direction to the desired position of the asset they wish to protect, thereby nullifying any adverse market movements. This works because with Options, they are guaranteed a method to buy or sell stock at a specific price, but with no obligation to buy, before or upon a certain date.

So, for example, should they wish to protect the value of a portfolio, of let's say, their very expensive Amazon shares (that they own). Then they could do so by buying a relatively cheap Option that worked in favor of falling Amazon stock prices – i.e., its value increases as Amazon prices fall. In this way, even though their prized Amazon portfolio dropped in price, their Option would be increasing in value and vice versa so together they would counter-balance any price fluctuations in the market.

This form of Hedging is often performed in order to protect against the risk to a position or an asset. Institutional stock traders have always had in place complex and often costly methods of risk management. However, it was only in 1973 when there was the standardization of stock options that it finally made risk actually manageable and very cost effective.

Using options in this way allows institutional investors to ensure price changes and is known as hedging. Institutional traders are willing to pay the price, known as a premium, to obtain this insurance.

Trading Options Basics

Learning Options trading is not trivial, but it can be very rewarding if you learn the basic principles well and stick to good trading practices. The most important thing to learn as a beginner, as with all forms of financial trading, is the necessity of protecting your capital. The most profound way of doing this is by only paper trading – or using a test simulator – when you first start out. It is vital that you test your strategies and trading tactics with virtual money before you ever trade with real money.

Options trading, though is still deemed to be complicated and very risky, it is actually a good place for beginners to start out financial trading as it provides several safety nets. For example, in Options trading, a beginner, if they follow the correct strategies, will find that their risk and losses are limited but their potential profits are unlimited. This is simply down to the nature of Options in so much as you as a beginner will be trading in contracts called premiums rather than buying the underlying stock. Hence the extent of your losses is limited to the price of the premium – don't worry we will explain all this in detail later – for now it is enough to know that when trading options we can show you how to limit losses and risk while chasing unrestricted profits.

As this book is targeted at beginners, it would be helpful first to give you a high-level summary as to why trading in options is advantageous. And the best place to start is to explain the mechanisms behind Option trading and how they work.

What is Options Trading?

When you trade in options, you are trading in a contract based upon an underlying asset – typically a stock in a company. An Option is a contract that gives the holders the right but not the obligation, to buy or sell an asset in the future at a price determined today.

That definition is hugely important to understand as it is the basic concept of Options Trading – basically, you are buying the right to buy the underlying shares but are under no obligation to do so. So should the price go against your position you can simply walk away, albeit you will lose the cost of the option but no more? Hence, despite the common belief of it being a high-risk pursuit, trading in Options is much less risky than buying stocks outright where losses and profits are unlimited.

However, there is another attractive characteristic of trading in Options, and that is due to the fact that you can as a beginner trade safely in high-value stocks that would generally be out with your budget. This is because when you buy an Option, you are not actually buying the stock but the future right to buy at a fixed price. Therefore, the option is priced at only a fraction of the actual stock price.

This means that you can buy an option in high volume, volatile stock such as Apple, Amazon, etc., which would give you the control over 100 shares for perhaps $100, whereas to buy 100 shares of these premier stocks would set you back thousands of dollars. Remember, as there is no obligation to buy the shares, you can simply take your profit and walk away – no questions asked.

Indeed as there is no obligation to exercise the Option itself, it also becomes a tradable asset – and this is what came about. Instead of traders exercising their rights to buy the underlying asset, many simply bought the Options to trade on the open market. However, for every deal, there must be a buyer and a seller – so other traders soon began writing Options in order to fulfill the market demand. Hence the flourishing market in Options we see today.

Options are extremely flexible so are used as both a form of insurance and as a source of speculative profits. The value is largely derived from the value of an underlying asset or financial instrument, but it also has additional components such as time till expiration and a locked-in price that provides additional value. So the value of the Option is not solely determined by the current value of the underlying asset or security as there are several other factors that come into play.

Moreover, Options provide the beginner the right level of entry into the market if they have only limited funds and trading knowledge. Furthermore, the beginner can, despite their lack of experience and trading skills also trade well above their budget and leverage their account to trade diligently in a low risk and high reward strategy. But Options are not just attractive to beginners with limited funds for in financial trading Options provide ways for experienced traders to add options on individual stocks, indexes, and exchange-traded mutual funds (ETFs) to their investment portfolio.

Nonetheless, the best reason for a beginner to start trading in Options and an intermediary level trader to add options to their trading or investing strategies is that Options trading allows you to both manage risk while at the same time allowing you to optimize profits. And because there are so many different methods and techniques to trade in options there is a wide market for both buyers and sellers – i.e., just about anyone can benefit from trading them, so let look at some traditional examples.

If we contemplate the traditional buy and hold strategy for stocks, which is a good example, as that is the way that long term investors operate. In this scenario, we can consider it to be akin to you owning (real estate) apartments and then taking income as rent through properties per month for long periods to generate year-on-year income.

Now, this is a good way to generate long term safe income. However, this patient strategy may not work so well when you want short term profits and large gains. In which case, the way to generate quick returns would be to rent out your apartment short term at higher rates via Airbnb. In which case, a financial trading metaphor would be to shift away from trading in stocks and mutual funds to invest in writing (selling) short term Options based upon your stock portfolio.

Comparing Options to other Securities

Options are a form of financial derivative, and all that means is that it derives its value from an underlying security. For example, a common type of Option is the Stock options - which this book focuses on – and they derive their value from the underlying company stock's market performance. However, Options can and are traded using other derivatives such as commodities and exchange-traded mutual funds

- Commodities and futures (ETF):

The provenance of financial Options is in the trading of Commodity and Futures contracts as these were agreements between two parties, typically farmers and traders looking for a future price for their next harvest crops. The futures markets developed to help traders hedge and speculate on commodities, especially in the agricultural market. The options market, in turn, evolved from the futures market, hence, the similarities and the shared concepts. But, because commodities and futures deal with a physical asset, there are slight differences as to how they work. The seller of a commodity or futures option is still obligated to buy or sell the stock. However, exercising the contract is different as commodities and futures contracts set the price for delivery of a specific quantity of a physical item – a bushel of wheat, for example - to be delivered to a particular location on an agreed date. There is nothing similar in stock options as there is no need for physical delivery of anything. Commodity options are options listed on such things as corn, oil, gold, or interest rates. Futures, on the other hand, are options trading on the underlying value of futures contracts, typical futures on commodities and currencies. Futures contracts are therefore derivative contracts – their value is derived from the underlying commodity/asset - that give holders the obligation to buy or sell an asset at a specified future date for a specified price. Where there is a similarity between stock options and commodities and futures contracts is that they lock in the price and quantity of an asset and have predetermined expiration dates. But in both cases, they are in themselves tradable assets, which means you can trade away your rights and obligations if you wish to exit the contract early.

- Equity options

An equity option is an option based on the price of a share of stock of a company. However, options are not available on all stocks, but some do not have options attached to them. It is up to the exchanges to determine whether or not to offer an option – based upon perceived demand – it is not up to the companies that issue the stock.

Most equity options are priced at 1 contract per 100 shares. Equity options are what most people think of when they contemplate Options.

- Index Options

The concept behind trading options in indexes is that if you can buy an option on a stock of a particular company within a sector says technology then why does the exchange not make available an option on that market sector as a whole? That's the idea behind index options you can bet on the sector performance and not have to drill down to a specific company.

The result has been a proliferation of Index options based on the performance of different market indices. There are options on the S&P 500, NASDAQ, and FTSE. Trading in indexes has become a very popular alternative to trading in stock options as they can represent a collection of diverse assets. This means that a trader can spread their investments across several sectors of interest. The index works by pooling together several stocks in the same sector or across diverse sectors, and the performance aggregate is used to measure the price of the group. There are many indexes, and these include stocks, commodities, and futures as they are all used as components of an index. But an index is just a logical category a convenient grouping of other securities so you can't buy an index directly. Instead, you buy a security that tracks the value of the index. An example of such an option would be one that tracked a particular ETF that owned the stocks in a particular index such as Standard & Poor's (S&P) 500 Index.

- Exchange traded funds (ETFs)

ETFs are mutual funds that have become very popular trading vehicles as they can be traded like stocks on an exchange. Most ETFs are designed to track an index or an underlying sector so technically ETFs are not derivatives. However, they are often referred to as quasi-derivatives. This is because, unlike other indexes, they can be traded and also because they are not necessarily holding exactly the same securities of the index that they are tracking. For example, some leveraged ETFs use swaps to mimic the action of the underlying index while adding leverage. ETFs allow you to trade on their underlying indexes, directly or through options. One of the most popular and well known ETFs is the S&P 500 SPDR (SPY).

- Stocks and bonds

Buying a company's stock gives you part ownership in that company, whereas buying bonds makes you a debt holder. Each position has its risks and rewards. However, when we bring Options into the equation, we can see that the three assets, stocks, bonds, and options, have very different risk and reward profiles. For example, although stocks give you a piece of the company, and bonds offer you income, options offer you no ownership of any tangible assets, but all three can lead to a total loss of investment. In the end, stocks offer indefinite holding periods, and bonds have a maturity date, whereas options have a limited life based on their expiration date.

- Interest Rate Options

These are sometimes better known as yield-based options, as they trade on the interest rate on a specific type of bond. With this type of Option, calls (buying) become more valuable as interest rates rise, and interest rate puts (selling) become more valuable as the rates fall. Importantly, the underlying value is the interest rate and not the value of the bond itself. Because interest rates aren't securities and can't be traded or exchanged as such the settlement is in cash.

- Miscellaneous Options

The way that the different options exchanges make money and compete with one another is when they develop new innovative types of contracts that capture the imagination of hedgers and speculators. As an option is just a contract, which is based on the price of another asset options can be drawn up for just about anything where someone might want to guarantee a price and someone else might want to speculate on that price. As a result, exchanges are always trying out new option types so you can find options on different measures of market sentiment, i.e., whether it's optimistic or pessimistic about different economic outcomes.

- A swap

This is a type of insurance contract whose terms are privately agreed upon by the participants. It is an over-the-counter style option as they are non-exchange traded options. They are often used to bet on the direction of just about anything, including the weather, that the two parties agree upon. Swaps are by sophisticated design securities, and so they are not available to individual investors. This is due to the lack of regulations and the often complex financial and legal requirements required to be signed before you can trade them.

Trading in Options

As opposed to investing in stock or assets, trading Options is often a decision based upon a short term analysis. An Option having a predetermined time period, a time-to-live, will have by design an expiry date. As a result, Options are renewable and can be resold many times. This makes them suitable for both trading's over the short term or over longer periods delivering income when the value of the underlying stock rises, falls, or even moves sideways.

Trading Options for Profit

Now the whole purpose of trading is that you want to have more money in the future than what you have just now. Therefore, to increase your wealth, you are trading Options supplied by the markets. But here is the thing, regardless of the time frame — the question will come down to whether you have a tendency to hold a position for a short or long time — your objective, after all, will be the same too make more money.

But here is the problem because that hunger to make a profit makes traders and especially beginners impatient. Therefore as a beginner, you should consider that every time that you contemplate a new trading strategy; you will also have to contemplate a new learning curve. As a result, be prepared to realize that every change in strategy or trading tactics will begin with a deep study and analysis of trade conditions. This is where paper trading or virtual trading becomes invaluable as it lets you experiment with virtual cash and practice tactics with zero risks. Always be careful that when you start to trade with real cash those losses can be amplified so always be patient and be prepared to spend the time diligently required learning how to trade safely or you will likely lose a lot of money on worthless premiums.

Regardless of the type of financial trading that you are undertaking, there are some simple steps that you should adhere to in order to trade safely. It doesn't matter if you are a beginner or an intermediary trader; it is always sensible to ensure that you protect your capital. This means that even if you are experienced in other forms of trading or investing, or even have experience with options but with different assets, you should always seriously contemplate the following:

- Check your financial health

This means simply to check your financial balance sheet and your disposable income. This is hugely important as before you start trading in Options or any other financial instrument; you must realize how much you can afford to lose. Therefore you must go over your finances diligently, and make sure that the amount that you have as trading capital is indeed disposable income. This means reviewing your current loans, mortgages, and life and health insurances as well as school fees or college funds.

- Draw up a financial net worth statement

The purpose here is to ensure that you are aware of the amount you could lose and the desire to make profits – be sure you are comfortable with the risk/reward ratio. Also, try and make sure that your finances are healthy and understand why you are taking on extraordinary risk.

- Be realistic

Don't chase unrealistic goals and trade beyond your experience or safe capital levels. Furthermore, never risk more than 5% of your capital on any one trade – for beginners, 1%-3% is the recommended maximum.

- Know your own risk appetite

If you are a typically a cautious trader or a gambler, that may indicate that you may not be a good options trader. Nonetheless, there may be many trading option tactics and strategies that will suit your risk appetite. The thing to remember is that once you understand the built-in safety nets that trading options provide, and then it will decrease your risk. An important caveat is that just make sure you read through the book and stick to the beginners' strategies and tactics and find the ones that make you comfortable before you jump in.

- Analyze the Data

Stocks trading place a lot of emphasis on technical analysis, fundamental analysis, and Charts in order to maximize your chances of trading options successfully. Option trading rides upon the underlying stock, so it also places a high emphasis on improving your technical and fundamental analysis skills. Therefore, you should be a diligent analyst, especially in identifying and following the dominant trends, as well as being able to analyze charts and the behavior of the underlying assets in your options.

- Always test your strategies before putting them into practice

Testing out scenarios and tactics beforehand through paper trading before you take real-life risks is essential. Testing out theories before committing them with real money is always an excellent idea that is certain to provide both practices as well as saving you a lot of money

- Never trade with money that you aren't willing to lose

This might seem strange as Options are often seen as being risk management tools. But even though options are often deemed to be risk-management vehicles, you can still lose money trading them – sometimes in the case of insurance that is the whole purpose. And if you should adopt more sophisticated and riskier option strategies; your potential losses should always be identified and accepted as they could be significant if your trades – especially- sell- if they are not thoroughly investigated and analyzed beforehand.

Chapter 1) The call and also put short and long options and how to speculate

In general terms, a financial option is a contractual agreement between two parties. Options can be personalized agreements between two private individuals, and these are known as over-the-counter options. However, options traded on exchanges in Options trading are standardized contracts known as listed options.

Options contracts have a few characteristics that we must be aware of when beginning trading. For example, they have a limited lifetime determined by the expiry date. The expiry date is hugely important because once a contract expires, it becomes worthless. What this means is that if you don't exercise your rights on or before the expiry date they will expire and you will lose your premium along with the entire value of the Option. This may well be what you intended as many Options are bought as insurance cover for that time period. However, you would not want to lose out on a valuable Option with inherent profit just because you forgot to exercise your option on the correct date. Fortunately, many online broker platforms will track and notify you well in advance of any options due to expire so that shouldn't be the problem it once was.

We use stock options for the following objectives:

•   To benefit from the leverage that allows us to profit from large stock movements using less money

•   To benefit and gain profit from a bear market when there is a downward trend and falling prices in stocks without the risk of short selling

• To protect the overall value of a stock portfolio against persistent falling prices or sudden market downturns

To accomplish these tasks, there are fundamentally two main categories of Options - Puts and Calls.

Long and Short Puts and Calls

In general terms, an option will give you the right to buy or to sell an asset. Thus there are two main types of options - call and put – whereby the call gives you the right to buy, and the put gives you the right to sell.

An important thing to understand is the difference between Buyers and Sellers as this is fundamental to the way Options work. The Rights of the owner of an options contract is dependent on the type of contract:

• A call option gives the holder (owner) the right to buy the stock before or at an agreed date at a locked in price. A put option gives the owner the right to sell a specific number of shares of stock at a locked in price.

• Option writer or seller obligations: The writer or sellers of call options have an obligation to sell shares of the underlying stock at the agreed locked in price. Sellers of put options have an obligation to buy from the option holder the pre-agreed amount of stock at the locked in price.

To see how this works in practice, let us consider why traders buy call options. Traders will buy call options when they predict an upwards or bull market, i.e., they forecast that stocks will go up in price. This is because the call option gives them the right to buy the shares at a lower price than they would otherwise. Now that is straightforward enough, but why do they buy put options? Traders will buy put options when they expect the market to go down, i.e., they will be buying options when they expect a downward trend in the market.

Going long or going short

Another confusing term for beginners and especially those familiar with other stock trading methods is the trading terms, long and short. In general trading terms to take a long position is to buy to own it, and to take a short position is to sell it.

Nonetheless, in Options trading, these terms take on more nuanced meanings. In Options trading, the terms of long and short are more complicated because you are also dealing with whether they are related to puts or call options.

Trading Long on a Call

If a Trader speculates that a company ABC's stock will be trading above $40 at expiration, which is within a month. The best premium for each Call option with a $40 strike price is $0.85.

Now, if ABC is trading at $45 at the expiration date, then all is well, and the trader can exercise the option and buy shares at $40 each, for a profit of $5 less the $0.85 premium - $4.15. But if ABC's stock price has remained at or around $40 or less, then the Trader is out the $0.85 option meaning they have lost $0.85x100 =$85.

Trading short on a Call

Another use of a call can be demonstrated when a Trader thinks Company ABC stock will be trading below $50 at expiration date in a months' time. However, in this scenario, the premium for each call option with a $50 strike price is $2.00. What the Trader can do is writes (shorts) call options at the $50 price, and they will receive $2 for each option.

If the price of Company ABC stock at expiration is $40 or below, the Trader is successful and gets to keep the $2 premium per option.

However If the price goes up to say, $54, the Trader will lose $54 – $50 = $4 per share; however, the $2 premium offsets half the total loss to $2.

Trading long on a Put

In a third scenario, we can see another way of using options when another Trader is confident that Company XYZ stock will be trading below $30 per share at expiration, in 3 months they use a put option.

The premium for a put option with a $30 strike price is $0.75.

If all goes as expected and the price of Company XYZ stock at expiration is $27, then the Trader will make $30 – $27 = $3 per share, less the $0.75 premium for a profit of $2.25.

However, should the price at expiration be $31 or higher, then the Trader is out of the money and the premium for a loss of $0.75.

Trading short on a Put

Another Trader thinks Company XYZ stock will be trading above $70 per share at expiration.

The premium for a put option with a $70 strike price is $1.02, so the Trader writes options at $1.02 each.

At expiration, the stock is at $72 per share, so the Trader gets to keep the $1.02 premium per share.

However, if the stock were to go to $68, then the Trader would then lose $68 – $70 per share, plus the $1.02 premium for a loss of $0.98.

The following table gives you a short summary of what happens to different types of options positions as the underlying asset's price changes.

Basic Put and Call Matrix

Option	Stock price goes up	Stock price goes down
Long call	Profit	worthless
Short call	Loss	Keep the premium
Long put	Worthless	Profit
Short put	Keep the premium	Loss

Writers & Buyers

The trader who decides to short an option—in effect, sell it to someone else—is also known as the writer. For every trade that is made, there is a writer and a buyer. Exchanges need both buyers and writers to create the market depth. This is simply because writers construct options to sell to those in the market to buy. In every trade, the option writer goes short, and the buyer goes long. Nonetheless, the interesting thing is that even if every trader in the market had a common perception of a stock's behavior, there would still be those that go short when the market as a whole is going long.

The reason for this is that there are always those trading for the purpose of speculation and those looking for insurance. These traders have conflicting interests and objectives, so they will have to take contrary positions in order to achieve their goals.

For example, Options that are bought for insurance purposes will take the opposite perspective of the market trend. This is because an investor holding a valuable asset; for example, 100 Apple shares may want them to go up in price but will still need protection against their price falling. Hence the need for a put Option with a low strike price that will counter-balance any sudden decline in value.

It is this ability to mix and match long and short, puts and calls in a few different ways that are the foundation in developing options trading strategies and cycles.

Setting the Strike Price

The strike price of an option is the predetermined and locked-in price where the option can be exercised at any time up until expiration. For example, a call with a strike price of $70 can be exercised if the

27

underlying price is at $70 or above. At exercise, the trader who wrote the call will receive $70 per share in exchange for a share of the stock. If the trader does not own the stock – remember they do not have to – the required stock will have to be purchased at market price. Whatever, the trader who bought the call has the right to buy the underlying for $70, whether it's worth $70.01 or $876 dollars in the market. The Option writer is obliged to sell the stock at $70 regardless of whether he has to go out to the market and buy it at $70.01 or $876 dollars in order to fulfill the contract.

Similarly, a put option with a strike price of $40 can be exercised if the underlying price is $40 or less. At exercise, the trader who wrote the put will have to buy the stock at $40 per share, whether it is worth $39.99 or $0.00. The holder of the option will receive the difference between the market price and the exercise price.

The following table shows what happens when a call or put expires in the money—that is, when the market price is above the strike price for a call or below the strike price for a put.

	Older	Writer
Call	Receives cash or security	Delivers cash or security
Put	Delivers cash or security	Receives cash or security

You'll notice that the receiver and deliverer are different for puts and calls, holders and writers. This allows for the structure of many different strategies.

To exercise an option, the holder notifies their broker, which then notifies the market clearinghouse, which then, in turn, notifies the seller that it is time to settle up.

Expiration Date

The expiration date is not as straightforward as you might suspect, albeit it does mean the day the option is no longer valid. However, the way the date is determined is by the month on the contract and the day is the third Friday of the month. Thus an Option will be dated 2019 Dec, and the expiry date will be the date on the third Friday of December 2019. By the expiry date, the holder must either exercise their rights, and the writer has to settle up by that date, or the option will expire and become worthless.

American and European Options

There is some ambiguity between Options as there are two distinct styles an American and a European style. The only real difference but it is a significant one is that an American option gives the holder the right to exercise the option at any time after the sale and before the expiration date. On the other hand, a European option can only be exercised on the expiration date. This is a major difference in terms of trading so you must make sure you know which option style you are trading in.

To compound the problem exchanges issue both types, it is no longer the case that American exchanges only issued American style Options and European only issued European style options now there is a mixture of both. You need to know which you are trading as it can have a large effect of the Options value and ability to be traded.

Chapter 2) Greeks and their importance

When it comes to trading options successfully, it is vital that you understand the multiple types of risk that come into play. To make them easier to discuss in detail, they have been broken down into different variables, each of which is labeled with a letter of the ancient Greek alphabet. Trading without taking the time to learn this valuable way to avoid as much risk as possible is akin to driving in a foreign country without first learning the rules of the road or even the language.

Regardless if you are placing a put or a call, or even just planning your strategy, it is crucial that you look at your various risks and rewards in terms of three key areas. First, the amount of change the price is likely to experience, second the amount of volatility currently at play, and finally, the amount of time the option has left until it expires. If you are holding a call, you will all need to consider if the price is moving in the wrong direction, if the volatility is decreasing or if there isn't enough time left on the option in question. On the contrary, sellers face the risk of prices moving in the wrong direction and an increase in volatility but never when it comes to the time value.

When options are combined or traded, you will then want to determine the Greeks related to new result, often referred to as the net Greeks. This will allow you to determine the new difference between risk and reward and act appropriately. Understanding what the Greeks can tell you will allow you to better tailor your strategy based on your desired level of risk. You can think of them as guideposts to keep you on the right track when it comes to seeking out the right options for you.

Delta: When dealing with individual options, Delta can be thought of as the overall amount of risk that exists between the price of an underlying stock at the current moment and where it is likely to move. If the strike price of an option is the same as the current price of the underlying stock, then that stock has a Delta of .5. If this is the case then is means that if the underlying stock moves 1 point, the price of the option will shift .5 points, assuming all other factors remain even. The total range Delta can possibly be anywhere from -1 to 1. Puts can be anywhere from -1 to 0, and calls can be anywhere from 0 to 1.

Delta is likely the first measurement of risk that you will always want to consider when it comes to choosing the options that are right for you. It can be particularly useful when it comes to deciding the right time to buy into a put option as you want it to be at just the right point in order to maximize its potential for profit. In this instance, it is beneficial to know the expected results of paying less in exchange for knowing the Delta is going to be lower as well. This difference can be seen by simply looking at the strike price and watching how it changes in relation to the put price.

Generally speaking, the cheaper an option is, the smaller its Delta is going to be. This is due to the fact that delta is often linked to the odds that a specific option is going to be worth a profit by the time it expires. As an example, if you are looking at an option with a Delta of .32, then you can assume, all things being equal, that buying into that option is going to pay out successfully about a third of the time.

Vega: Whenever a position is taken, regardless of what that position is, the risk of change that comes from the volatility of the underlying stock is known as the Vega. The level of volatility that an underlying stock has can change even if the price of the stock in question doesn't. This means that it has the potential to affect their profits significantly. Successful strategies can be built around both low and high volatility choices, as well as neutral volatility choices from time to time.

As a general rule, the more time standing between an option and its expiration date, the higher that option's Vega is going to be. This is because time value is proportional to volatility as the longer the timeline, the higher the chance that the volatility will manifest itself. As an example, assume an option is currently worth about $4 with an underlying asset that is worth $90. Further, assume that it has a Vega of .1 with 20 percent volatility. If the volatility increases by just one percent, this will equate to 10 cents worth of increase in the price for a total of $4.10. The amount of change that is seen in an option with a shorter period is often going to result in larger changes because there is ultimately less time the option will destabilize.

Theta: Theta is the measure of the rate at which the time the option has left disappears or decays, which means that this number will often be negative when you are dealing with it. The instant you purchase an option, that option's Theta starts to decrease along with the total value as both decreases the closer the option is to its expiration point. If the Delta of a given option is greater than its Theta, then the option will benefit the holder, and if the Theta is greater than the Delta, then the option will benefit the writer.

As an example, consider an option with a Theta of .015 that is going to decrease in value by 1.5 cents in 24 hours. Puts have negative thetas and calls have positive thetas. This is because puts are worth the least when they are about to expire, and calls are worth the most because the difference between the starting and ending amounts is going to be at its highest. Additionally, Theta fluctuates day to day as it starts off slow and then builds in intensity the closer the option gets to its ultimate expiration. This explains why long-term options attract buyers, and short-term options are preferred by sellers.

If you are looking to make a trade when the market is neutral, then you will want to be sure to take Theta into account, but you can otherwise move forward confidently with your current strategy. Generally speaking, you are always going to want to buy into options with a Theta that is as low as you can manage it.

Gamma: If Delta is the amount of change that the option will experience in response to a change in the underlying asset price, then Gamma is the amount you can expect Delta to change over time. Gamma increases as options near the point where the price of the options and the price of the underlying asset overlap and will decrease even further below the strike price as the price of the underlying asset drops. The larger the Gamma, the larger the risk, but also the larger the return. Gamma is also likely to spike as the option in question reaches its expiration date. This can be taken a step further with the Gamma of the Gamma which considers the rate the rate the Delta changes at.

For example, if a stock is trading at about $50 and a related option are currently going for $2. If it has a delta of .4 as well as a gamma of .1, then, if the stock increases by $1 then the delta will see an increase of 10 percent which the Gamma amount is also. If volatility is low, then gamma is high when the option in question is above its strike price and low when it is below it. Gamma tends to stabilize when volatility is high and decrease when it is low.

Rho: Rho is the name given to the amount of risk associated with the odds that the interest rates that affect your option are going to change before it expires. Rho isn't going to come into play as frequently as the other Greeks as interest rates are typically going to increase in tandem with call prices while the price of puts will decrease, and the reverse is true when interest rates decrease. You can expect the Rho values to reach their peak when the price of the underlying stock crosses the price of the option you are working with. Additionally, this value will always be negative for puts and positives to calls. Rho values are more important when it comes to long options and virtually irrelevant for most short options.

Finding the Greeks

In order to determine how the Greeks are going to apply to any of the options trades you make, the first thing you will need to keep in mind that every strategy is likely to have a positive or negative value for each of the Greeks. As an example, if the Vega is positive, then the position will see gains if the volatility rises. Likewise, a negative Delta position will result in a decrease if or when the underlying asset decreases. Keeping an eye on the Greeks and noting how they change is key to options trading success in both the short and the long term.

In order to find the Greeks for your chosen option successfully, the first step is always to remember that the results you see are going to be theoretical as no one, and certainly not the Greeks, are able to predict the future. What you are seeing is just the results of a mathematical formula with several different variables plugged in as needed. These include the bid you are putting on the option, the asking price, the last price, the volume, and occasionally the interest.

Different Types of Options

We have already determined in the previous chapter that options are actually contracts that give buyers the right to purchase a corresponding security for a predetermined value for specific time duration. The premium, which refers to the price paid for an option, consists of a number of variables. These variables help options traders to make informed decisions about the best time to trade options.

Different Options Markets

While options are commonly found at the stock market, they are also found across other markets. These include Forex, commodity, and futures markets. For our purposes, we shall focus more on stock market options even though the concepts are similar across all markets.

Why do individuals and traders trade in options?

There are different reasons why traders and investors opt to trade or deal in options. One of the reasons is to hedge positions. Individuals, organizations, and institutions sometimes hedge their positions to protect themselves against any potential future disasters.

Traders often use options in order to generate huge profits at much lower costs compared to direct investment in stocks. Most options traders are speculators. They generally have no intention of exercising the options contracts that they invest in. Instead, they prefer to profit from the change in the price of the option.

Main Advantage of Options

One of the biggest advantages of trading in options is that traders are able to benefit immensely in the price movement of a stock without actually having to buy the stock. For instance, if a share of stock ABC costs $25 each and there's enough reason to anticipate a value increase in the next three months, then you will spend $2,500 to buy 100 shares. Alternatively, a call option entailing a strike price worth $27 with an expiry date of 2 months could be bought. This will cost you a mere $50 is a single option costs $0.5. This is because $0.5 X 100 = $50.

Different Types of Options

Essentially, options consist of two general types—the call options and the put options. As previously defined, put options give the investor an opportunity to sell stocks at a specified price while call options give you the option to buy stocks at a certain price.

Underlying Asset

Every option contract is based on an underlying asset. Most options are based on stocks of companies that are listed at the stock market. In recent years though, other securities have been used. These include REITs or real estate investment trusts, ETFs or electronically traded funds, foreign currencies, and stock indices. Some are even based on commodities like minerals, industrial, and agricultural products.

Generally, 100 shares of a corresponding stock serve as the basis for stock options contracts. Some exceptions are made in special cases for instance where mergers occur or when there is a stock split. Also, buying options is completely different to investing in shares. Here is a look at different types of options.

Different Types of Options

- **Weekly Options- Mini Options**
- **The Protective Put- Stock Options**
- **Futures Options- ES Weekly Options**
- **Index Options - Mini Index Options**
- **Binary Options- E-Mini Options**
- **IRA Accounts- ETF Options**
- **Near month in-the-money options**

1. near Month In-the-Money Options

Some options are best suited for day trading. One such example is the near month in-the-month option. This option basically refers to options contracts that are set to expire at the close of the next month. Such options are usually past their strike price so investors are free to exercise them.

The inherent value of this options contract is one of the determining factors of the premium especially when it nears its expiration date. Such options are often traded in large volumes and this causes a smaller gap between the asking and bidding prices. As the option nears its expiration date, its time value diminishes.

2. Protective Put Option

A protective put is an option that is used by traders who wish to purchase both an option and its underlying securities. This is the preferred strategy anytime that the underlying stock is expected to undergo periods of high volatility.

There are instances when day traders will continually buy and sell the same stock option for a long time, maybe a couple of months, in order to benefit from a short-term upward trend. At other times, day traders make use of a strategy of purchasing put options on the same underlying security just so they insure themselves against any sharp losses in the price of the stock. This is then considered as a risk management technique. While there are certain small loses paid in order to protect the share, the opportunity to minimize losses on a downward trend is absolutely invaluable.

3. Stock Options

Traders acquire a technique in upping their earnings through straightforward stock options through just purchasing or shorting shares for a certain predetermined price at a set time at the options market. Day traders have specific upper hands when it comes to stock options because the parameters are applied to stock options. Since both stocks and stock options are traded on an exchange, the market will have the same liquidity and will enable fast execution of orders. Sophisticated investors can use options as an effective hedge against risks.

Stock options have the potential to cost you 100% of your funds. Brokers only permit sophisticated traders to deal with complex options systems like stock options. You can be exposed to enormous amounts of risk and it is crucial that you avoid strategies that require substantial experience. However, it's good to note that day traders rarely sell options.

4. Weekly Options

Weekly options are also popularly referred to as weeklies. Such options are generally listed with only one week left to expiration. Most options often have several months and sometimes even years to expiration. However, weeklies are generally available to day traders. They are found on ETNs or exchange-traded notes, broad-market indices in the US, and ETFs or exchange-traded funds.

A lot of traders view traditional options as a huge setback largely because of the long time duration. These traders very much prefer weeklies and view them as major game changers. They get to apply the leverage of options even as they engage in more short-term strategies.

Created on Thursdays

Weekly contracts are usually created once each week on a Thursday. They remain valid until the following Friday for ETNs, ETFs, and equities. Weekly index options, however, often close their final trading sessions on Fridays or Thursdays depending on the index. These basically have a total lifetime of seven trading days or one week.

As a day trader, you can benefit hugely if capitalize on the increased volatility that comes with the time decay and expiration that is associated with options. Weekly options have 52 expiration periods throughout the year and this increases your chances of benefiting from expiring options.

While weeklies provide a couple of advantages to day traders, they have some possible disadvantages especially due to the time factor. Option buyers generally pay less for the cost of a weekly option relative to regular options they usually experience a hugely limited opportunity window especially when trades move in the opposite of

41

the intended direction. There is generally very limited opportunity for price recover and it is hard to fix a trade through strike adjustments.

5. Mini Options

Mini options are actually options that let traders and investors trade in options that are based on 10-share sets rather than the standard 100-share sets. Mini options have expiration dates that are similar in nature to regular expiration dates. This expiration date is also similar to quarterlies and weeklies.

Other features like the bids, strike price, and offers are also similar and correspond to features of regular options. However, they do offer certain benefits. As a trader, you stand to enjoy the following benefits by simply trading in mini options.

Benefits of mini options:

- You are able to hedge a position for very little money.

- Mini options are more affordable per transaction.

- They can be exercised on any business day as long as they are not expired because they are American style in nature.

Sadly, they also have some drawbacks. For instance:

- Mini options are available for only limited securities.

- They have much lower liquidity.

- The bid-ask spreads are much wider.

- They charge a higher commission based on a percentage.

In general, mini options act as a great tool for hedging highly valued securities and for day trading. However, their use in day trading is limited unless they are available on a bigger variety of ETFs and stocks.

6. Index Options

We also have another type of options contract which is known as the index option. These options let you make use of put or call options to speculate on the movements of a whole stock market index like the S&P 500 or the Dow Jones instead of individual stocks and shares.

A trader who trades index options can capitalize on their predictions based on volatility or direction of an entire market without any need to trade options based on individual stocks. One of the main challenges that traders encounter when pricing index options is accurately calculating dividend estimates.

Features of index options:

- **Basically, index options are less vulnerable to volatility compared to stocks in general that constitute an index.**

- **Index options are well able to handle fluctuations that individual stocks could be exposed to and as such, they tend to be more stable compared to other kinds of options.**

- **A lot of index options are exercised in a European style. This is because they cannot be traded until** they expire. However, the trader or investor will not necessarily be stuck with them as they can be sold or bought as long as they haven't expired.

- Index options often trade in large volumes because they are largely traded by investment firms, hedge funds, and individual traders.

- Unfortunately for day traders, large volumes minimize the spreads quoted at the markets.

7. Mini Index Options

The mini index options happen to be quite similar to ordinary index options. However, they cost 10% less and are only 10% the normal contract size. Traders and investors with limited capital are easily able to trade this option type and benefit from trading on the general market. Day traders benefit from this option type as they are able to have a wider strategy scope.

There are certain benefits or advantages of the mini-index options.

Here is a look at some of these benefits:

- They are a lot cheaper compared to ordinary index options.

- They resemble the underlying index perfectly.

- They generally offer a partial hedge against ordinary index options.

There are some disadvantages as well. Some of these disadvantages include:

- Mini index options have a large bid-ask spread.
- They usually have a higher extrinsic value due to lower liquidity.
- They are a lot more expensive compared to others.

8. Binary Options

Binary options are among the most commonly traded options. They are known by different names depending on the platform where they are trading. For instance, binary options are referred to as FROs or fixed return options when traded on the American Stock Exchange. On the Forex markets, they are referred to as digital options and sometimes as all-or-nothing options on the ASE or American Stock Exchange.

The reason why they are known as binary is that this options class offers returns or profits in two outcomes. This means you get something or nothing. In this instance where you have binary options, the profitability is usually a pre-set amount such as $100.

There are certain assets that can be traded as binary options. These assets include:

- **Stocks**
- **Commodities**
- **Currencies**
- **Stock indices**

While there are plenty of different types of binary options, only two are commonly used by day traders. These popular binary options are:

- **Asset or nothing binary options**
- **Cash or nothing binary options**

The asset or nothing binary option pays the entire value of the underlying security. The cash or nothing binary option pays an investor a set amount of money should the option be in-the-money upon expiry. This is the reason why this type of options is referred to as binary. You can expect to receive only one of two outcomes investing in this particular options class.

The reasoning behind binary options day trading is pretty simple. As a trader, the aim is to enter a trade position and exit before the close of the trading day. All binary options contracts come with expiry times and dates. This means that most binary options contracts have a set expiry date except on trading platforms where traders have a variable expiry on options.

As a day trader, you should identify expiry dates that will conclude trades within the same day. This is because once you enter a trade that has an expiry date, you will not be able to exit manually the same way that you do with all other options trades.

Predetermined profits

When trading in binary options, you will already know what your potential profit will be. This is because the potential profit is always already pre-determined. Also, binary options can be applied to almost all types of securities and financial products as puts or calls.

This is why day trading with binary options is considered easy and quite profitable. As a trader, you can expect high returns that are paid out almost immediately. Apart from the high profitability of binary options, there are other advantages that they offer.

- As a trader, you get to select variable expiry times to fit with your strategies.

- There are no brokers so you will manage your own trading account.

- You can trade diversified options at the same time.

- You are allowed to make multiple small investments, which is similar to day trading but with limited risk exposure.

- One trade can be sufficiently profitable to counter previous losses.

- As a trader, you have trading opportunities throughout the day with no downtime.

- With binary options, the potential to make profits is high and the turnaround times are remarkably fast.

- Day traders have constant new opportunities as binary options markets keep expanding.

- Security is high on these platforms largely due to the nature of private trading in the options trading market.
- Volatility is not a big issue because risks are transparency and also options have short time frames.

If you want to be a smart trader, then you should ensure that you follow patterns and trends in the market. When you can identify a true trend, then you will be able to attain profits regularly on a continuing basis and with the need of changing strategy. However, should the trend fail to work because it was false or due to brief trading times, you must then exit the trade to minimize losses?

9. Futures Options

Options on futures are contracts that are focused on one futures contract. As a buyer, you reserve the right to choose a futures position on an index, currency, commodity, or another financial price. The options trade is at a specified price known as the strike price and you maintain your right until the expiration of the option.

A future options seller is obligated by the contract to assume the reverse futures position as soon as you exercise your right. These options trades are dealt on the same exchanges with traditional futures contracts. The options contracts concisely match the underlying securities, which in this case are futures contracts. The matching is in terms of strike price, expiration dates, and quantities.

There are certain differences between futures and options futures. As an example, buyers and sellers have different obligations. It is advisable to find out more about the differences between options on futures contracts and futures contracts.

Futures contracts

When it comes to futures contracts, then you as the buyer will take on the obligation of purchasing a particular asset at a set date in the future. Your seller is obligated to sell and then deliver the specific asset at that future date unless your position closes well before the expiration date.

Futures contracts generally do not have any initial costs. This is in contrast to other options contracts that have some upfront costs. Also, the underlying position has a much larger size. Any profits earned are credited to the futures account right at the close of trading day. As such the value of the asset gets recorded based on its market price.

Options based on futures contracts

Options that are based on futures grant you, as a buyer, the right to sell an underlying security at a price that is predetermined. As a buyer, you are allowed to exercise your right to sell this asset as long as the contract is valid and not expired. However, in this instance, the underlying position's size is usually smaller compared to that of a futures contract.

How to make gains:

- **Consider this position as a great opportunity to hedge.**
- **Exercise the option as soon as it is deep in-the-money.**
- Hold your position until it expires then benefit from the size of increase between the strike price and the asset price.

10. ES Weekly Options

This type of options contract is commonly referred to as weekly options on futures. It is mostly used by day traders for short-term swing trading as well as day trading. The weekly options on futures provide an additional day trading opportunity with even more benefits. Here is a look at these benefits:

- These options expose you to limited risks.

- You do not need to have a futures account in order to deal with them.

- Common rules such as pattern day trading are not applicable in this case.

- Options increase in value much faster when you go long due to the option Greek.

Even then, there are some cons or negatives related to this trading type. Here is a look at some of these negatives:

- They have a very brief time period before expiration

- You need a lot more effort in order to place it

- It is challenging to set limited orders if you're expecting to enter or have a target

Just as it is with futures trading, when trading the ES Weekly Options as a day trader on the 15-minute charts, you get access to more valuable intraday opportunities in relation to the daily chart.

11. E-Mini Options

One of the least known options contracts is the E-mini contract. This is an option that is electronically traded. It is viewed largely as a mini version of the ordinary futures contract. The E-mini contract, just like with other mini options, is in line with the structure of the standard counterpart just smaller in size and cheaper in price.

These contracts offer investors great leverage especially when investments are relatively small. The only challenge is that any potential losses are exponentially large. While these E-mini contracts were first made available for the S&P 500, they are today readily accessible on other indices such as the S&P Midcap 400 and the NASDAQ 100.

These options are sometimes used by day traders to hedge or even as a leveraging tool. Traders and investors can also use E-mini options to increase their profits on other future trades. They are also popularly used to protect or safeguard a position that is perceived to be vulnerable to market movements.

12. ETF Options

An ETF option is an options contract that is derived from the ETF or exchange-traded fund. ETFs are basically investment pools that are then traded at the stock market. Electronically traded funds contain a specific number of underlying assets that include bonds, commodities, and stocks. They trade very near to the net asset value throughout the course of the trading day.

The shares and other financial instruments are traded in much the same manner as regular stocks at the course. This way, a trader is easily able to purchase and sell shares and even options of an electronically traded fund via a brokerage account. You will find ETFs across all the common stock indexes such as the Nasdaq 100 composite (QQQQ) and the Dow Jones Industrial Average.

Sometime traders will choose a specific industry because chances are high of finding stocks of major industries across most ETFs. This way, traders are able to focus more on determining and predicting movements in a specific industry rather than a mixed choice of stocks as offered by standard index ETFs.

ETF options come in very handy as their related options trade throughout the day. As a day trader, if you actively trade ETF options and make use of hedging strategies, then you need to ensure that you are well informed regarding the background information of the underlying stock. If you feel confident about this information, then you will gain from the tax breaks and low costs associated with trading ETF options.

13. IRA or Individual Retirement Accounts Options

Yet another options account that is out there is the IRA options contract. However, IRA accounts are generally unavailable to the general population because of rules put in place by the SEC or US Securities and Exchange Commission.

The SEC demands that any day trader have the appropriate designation and should hold margin brokerage accounts. However, this is not the case when it comes to an IRA account. Such accounts cannot be margin accounts and are limited to only cash accounts.

In simple terms, day trading of stock options and stocks needs traders to operate a margin account and any IRA account used should have only a cash account status. The only alternative that you can have is to create your own IRA account via a commodity futures broker.

Useful Options Terminology

As you learn about options and get to understand how they work, it is extremely useful that you get to understand the terminology involved. We have the general options terminology and then we have terminology specific to pricing.

When it comes to options, the terminology is very similar to that used in futures in many respects. Here are some useful definitions that you need to acquaint yourself with.

Options Pricing Terminology

It is advisable to learn as much as possible about options pricing especially at the basic level. Below is a review of some of the most basic terminology that pertains to options pricing.

At-the-money options: These are options contracts with a strike price that is exactly the same as that of the market price of the underlying commodity.

Contract: This is an option that consists of 100 shares of a specified underlying security.

Covered Put: This is an options contract where the option writer has a short position within the underlying security based on a share for-share basis.

Covered Call: In this instance, the option contract writer has a long position on the underlying security based on a share-for-share term.

Covered Writer - This term refers to an options seller who also owns the underlying security. The owner hedges the security against the option.

Date: This is the date when an option contract expires and becomes null and void. A lot of options contracts expire on the third Friday at 4.00 pm on expiration month.

Derivative: This is a security that derives its value from another security referred to as an underlying security. Options contracts are a type of derivative because they derive their value from an underlying security.

Early Exercise – When you decide to exercise an options contract before it attains its expiry date. This can happen with American style options.

European Options: This term refers to a specific type of options contract which can only be exercised at a particular period of time just before it expires.

Holder: A trader who purchases an options contract then pays the writer a premium.

LEAPS: Long-Term Equity Anticipation Securities – these are options contracts that are publicly traded with expiration dates that extend beyond a year.

In-the-money: We say that a call option is in-the-money when the value of the underlying security is greater than options' strike price.

Listed Option: This is a call or put option that is available for trade at the options exchange. Some of the terms pertaining to the option are determined and standardized by the exchange.

Open Interest: The sum of all outstanding options at the options market on a specific day.

Naked Option: This refers to an option's position that does not include the writer's offsetting position with the underlying security. This means that there is no protection in case the price moves in the opposite direction.

Option: An option is a financial instrument and a derivative. This derivative grants its buyer the right to an asset or security without any obligation to sell or buy. However, this is usually for a specified period of time and at a set price.

Out-of-the-money: An option that has no intrinsic value and that will expire worthless at the close of the trading day. For call options, this is the case when the strike price exceeds the underlying security's market price. For the put option, this is when the strike price is below the market rate of the underlying security.

Over-the-counter: This term refers to options contracts that are not traded at an exchange like other options. Such an option lacks standardized expiration dates and strike prices.

Premium: This is the overall cost of an options contract. When you buy an option, you pay an amount known as the premium. This amount combines the time value of the option and its intrinsic value.

Put: This refers to an option contract that awards a buyer the right to sell an underlying security without the obligation of doing so. This right is pegged within a certain time frame and an agreed price.

Strike Price: this is the price that is agreed upon between parties at which you can exercise your options contract. For a call option, the strike is generally the price at which you can buy the contract. For put options, it refers to the price at which you can sell the option. Sometimes this price is known as the exercise price.

Terms: An options contract has conditions. These include an expiration date, strike price, underlying security and so on. These are collectively known as terms.

Writer: This is an investor who writes and sells options contracts and collects a premium as payment for the effort. As a writer, you are obligated to sell or buy the underlying security should the holder decide to exercise the option.

Underlying Security: This term refers to a financial security that will be sold or bought should an option be exercised.

Trading Options vs. Stocks

Options and stocks are used by traders and investors in order to benefit financially from the movement of stocks. However, these financial securities have major differences in the way they are created and the mode of operation.

Options are sometimes used for hedging positions that have been established by traders. However, equities are also widely used to determine a company's directional view.

Options Contracts

Investors have plenty of financial and strategic leeway with options compared to simply investing in stocks. By investing in options, traders not only hedge to protect against losses but also gain access to stocks at a fraction of the normal costs. Options contracts lower your risk in all market conditions on speculative bets and increase your profits on any new or existing positions you may take.

Trading in options has a lot of positives compared to trading in stocks only or other securities. However, there are some inherent risks that you need to be aware of. As a potential trader, you need to be aware of the great benefits as well as inherent risks related to trading options.

Pros of Trading Options

1. You require much lower upfront financial resources than with stocks.

The cost of buying options, which includes the premium amount and trading commission, is much lower compared to the amount you will pay to invest directly in shares.

As an investor or trader, you will pay far less money to invest in the same number of shares compared to one who invests directly in shares. However, if the trade is successful, then you will benefit just as much as a direct investor percentage-wise.

2. Limited losses when you invest in stocks and options.

When you purchase stock options, you are not required to exercise your right to buy or sell the underlying stock. If your estimations or speculation about stock movement are right, then you make a large profit. However, should your speculations not follow through, and then your losses are limited only to the cost of the premium and brokerage fees.

3. Options offer traders flexibility on their trades.

There are a couple of strategies that can be implemented by investors or traders before the expiry of the contract. Here are some of these strategies:

- You can exercise an option and purchase the underlying stocks then add these to the portfolio.

- You can also exercise an option contract, purchase shares and then sell them for a profit at the stock market.

- You can make back some funds that were spent buying an out-of-the-money option. This is by selling the option to another trader before it expires.

- You can also exercise options that are in-the-money to other investors.

4. Options can help you to fix the stock price.

Option contracts act similar to lay-away in stores because they let investors fix the price of a stock at a specific value which in our case is the strike price for a couple of days, weeks, or months. This guarantees you that an investor will be able to sell or purchase the underlying security at the strike price before the option expires.

5. You have plenty of leverage.

Using options contracts, you are able to invest a significantly tiny amount of money yet control a large number of shares. For instance, a single options contract enables you to be part of the movement of 100 shares of a stock. In this case, your risk will be limited to a certain level and the costs will be extremely low.

Setbacks of Trading Options

1. Sellers are exposed to large and sometimes unlimited losses.

Option buyers and holders are only exposed to small losses. However, the option writer's risk is almost unlimited. The losses that they stand to incur are so much greater than the cost of the options contract. The reason is that they have obligations of purchasing or selling stocks or the underlying stocks if a buyer or seller chooses to exercise their right.

2. Time is always limited for the investor to make a profit.

Options are short-term in nature. Investors who use options often seek short-term or near-term price movements that they can capitalize on. These price movements need to take place within a matter of a couple of days, weeks, or months for the payoff to happen.

As such, it is crucial to make a number of assumptions. These are deciding when to buy an option and when to exercise it or walk away from the contract before expiration. This contrasts long-term stock buyers who have really no time limit. They are able to invest and wait for years and even decades.

3. Traders have to qualify to trade.

As an options trader, there are certain essential criteria that you must meet if you are to start trading. For instance, you must be approved by a broker. You do this by answering a couple of questions or going through a similar screening process. The broker will need to find out about your personal financial situation and your knowledge and experience with risk and understanding how to trade options.

After the screening, then you will most likely be assigned a trading level based on your skill and experience. The broker will also take into consideration your understanding of risk posed by options trading. This level will dictate the kind of options trades that you will be allowed to place.

As a trader, you will generally be expected to maintain a minimum balance of roughly $2,000 in the brokerage account. This is the general requirement within the industry and this is a cost that you need to seriously consider.

4. Options traders can incur added costs that affect returns.

There are certain strategies that need you to set up a margin account. For instance, when you are selling a call options contract on securities that you do not own. This margin account provides a line of credit that is held as collateral in the event the trade moves against you.

There are different minimum requirements across the various brokerage firms for account opening and so on. The interest rate and amount will depend on factors such as how many securities and cash are present in an account. You can get access to margin loans with interest rates ranging from the low single digits to the low double digits.

In the event that you are unable to repay the margin loan advanced to you by your brokerage firm, then the broker will issue a margin call then liquidate your account should you not add some funds or securities to it. This can also happen if your account falls below a certain percentage which is very possible in the course of a trading day.

You can learn detailed information about the risks and characteristics of standardized options contracts at the Options Clearing Corporation of the USA. There are also income tax regulations that you need to familiarize yourself with if you are going to trade in options and other securities.

Pros of Trading Equities

1. Equities have significantly high liquidity.

Compared to options markets, equity markets are significantly more liquid. For most traders and investors, it is easy to enter and exit positions. This can happen within minutes in most cases. Exiting positions within a matter of a few minutes is especially easy for stocks that constitute major indexes such as the S&P 500. This liquidity often comes from mutual funds and passive index funds that are invested in the S&P 500 stocks. These funds are regularly seeking to invest in stocks contained in the fund in order to own larger percentages.

2. Time is on your side.

Options give you very little time to profit from market movements. This is not the case when it comes to stocks. In fact, stocks have no time limit which means you can hold them for as long as you see necessary.

As a stock investor, you have plenty of time within which you can enter and exit trades. You will not be punished for early or late entry into trades. However, options traders really need to factor in time because options contracts are limited by time.

3. Stocks generally have a lower risk.

Both stocks and options have their own pros and cons. However, in general, traders and investors view stocks as being generally less risky. The volatility of any given stock is generally much lower than that of options. Also, stocks have no risks due to time decay.

Disadvantages Associated with Stocks

There are certain downsides of equities trade compared to options contracts. We will examine some of these disadvantages and see how they compare to options.

1. Stocks have limited upside.

Most stocks move in tandem with respective indexes. Stocks rarely move above 20% in any given year. Traders with limited finances or small capital will be frustrated to discover that even with all the time in the world, their income potential is limited. This contrasts traders who focus on other instruments such as options who are able to double their income in just a few short months or even weeks. Just a few well-managed options trade and good risk management techniques, it is very possible for multiple investments within a short time period.

2. Stocks have limited leverage.

Investors in stocks can only access limited capital through borrowing of only up to 50% of the total value of securities they have purchased. This refers to margin loans that are advanced by brokerage firms to clients.

This limitation is placed by the federal government through the Federal Reserve's regulations. This regulation applies only to equities markets but not the derivatives markets. The use of excessive leverage is discouraged and generally frowned upon. However, investors with capital amounts totaling about $5,000 can access marginal loans of up to $10,000 which they can use to invest in trades.

3. Higher risks for lower profits.

It is possible to put money in a stock and actually lose the entire amount. While this is very rare and hardly occurs, it can happen should the asset's value tumble down to zero. When it comes to options, you only stand to lose your initial investment only which in most cases is the premium paid for the options contract. While the losses may sound similar in both cases, this is not so. The amount of capital needed to invest in stocks is vastly different from amounts used in options trading.

Other Crucial Considerations

In order to make informed decisions about whether to buy, sell, or hold stocks, you need to understand more about a company's operations and business. You also need to understand the company's vision and have a sense of direction where the asset is heading. This is crucial, especially for options traders.

To be successful, options investors should have an excellent understanding of a company's intrinsic value and also affirm thesis regarding the foundations of a business and how near-term events will affect its performance such as macroeconomics. Numerous investors can choose to think options just add complexity to their basket of investments. However, if you really want to earn big profits and enjoy attractive returns on your investments, then options trading and investments is really the way to go. It is crucial that you learn how to trade options and how to limit your downsides. Fortunately, these are some of the things that you will learn in this bok.

Choosing Options Over Stocks

Leverage

When you buy options, your potential gains are virtually unlimited while any potential losses are limited to your original investment and any additional costs incurred such as the brokerage fees. Therefore, in theory, your potential gains are limitless while losses are capped to the amount paid as premium.

Also, you spend significantly less to invest in stocks through options compared to direct stocks investments. For instance, to buy $10,000 worth of stocks, you will need to fork out at least that much money.

With options, you will pay a tiny fraction of this amount. However, you stand to gain the same returns in both cases.

Fine-tuning Strategies

When you invest your funds in shares, your options are pretty much limited to buying or selling shares. However, with options, it is easy to identify a strategy that does fit your expectations. Stock options can be purchased and exercised in numerous combinations that enable traders to fine-tune strategies so that they can match market conditions whether bearish, bullish, neutral or in-between.

For example, as an options investor, you can opt to select a variety of expiration dates. These can range between about-to-expire monthly options with LEAPS that have close to three years before expiration. It is possible to find a strike that is based on both your risk tolerance and stock performance expectation.

With this approach, you are also able to benefit significantly from high market volatility simply by choosing a strategy that will benefit you from major movements in either direction like the short straddle. Options are also widely used for hedging positions such as the protective put and for managing risk such as with the stock replacement strategy.

Chapter 3) Managing costs

The Bull Put Spread

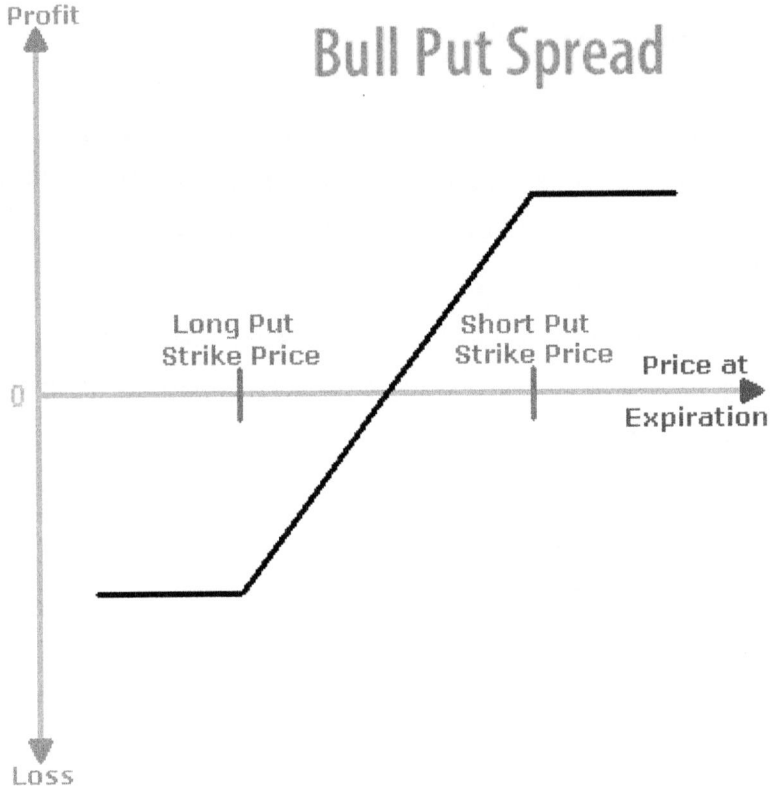

You can apply a variety of strategies when it comes to working in options trading. The first strategy that we will take a look at is the bull put spread. This is considered a directional strategy that you will want to use when a stock is showing signs of reaching its support level and is unlikely to fall down further. When the stock reaches this stage, it is either starting to trade flat, which means that it isn't moving much in either direction, or it is going to rise again.

If you would like to work with a bull put strategy, some of the things that you will need to do include:

Select the stock or the index that fits the criteria for trading on this strategy. This is going to be based on your medium or short-term outlook for that stock.

You will then sell one OTM put option of this stock. Buy one OTM put option that has the same expiry date and the same underlying stock as the put option that you did in the second step, but you will pick a lower strike price.

Once done with the above steps, you should make sure to monitor your position the whole time and then close both the options at the same time once the trade has made a good profit. Alternately, you can choose to hold onto the trade until both of the options reach their expiration, which can help you to get the maximum profit. You will only want to go to the expiration day if you feel confident that the stock does not have any threat of following below the strike price of your higher strike put option ahead of time.

When should I use this strategy?

The first question that you may have about this strategy is when you would choose to use this kind of strategy. You will want to use this kind of spread when you believe that your underlying stock has gotten to a strong support level and there isn't much of a chance that the stock will go down much from that level, at least before the chosen expiration date.

A good time to choose this kind of trade is when the stock has just gone through some expected correction or a profit booking. For example, it may be a strong stock that underwent a decline of about

5%, and then it started to show that it was stabilizing again at the lower level. You do need to make sure that the buying volume and the number of buyers is the same or increasing so that the stock is likely to go back up rather than down. Or you can pick to start trading when a stock is slowly climbing up and it doesn't seem likely that it is going to fall back down in the near-term.

For this strategy, it is preferable for you to trade options that are historically low in volatility. This is a credit spread strategy that will exploit the time-decay. When working with low-volatility stocks, a price fall is only going to be small and this makes it unlikely to overcome the time-decay of the options. Basically, this keeps the trade pretty profitable, even if the stock doesn't move with your expectations. This strategy can sometimes work for the higher-volatility stocks as well if the opportunity presents itself, but this is not always the best choice to go with.

Advantages and disadvantages

The biggest advantage of using the bull put spread strategy is that it will make sure that the time-decay will work in your favor. Even if your stock doesn't go up after it hits the support level and it stays pretty stagnant, you will be able to get some kind of gain because of the time-decay. In addition, if you use this strategy in times of high volatility in the market, any drop is going to act like a catalyst in making the trade profitable at a faster rate.

The biggest disadvantage of using this kind of strategy is that the maximum amount of profit that you are able to earn is less than the potential that you could use if the stock doesn't go the way that you would like and your positions get into losses.

The Iron Condor

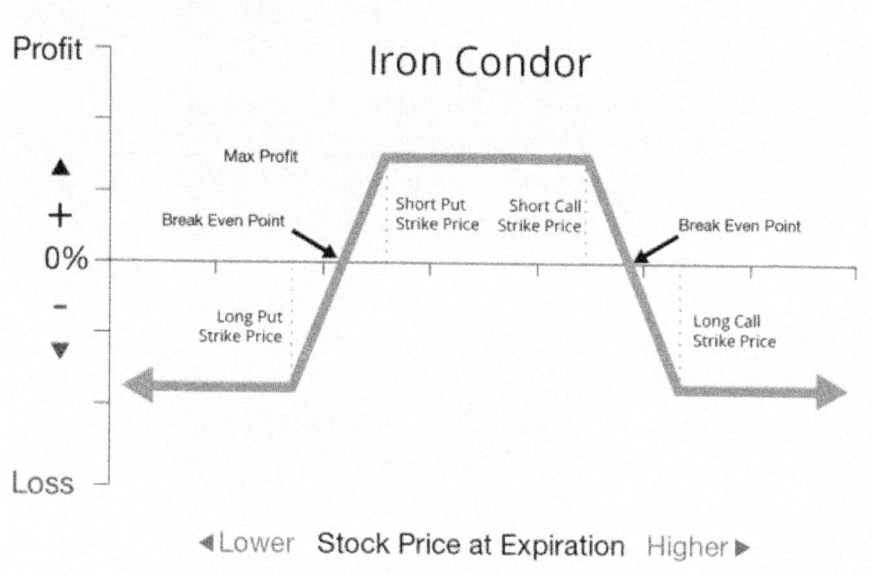

The other strategy that we talked about was directional strategies but the iron condor is going to be a non-directional strategy. This one is going to limit your profit a bit but its probability of success is pretty high for the traders that are able to trade it well. When you are working with an Iron Condor trade, no matter which way the stock or the index ends up moving, the trader is going to become profitable as long as the movement stays inside the boundaries that the trader sets, at the time of expiry. Out of all the strategies that we are going to discuss in this guidebook, this one has the highest potential to give you profits and it has the least amount of risk as well.

You will use the iron condor to trade on stocks with very low volatility. It is not a good idea to go with a stock that moves around quite a bit and has big highs and lows that go all over the place. You will find that this is a credit spread strategy that will be viewed as a combination of the bear call spread (which we talk about in the following chapter) and the bull put spread.

You can consider the iron condor as a type of evergreen strategy, one that a lot of traders are going to use when they find a stable stock. As a trader, if you are able to choose any strategy and you want to go with one that is pretty easy to follow and will give you a higher probability of doing well, then the iron condor is the best option for you to choose.

The iron condor is going to be a little bit more difficult to work with because there are four legs to go with it, rather than the two legs on the other trading strategy. For the first step, you need to go through and find the stock that you would like to work with. Remember that for the iron condor to work, you need to have a stock that is pretty stable and is not going to go up or down too much in the process.

The next step is to sell one deep OTM put option of the stock that you selected. Then buy one OTM put options with the same expiry date and with the same stock that you sold in the first step, but make sure that this one has a lower strike price.

After those steps are done, it is time to sell again. This time you are going to sell a deep OTM but it needs to be a call option. You want this to use the same stock and have the same expiry date as what you used in the last part. And finally, you can buy an OTM call option that has the same stock and the same expiry date as all the other steps, but this one needs to have a slightly higher strike-price.

One thing to note is that there is going to be a difference between the strike prices the two put options need to be the same as the difference between the strikes of the two call options if you want to accurately create this strategy. Throughout the time until the expiry, you will want to monitor how your position is doing. Unless you are certain that your stock is going to keep within the limits that you have placed, you will want to consider exiting out of the trade when the position is making 50% or more of the maximum profit that you want out of this trade. If you find that the market goes against your expectations and there is a big directional movement of your stock, it is time to close out all of the positions and wait until that stock has time to stabilize before entering again.

You would choose to go with this strategy any time that your stock is showing a really low amount of volatility. This means that the stock is not moving much or if it is moving within a range that you are able to define easily. For the most part, index options are going to be the best for executing this strategy compared to stock-based options since these indexes are often less volatile. If you are working with a market that is pretty stable, you will find that iron condors are the safest option for winning.

The biggest advantage of using the iron condor is that it is considered a neutral position and you are likely to get some kind of profit as long as you execute this strategy the right way, no matter which way your chosen stock or index ends up moving. And since this is a net credit strategy, it will be able to help you work against the issues with time decay.

The biggest disadvantage that you are going to find with the iron condor is that the returns that you will get out of it are quite a bit less than what you can get from a directional strategy. In addition, the maximum loss that you can incur is going to be quite a bit more than the maximum profit that you would be able to gain in this position if you are not careful with the stocks that you are using. However, when looking at the statistics for success with the iron condor, you will notice that the probability of a win is going to be much higher than that of a loss, which helps to make this a great strategy to work with.

The Bear Call Spread

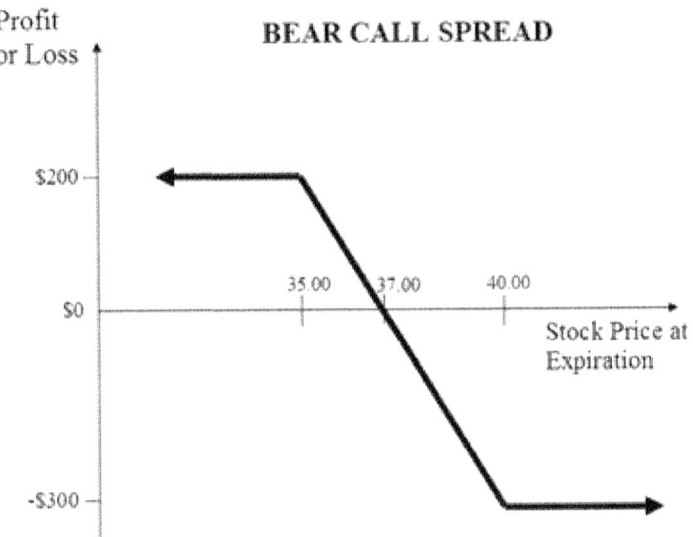

Next on the list is the bear call spread. This is another directional strategy that will be used by a trader when they believe that their underlying stock has reached its upper resistance level and they do not believe that the underlying stock is going to go up much more at this point. They usually believe that the price point of the stock is going to stay flat and not change or it is going to go back down. Basically, this is going to be the opposite strategy that we talked about earlier with the bull put spread.

Like the bull put spread, the bear call spread is also a credit spread. What this means is the premium that you end up receiving while selling one leg of this trade is going to be greater than any premium that you end up paying for the second leg of the trade. You will end up receiving a net credit to your account when you decide to go with this position.

First, create your bear call spread is to select the right stock that fits this kind of strategy. You will find that there are a variety of stocks that you can choose from, but you will need to pick based on your outlook for this kind of index.

Next, you will need to sell an OTM call option of the stock that you selected. And third, you should purchase an OTM call option that has the same expiry date and the same underlying stock as your id with your ATM call option, but the second one needs to have a higher strike price.

Once you enter the market, you will want to constantly monitor your position each day. Once you have made a considerable profit, which is about 50% of your max profit, it is time to exit your position. Or, once you have started to recognize some of the signs of the market and you are sure that the stock is not going to end up reversing, you could wait until the stock reaches its expiry and then take the maximum amount of profit.

Sometime spans are crowned as better for entering a bear call spread than others. You would want to choose the bear call spread any time that you believe that your chosen stock is not likely to rise in price in the near future and that this stock is probably going to decline from its current price rather than go up. This can happen when the stock from a particular company that had big market expectations posted their results and these were way below the expectations of the market. In addition, the index option could hit a big resistance level and this could cause it to go down a bit.

This method is not going to work that well if the stock is really volatile and it has the potential to rise quite a bit over the short term. You want to pick out some options that are not likely to go up anymore. You would then be able to use the bear call spread and make some profit whether the stock stays stagnant or the price goes down.

The maximum profit that you will be able to make with the bear call spread is when at the time of expiry, the stock price is trading below the strike price of the call option that was sold. To get the maximum profit, you will need to take the premium received or selling the lower-strike call option and minus the premium paid for purchasing the higher-strike call option. Then you can multiply both of these by the lot size.

The biggest loss that you would incur with this kind of spread is when at the time of expiry, the stock price is trading above the strike price call option you bought with the higher strike price. This is why you want to make sure that you are picking out stocks that are going to go down or remain steady. If the stock goes up with this option, you will end up losing money in the process. This is why this strategy is a good one to choose if you think that the market is about to go down or you want to work with a stock that is not really increasing at the time.

The biggest advantage of working with the bear call spread is that it is going to ensure that the time-decay is going to work in your favor. As long as you go with a stock that is able to stay below your lower strike-price when the expiry happens, you will get the benefit of keeping your entire credit that you received when you entered into this position and you have the potential to make a good profit.

However, there is a disadvantage of working with this strategy. With this position, if you see that there is the possibility that the stock will make a big movement that goes against your expectations. This means that the stock starts rising in price quickly rather than remaining stagnant or going down as you had predicted. If this does happen, the maximum amount that you could lose can be a lot more than the maximum profit that you might have been able to gain with this strategy so there is some risk.

The Bull Call Spread

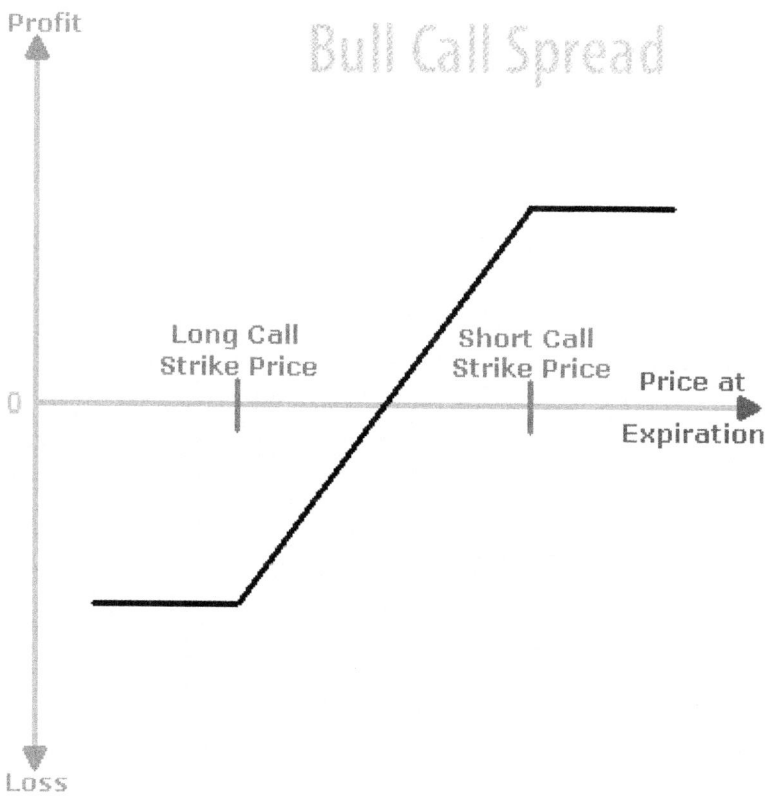

Now we are going to take a look at the bull call spread. This is another directional strategy that you are able to use any time that you have a positive outlook on your stock and you think that it is going to have a moderate rise in the short-term. As you will find with any of the other strategies that are spread based, both the potential losses and profits are going to be capped when using the bull call spread. However, the best advantage of using this spread is that the maximum amount of profit that you will be able to gain from this strategy will exceed the maximum amount of loss that you may incur.

The bull call spread is a bit different than the other strategies that we looked at because it is considered a debit spread. This means that you must pay what is known as a net debit to enter the position. This spread, as well as the bear put spread that we will talk about next, are the two strategies that you can choose that provide a high percentage of returns because they can be used to capitalize the momentum of the market while still making sure that the risk is as low as possible.

How can you get started with this strategy? First, you will want to pick out the stock that will meet all the criteria that you need to trade successfully with this strategy. Once you have chosen the strategy, you need to make a purchase of one slightly OTM call option.

Next, you need to sell one OTM call option, but make sure that this call option has a strike price that is about one or two strikes higher than the option that you originally purchased. Both need to have the same expiry date and they need to be using the same stock.

After you have made both of the purchases that you would like, you need to make sure that you monitor your position and watch what the market is doing. It is a good idea to close up the position as soon as the trade has provided you with a good amount of profit. This is going to be when the profit reaches about 30-40%of the maximum amount that you can make on this trade.

You may be wondering when you should choose to use this kind of strategy when it comes to options trading. You will want to trade using the bull call spread whenever the market has a good outlook on whatever your chosen stock is. For example, if the stock of a company has received some positive news, like a good strategic move by the company, good earnings result, or some other news that would increase the growth of the stock.

You can also choose to work with the bull call spread on stocks that have been overcorrected and then have started showing strong signs of reversing. One thing to notice with this strategy is that since it works as a debit strategy, the time-decay is going to end up working against you. the decay will be much slower compared to working with a naked long call position, but the time-decay is not going to work as well as it did with the other options. This means that it is not the best idea to hold onto this spread for more than two or three weeks unless you see that the position keeps on gaining after the two weeks and that it is gaining a lot more than you expected.

If you enter this trade and notice that there really isn't any momentum for the two weeks or more, it is best to exit out of the trade. You may end up taking a small loss when doing it, but at least you are able to free up your capital to use on other trades and you won't have to worry about losing more money out of the profit.

The main advantage of using this type of strategy is that there is a good ratio for your reward to risk and even a moderate move up in your stock could help you to make some good profits. You are also able to increase your potential for profits by widening up your spread, which means that you would increase the strike prices between your two options. You can also choose to reduce your risk a bit more by decreasing how many strike prices are between the two options. The method that you choose is going to depend on how much risk you would like to take and how favorable the market is.

You have to remember that you have to work against the time decay when you are working with this strategy. Despite the limited amount of loss potential with this strategy, if you are working with a stock that stays stagnant for a long time, the position will lose you money.

The Long Straddle/Strangle Strategy

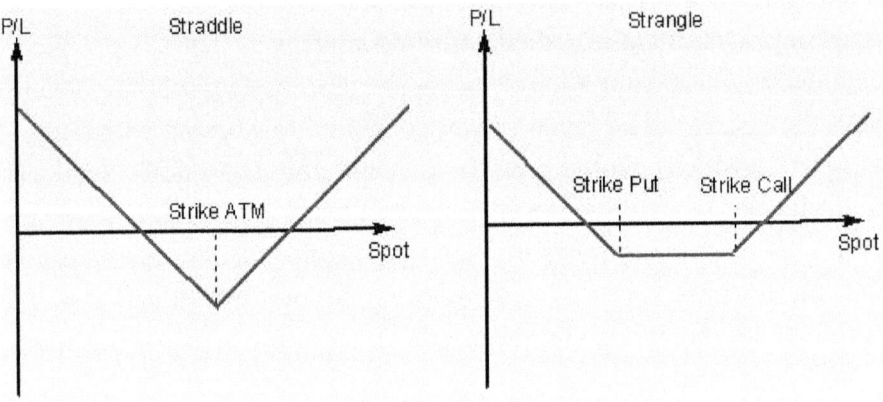

Another strategy that you can work with is the long straddle and strangles strategy. This strategy is nice because it has the potential to make the trader unlimited amounts of profit but there is a limited amount of risk. You have to make sure that you are picking the right kind of stock to make this strategy work. For example, this is a good strategy to work with if you feel your chosen stock is going to deal with a lot of volatility in the near future.

Compared to the other strategies that we have talked about so far in this guidebook, the long straddle is considered one of the riskiest strategies and you will only want to work with it if you feel the movement in your stock or your index is going to be pretty big over the near future.

However, even though there is some risk that comes with this strategy, it does have the potential to help you earn the maximum amount of profits compared to some of the other strategies as well. This is because there isn't an upper limit on the amount of profit that you are able to make when you are working with the long straddle while the other strategies will have a limit on the profit.

There is also the long strangle. This one is similar to the long straddle but there are some modifications that make it slightly different. We will discuss the long strangle a bit more later on.

So, to execute the long straddle is going to be a bit different than what you were able to do with some of the other strategies that we have talked about. First, pick out the stock that you would like to do. To see success, you need to pick out a stock that is going to show a lot of volatility along the way in the near future, or you are not going to get good results.

After you have chosen the stock that you want to work with, you need to purchase an ATM call option of this stock. Then you need to purchase an ATM put option that has the same stock and the same expiry date as the call option that you purchased in the previous step.

When you complete the purchases, you will want to watch your trade pretty closely. When you see the large price movement that you were watching out for, it is time to close the legs at the same time. This is another strategy that is going to have to fight against the time decay issue and this time decay is going to impact both options, so it is best to not hold onto this kind of strategy for over a few days.

One thing to note is that the strike prices of both your put and your call options need to be the same when doing the straddle trade. This can be difficult to do when entering into a trade though and you may not be able to purchase the options when the market price of the stock isn't matching up to your chosen strike price. When doing this trade, you may find that the market price of your chosen stock might end up being slightly above or below the chosen strike price of your option. This implies that you have a likelihood of ending up with one option that is slightly OTM and the other one ends up being slightly ITM when you initiate this kind of trade. This is fine as long as you keep them as close to ATM as possible.

The long straddle and strangle is a strategy that you are only supposed to use on rare occasions and only when you think that there is going to be a sudden and big rise or fall in the stock you want to choose, usually following some external factor. Even in this kind of trade, when you enter into the long straddle position, you want to make sure that the volatile still isn't too high. Most traders are going to stick with a stock or an index that is less than 60%of historical volatility. The reason that you want to be careful with this is because if there is a big drop in the volatility of the stock, even after the price movement goes the way that you want, this drop-in volatility is going to end up harming how much profit you can make.

Ideally, the long straddle can be traded when there is a big decision making or policy change in the company, especially one that will have a big impact on the stock for that company and that could cause it to fall or rise really quickly over a few days. Some of the situations that may result in conditions being right for the long straddle include:

- The quarterly or annual results from a company will come out in the next few days and people have some big expectations from these.

- A big decision regarding the company that owns the stocks is going to come out soon. This could include a decision for the company to change their management or to do a merger with another company.

- A big announcement that will talk about a large dividend or a bonus issue is going to come out soon.

If you are working with a benchmark index, there are many situations that could make it rise or fall. Some of these would include the announcements of the annual budget for the company, when the company is going to make some new monetary policy decision when there are some major elections in the management of the company, and even some major socio-economic decisions. If you see that any of these are going to happen with the underlying stock, it may be time to work with this position.

On the other hand, if you see that your chosen stock is trading on a pretty narrow range, or if you feel that the outlook on that stock is pretty neutral (without much movement even if it is negative or positive) over the short-term, then the long straddle strategy is not the right one for you. It should also be a strategy that you avoid if the volatility is high, even if there is some potential for movement.

When you get into the long straddle position, it is a good idea to exit this position once you see that there is a big rise or fall in your position and you are gaining profit. It is common for many people to stay into the market too long with this strategy and if you hold onto that position too long, you could end up losing any profits that you earn, thanks to the potential of a drop in volatility or because of the time decay issue.

The primary advantage that you are going to see when working with the long straddle is that you do have the potential to earn unlimited profits as soon as the trade crosses pass the break-even point, no matter what direction it goes in. the straddle is often used to earn profits even when a stock is volatile in the market without having to worry about predicting which direction that the stock will move in and for how long. Volatile stocks often go up and down pretty quickly and it is hard to figure out which way you should go. With this strategy, you will have the opportunity to profit from a rise and a fall of your stock based on the points that you pick.

Another benefit that you can find with the straddle position is that it will limit how much risk that you are exposed to. The amount of risk that you will face is the total amount of premium that you paid when you decided to enter into the trade with this stock.

The biggest disadvantage that comes with using the long straddle is that you will have to deal with the time decay issue. In fact, the time decay issue could affect both sides of your straddle trade, the call and the put, so this issue is compounded and can cause you more issues than you would have with other strategies.

Another disadvantage of using this kind of position to earn a profit is that it can be a bit difficult. In order to earn a profit, you need to properly predict that your chosen stock is going to have a very sharp movement, either up or down, in a pretty short amount of time.

The long strangle

Before we take a look at how to make this strategy work, we also need to take a look at what the long strangle is all about. This strategy is very similar to the long straddle but instead of purchasing an ATM call and put with the same strike price, the trader will choose to purchase a slightly OTM put and call for the same stock and the same expiration date.

The advantage of going with this long strangle rather than the long straddle, is that the amount of premium that you will have to pay for your premiums will be less than what you have to pay with the long straddle. However, for the long strangle to work, you are going to need the move in the market to be much bigger in order to recover your costs.

Traders are going to profit using the long strangle any time that they see a sharp move in their stock, similar to using the long straddle position, and you still have a potential to make unlimited profits. However, with this strategy, the maximum loss is going to happen if the price of the stock settles between the strike price for the call and the put when you reach the time of expiry. The maximum loss though, in both the straddle and the strangle, will be the premiums that you paid for the put and the call options.

The Bear Put Spread

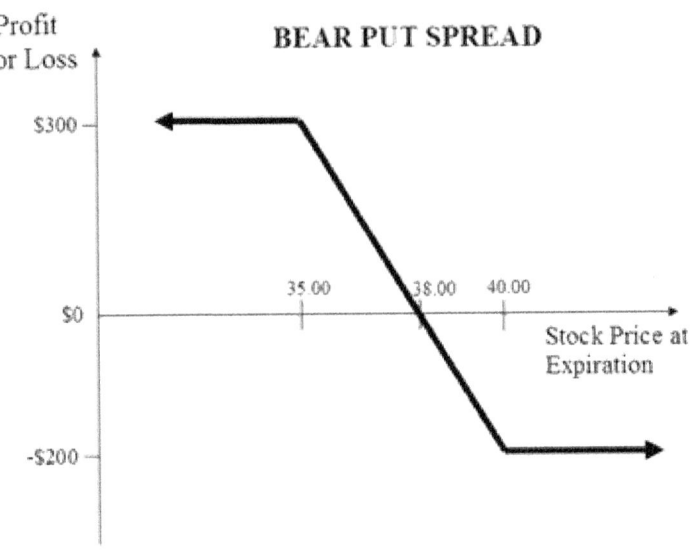

So far, this guidebook has spent some time talking about quite a few of the strategies that you are able to use in order to be successful when it comes to options trading. The next one that we are going to discuss is the bear put spread. This is another directional strategy that you will want to employ any time that you have a negative outlook on your chosen stock. This means that you are taking a look at a stock and you expect that in the near future, it is going to fall moderately. This is another debit spread; just like the bull call spread that we discussed earlier, which means that you will be in charge of paying a debit in order to enter into the position.

To get started with this kind of strategy, you will want to pick out the right stock that will fit into the criteria that are needed for this strategy. Remember that for this strategy, you want to have a negative outlook on the chosen stock. You want a stock that is going to go down for some reason, whether you have heard some bad news about the stock or there is something else that is going to bring the value of your stock down.

After you have been able to pick out the right stock, you will need to purchase one slightly OTM put option. You will also want to sell one OTM put option, making sure that the strike price ends up being about one or two strikes lower than the option that you purchased in the first step. Additionally, ensure that you are picking out ones that have the same stock and the same expiry date as what you did with the first step.

Once you are done with all of these trades, you want to make sure that you monitor your position and watch what is going on. You will then want to get out of both positions once they have helped you to receive significant profit, which is about 30-40%of the maximum potential profit.

This one is going to work similar to what you were able to do with the bull call spread. If you decide to increase the spread, you are going to increase how much potential profit you are able to make, but it also increases the risks that you are dealing with. In addition, you can choose to decrease the spread, the risk will also decrease, but you would also limit how much profit you could potentially make on the trade.

There are a few times when you will choose to trade using the bear put spread. You will want to go with this kind of strategy when the market has a pretty negative outlook on the stock that you want to use. This is usually going to happen when some development occurs, such as the company not making the earnings that it should or the organization has made some new changes or decisions that the investors did not look at favorably.

Some people choose to trade with this kind of strategy when the company is part of or is selling under pressure. They do not want to sell but there is something that is going on that will make them feel like they do need to sell. For example, there may be some environment or market conditions that are unfavorable to the company that surfaced and is changing the company.

Remember that since the bear put spread is considered a debit spread strategy, you will have to work with the time-decay and it is going to go against your overall position, even though this kind of decay is considered a lot of slower than what will happen with a naked long put position.

When it comes to the disadvantages and advantages, this spread is going to end up being pretty similar to the bull call spread. The primary advantage that comes with this trade is that the ratio for risk and reward is pretty good and even a moderate decrease in a stock can still help you to earn some good profits.

You will also be able to increase the amount of profit that you could potentially make by widening up the spread. To do this, you will want to increase the strike price that happens between your two options. You can also choose to reduce your risk in order to help you out as a beginner and to do this you will decrease the spread. In order to decrease the risk, you will want to decrease the number of strike prices that are going on between the two options.

The biggest disadvantage that comes with this strategy is dealing with the time decay that will work against the position. And while there is a limited amount of potential loss, if the stock ends up staying stagnant for a long period of time, the position is going to end up with a loss.

Chapter 4) Strategies and analysis

There are a lot of different market conditions that you could work with when you end up trading in options. Sometimes the market will rise a little or a lot, sometimes they will stay steady, and sometimes they will fall a little or a lot. And with options trading, you are able to make money on all of these conditions if you use the right strategy. This chapter is going to spend some time talking about the different strategies that you can use in many different market conditions to help you make a profit no matter what!

Strategies to use in every market

As a beginner, there are a lot of different strategies that are out there that you are able to keep track of and use the way that you want. But all of this information can be a bit confusing when you first get started out. To keep things a bit easier, we are going to take a look at some of the market scenarios that you may run into overtime and how you can pick out the right strategies that will handle these markets and still be successful.

Securities price rises a bit

The first thing that we are going to look at is if the price of your security ends up raising a little bit. There are a few options for strategies that are going to work here including the short put; the bull put spread, and the bull call spread. First is the bull call spread. The advantage of using this strategy is that you are able to reduce some of the costs that you pay upfront but the downside is that there are some limitations on your profits if the asset ends up rising quite a bit.

You can also work with the bull put spread. This one is similar, but you will write the puts on the asset while also buying this amount of puts. The good thing about this one is that you will still make a profit even if your asset doesn't rise during that time, but if the asset does see a significant increase in price during that time; your profits will be limited.

And you can choose to work with a short put. This is simply a sell to open order where you will write the puts on the asset you think will see an increase in price. The best move to do with this one is to write close to the money put options that are going to end up expiring soon. With this strategy, you get the benefit of using one that is simple but if the asset ends up going down quite a bit in price, you would lose out on your money as well.

Securities price falls a little bit

If there is something going on in the market and you think that the price is going to fall a bit, there are going to be three strategies that you can pick as well including the short call, the bear call spread, and the bear put spread. With the bear put spread, you get the advantage of having a cheaper option compared to just purchasing a put, but the profits are going to see some limitations if the security ends up falling quite a bit, instead of a little.

You can also work with the bear call spread. With this one, you would write out calls and then purchase calls that have the same asset with the same expiration date, but the ones that you end up purchasing should have a higher strike price. This is an option that is usually saved for some of the more advanced traders because it is difficult and if your asset falls quite a bit in that time, your profits will be limited.

The good news is that if the security doesn't end up moving at all, you will still make a profit.

The short call will be an option that you can choose as well. This is going to consist of the trader writing out call options at or near the money, using an order that is known as sell to open. Ideally, for this to work, the options should expire soon. With this one, even if your asset doesn't seem to move, you are still able to get a return, but you will lose out if the price goes down quite a bit.

Security goes up a lot

If you think that your security is going to see a dramatic increase in price soon, there are a few strategies that you are able to use including the short bull ratio spread and the long call. The long call is basically just a buy to open order to purchase calls. The advantage of going with this one is that you do have limitless profits if the price does go up quite a bit on your security. On the other hand, if the security doesn't change in price or if it ends up going down, you have nothing to protect you in this scenario.

The other option to go with is the bull ratio spread and it is usually another one that will be reserved for traders who have been doing this for a bit. With this kind of strategy, you would need to buy and write calls of the same asset that will expire at the same time. You will be in charge of buying more options that you write. The biggest advantage of this one is that you will have some protection if the asset price does start to fall or doesn't move at all, but it won't provide you with the same profit possibilities as some others.

Security prices go down a lot

If you are working with a security and you think that the price is going to go down quite a bit, it is possible to work on a long put or a short bear ratio spread to help you out. The long put is pretty simple and it is a good option for beginners. To start with this, you would need to work with your broker to use a buy to open order and then you would buy a put option on your asset. It is always best to buy at the money contracts, which basically means that the strike price is going to be the same as the market price. This helps you to keep a better handle on the risk that is going to be involved. If you feel that the security will fall soon, you can pick out a contract that has a close expiration date. The downside to this option is that if the price ends up rising or doesn't move during your time, you will not get the protection you need to cut your losses.

The other option is to choose a short bear ratio spread and it is a bit more complex. You will buy puts and write puts at the same time and they will have the same asset and the same expiration date, but you need to make sure that your written puts come in at a higher strike price and you must purchase more contracts than you end up selling. This helps you get protection if the security ends up staying constant or goes up, though you do end up with fewer profits compared to the other strategy.

Security rises to a certain number

If you have a number in mind that your security will get to and you think that it will reach that place within a certain amount of time, there are a few strategies to work with including the bull condor spread and the bull butterfly spread. With the bull butterfly spread, you will conduct three transactions, which is why it is considered more advanced. You will write calls that have the strike price of what you think the asset price will be when it expires. For each two calls that you write, you will need to purchase one call that is the next lowest strike price and then purchase another call that is at the next highest strike price. There can be a lot of profit from this option, but there are no limits to the potential losses.

If you want to get even more complex, you can use the bull condor spread that has four transactions. With this one, you will write calls with each strike price on the lower end of the price range that you want the asset to rise to, while also writing a few calls on the higher end. You can also buy calls at the higher and the lower strike price. The strategy can be great for profits, but since there are so many transactions in the process, remember that you will have to pay your broker more to complete this.

Security falls to a specific number

For this one, you believe that the asset you will invest in is going to fall down to a specific number. The best choice to do with this one is the bear butterfly spread, but there are going to be three transactions that have to occur for it to be effective. You will write the put options at whatever price you think the asset is going to fall to, and then, for every two puts that you end up writing, you are also going to purchase two put options. One of these needs to be a higher strike price and the other should be lower with them both expiring at the same time. The advantage of doing this one is that you won't end up losing as much money if the asset doesn't move in price the way that you would like. However, commissions can add up because you are ordering three different transactions.

The security moves up or down in price

Sometimes the market may be a little volatile and you are not sure if it will see a rise or fall in price, but you are fairly certain that it is going to go one way or the other in a big way. There are a few strategies that work well with this one including the short butterfly spread, long gut, long strangle, and the long straddle depending on what you would like to see happen.

Using a long straddle can be good because you can increase your potential for how much profit you are able to make; however, if there isn't a big change in your asset, you are going to experience some losses. The long strangle is going to be cheaper than the other option, but you do need to see a larger change in the asset price for it to do you any good.

You can also choose to work with the long gut if you are a beginner because it will involve buying in the money call options while also purchasing in the money put options. All the things that you purchase should end up with the same expiration date and you should end up with the same amount of call and put options when you are done. If you think that the asset will move soon, you want to pick out options that have a short expiration date.

If you are a more experienced trader, the short butterfly spread can be a good option for you. There will be three separate transactions for this one including selling in the money calls, selling the same amount of out of the money calls, and buying twice as many at the money calls. All of these options need to end up with the same expiration date. For the strike prices, you're out of the money calls should end up proportional to the amount that your money calls at in the money. If you are with a strike price that is pretty close to the asset price, the asset won't need to see much movement for you to see a profit, but the profit will be smaller.

Security doesn't see a price change

And finally, what are you going to do if your asset ends up not moving at all. Luckily, you can try out a few different strategies to make this one work include the butterfly spreading, short strangling, and the short straddle. The short straddle is going to be a higher level of trading because it involves using a sell to open order so that you can write at the money calls and then you have to do the same number of puts on that asset. Both should end up with the same expiration date if possible.

With the short strangle, you will need to write call options as well as the equal number of puts. They need to be out of the money. If you go with contracts that are considered really out of the money, the price of the asset will need to have a huge amount of movement before you would lose anything. And if you go with shorter term expiration for the options, it means that you will have a better chance of receiving a profit from this.

Most beginners are not going to choose the butterfly spread on this one because it is going to be difficult and more expensive than the other options. It does have a lower upfront cost, but there are quite a few transactions to make it happen and the commissions are going to add up quickly.

Option Trading Strategies

No matter what type of investment you choose to work with, there are always going to be some risks that come with it. One of the best ways that you can ensure that you reduce those risks is to find a good strategy that will help you to pick out the right options and earn money in the process. Many beginner investors who do poorly will often fail because they either didn't pick out an investment strategy in the beginning, or they didn't understand and use that strategy in the proper way.

Often, picking out a strategy is going to help you to choose which options to go with because all the strategies won't work with all of the options. The right strategy can also help with determining how much risk you are willing to take on when you first get started. This is why it is so important to pick out a good investment strategy right in the beginning before you even talk to your broker or pick out any options to trade in.

So, at this point, you are probably curious as to which options you should work with to see a good profit. Some of the best options trading strategies that you can pick include:

Covered call

This strategy is going to involve actually going in and purchasing the assets. Once you own the assets, you would write out a call option for them. This is a good strategy to use when the trader wants to earn some profits from their call premium, while also being able to protect against the possibility of the asset losing some value. With this one, if the volatility increases, the trader stands to lose, but if the volatility decreases, the trader stands to gain.

Naked call

This is a riskier strategy to work with so if you are just getting started and want to keep your risks pretty low, this is probably not the best option for you to choose. With this option, the trader is going to sell a call option on the open market, but they don't really own this asset. It can cause you to lose a lot of money if the trade doesn't work out, but there are a lot of gains as well if it is done in the proper way.

Married Put

This one is going to be a bit different because you will do a combination of the two above to help protect yourself. In this kind of option, the investor will make the purchase of the asset they want to use while also doing a put option for them. This is a good choice to go with because it will protect them against any short-term losses that may occur.

Bull call spread

Another strategy that an options investor can choose is the bull call spread. With this particular strategy, the trader is going to buy call options once a specific strike price is reached. Then when that strike price gets a bit higher (they will need to choose the right strike price that they want to use here), the trader will turn around and see the option and make a profit on the difference. This is a good strategy to go with any time a trader is looking at an option and thinks that the asset may soon go up a bit in the near future so they can make a profit from this.

Bear put spread

You can also work with the strategy that is known as the bear put spread. This one is similar to what we say with the bull call spread, but a bit different because it goes the opposite way. This particular strategy is going to involve making a purchase of a put option instead of at a certain strike price. Then when the strike price goes lower, they will sell the option. This is a strategy the trader would work with any time that they think the price of the asset is going to go down. They can still make a profit from this as long as the price of the asset goes down. If it goes up, they stand to lose.

Protective collar

The next strategy that can be used is known as a protective collar. For this one, the trader is going to purchase an out of the money put option and then at the same time they will write an out of the money call option. This strategy is one that the trader will use when they see that the long position they have chosen is doing well. The protective collar is going to allow the trader to lock in the profits that they want without needing to sell the asset's shares in the process.

Long straddle

The long straddle strategy is one where the trader is going to pick out an option that they like and then they will buy a put and a call of this asset. Both orders are going to work on the same expiration date and strike price. This is the strategy that you would want to use when the trader knows that the price of their asset will make a dramatic move sometime in the future, but they may be uncertain about which way the move is going to occur. This allows the trader to make money no matter which way the trade ends up going.

Long strangle

This one may look similar to the option that we had before, but there are a few differences that will make it unique. One difference is that while the put and the call options are going to still be the same asset and will use the same expiration date, they will come in with different strike prices. The price that is used with the call option will usually end up higher than the price of the put strike, but both of them are going to be out of the money. This option is often less expensive compared to the long straddle, but it is a choice to go with when you think the price of the asset is going to move up or down quite a bit soon.

Butterfly spread

This one is going to be kind of a combination of a few strategies and you may recognize a few points from the bear spread and bull spread that we talked about earlier, which makes this one a bit more complicated. One method is going to purchase a call option at the strike price that is as low as possible while, at the same time, selling two of your call options at a much higher strike price. Another option is to sell another call option that has a higher strike price compared to the other two calls.

Iron Condor

For this strategy, the trader is allowed to hold the short and the long position at the exact same time, but there has to be two strangles that are separate. It is a good way to get started with selling your options because you won't be able to experience a loss on both sides when you do this trade. This means that you will only lose on one side while you win on the other and this is a great way to get into the market.

Iron butterfly

This is a good strategy to go with as a trader when you want to have control over limiting your profits and losses within a range that you get to specify. To help cut your losses and make sure that you are limiting your risks, the trader will use what is known as an out of the money option. To work with this strategy, the trader is going to combine together either a long or short straddle with a purchase or they will do a sale of a strangle at the same time. This one is a bit different than the butterfly spread we just talked about because it will use both puts and calls.

Chapter 5) Creating an options trading Plan

Now that we have taken some time to learn more about options and the benefits of trading in them, it is time to get started on the actual process of trading with them. We will make this easier by breaking things down into steps so that it is easier to understand. Sometimes as a beginner it is confusing to know where you should begin or what steps to take, so we are going to try to make this as easy as possible so you can be successful right from the beginning.

Getting ready

Before you start with the actual process of trading, there are a few steps that you can take first. You need to have a good understanding of some of the basics, which we have covered a bit, such as the types of options available. The more information you have about options and what they are, the more prepared you will be to begin this journey.

Once you are pretty certain that you have a good grasp on trading and what comes with options, it is a good idea to think about why you want to go into trading? How much money would you like to make and what other goals are important to you during this time? It is always a good idea to be precise in your goals because you can develop your strategy around this. It also helps to break frustration and overspending from the start.

But the most important thing that you can do in this first step is to make sure that you create what is known as a trading plan. This is basically a plan that lists out everything that you want to accomplish such as your expectations, goals, and the guidelines that you will follow with your strategy. Those who don't go into this with a plan are the ones who add a lot of risk to the whole process.

Getting a broker

The second step is to find a good broker to work with. The broker is the person who, at your request, will make the actual trades. Remember that they will require some fees and a commission for the work that they do, so factor this in when figuring out the costs of getting started with options. Do some research on the broker that you would like to work with? There are some that will offer their services at a discount, but you have to determine if they are a good choice for you or not.

When you first get started with your new broker, they will probably sit down and discuss some of the things that they like to do with trading and they will go over a risk assessment with you since you are a new customer. This risk assessment is when the broker will figure out how much risk you will feel comfortable with based on your investment and financial history, and then they can assign you a trading level to keep you safe. This is a good place to start to develop your strategy and will help the broker to provide you with the best services possible.

Choosing your underlying assets

Since a contract with options is going to be a derivative of other securities, there are quite a few that you will be able to pick from. You are able to purchase and sell options contracts of things such as stocks, bonds, foreign currencies, commodities and so much more. This is great news because it allows you to work with what you are comfortable with and will give you a lot of flexibility in the process.

The key point here is to do your research before entering the market because it is never a good idea to just pick out a bunch of options that you have no idea about simply because you can.

Managing your money and your risk

The next thing that you need to consider when you get started with options trading is to know how you can manage your risk and your money. Like any type of trading, options are known to be risky and if you just jump in without a plan and you aren't careful, it is possible for you to lose a lot of money. When you are creating your own trading plan, it should include some guidelines on the amount of risk that you will take depending on the money amount that you are using.

Get this kind of plan in place right from the beginning and keep it there. Having this plan in place is going to help keep your emotions out of the game; if emotions get into the game, you may as well give up now because you will make bad decisions that will lose you a lot of money. This is true whether the emotions are excitement, greed, nervousness, or something else.

Before you make any decisions with trading, take a breath, look over your plan, and then make the decision that will stay closest to that plan. If you follow that good feeling that you have about a trade, you will often take on more risk and it could be disastrous.

One way to help you keep better hold on your risk and money is to use what is known as an option spread. This is when you will combine more than one position on your contract on the same security. This way no matter which way the market goes, you will end up making some money off the process rather than losing out.

Diversifying

Another thing that you need to work on when you enter the stock market is diversifying. This makes a lot of sense and is actually one of the best ways to limit how much risk you are taking on. There are some choices that you can make when it comes to diversifying in options trading. You can choose to work on a variety of strategies, pick out different securities, work on different orders, and even invest in different types of options.

Position sizing

This step sounds kind of fancy, but it is pretty simple. All that it means is that you will decide how much money, or how much of the capital that you are using, that you want to spend on taking a certain position while trading. It is similar to diversifying because you probably don't want to spend all of your money sitting in one position. When you stay in control of your capital, you are able to control your losses better and it is easier to protect yourself from big losses.

Planning out the trades

Once you have finished out some of the other steps, it is time to get with your broker and start options trading. Some of the steps that you need to do for this part include:

- Forecasting: in this step, you need to make predictions about what will happen with the security, such as whether it is going to rise or fall. Having this forecast is going to determine the strategy that you will use and the options that will fit into that strategy.

- Setting goals: in this step, you will have to decide what your goals are. You can ask yourself some questions for this one, such as how much you would like to make off the trade? This can help you determine whether or not the trade was successful when it is all done.

- Choose the right strategies: there are a lot of great options trading strategies that you can choose and we will discuss them a bit more lately. But having a good strategy in place is going to help you be successful. Before you contact the broker about making a trade, you need to choose what strategy you would like to use.

- Choose your position sizing: this is going to be the basic decision of how much money you would like to put into each option so that you have a good idea of the risks ahead of time.

Making the trades

Once the other steps are done, it is time for you to contact your broker and work with them to place the orders that you want to work with. You should have already set up the funds with the broker, so it won't be too hard to get the orders going quickly. This is the point where you are entering into a trade and you should also spend some time writing out what circumstances need to happen when you want to exit the trade. Will you keep going until the contracts expire? Will you close them early when you receive certain information? Or is there some other determining factor about when you will exit? This is important because it helps you to have a good strategy for all parts of your trading.

Monitoring the trades

After you place your orders and the broker has been able to make the trades for you, there are a few other things that you will need to do. it is not enough to just put in the money and hope that things go well. Instead, you need to spend your time monitoring the trades as they are in progress. What this means is that you have to keep good records about what is going on throughout time with your security so you can make good decisions about holding onto this option or whether it is time to close it or not. The choices that you will make during this particular stage will depend on whether you lose money or make a profit on the options that you chose.

And that is basically all that it takes to get into the options trading and start making the money that you want in the process. If you pick out a good trading strategy and a good process to work with along the way, this process can yield you a good return on investment without having to put in as much work as you find with the stock market. It can still be hard to do sometimes, but as you get better at your strategy and work hard to learn how this market works, you can make some good money in the process.

Chapter 6) Common pitfalls for beginners and how to avoid them

Inexperienced traders are often warned away from purchasing options that are out of the money as being a greater risk than the ultimate reward is likely to be. While it is true that a short expiration time coupled with an out of the money option will frequently look appealing, especially to those with a smaller amount of trading capital to work with, the issue is that all of these types of options are likely to look equally appealing which leaves them with no way to tell the good from the bad. As a more experienced trader, however, you have many more tools at your disposal than the average novice which means that, while risky, cheap options have the potential to generate substantial returns, as long as you keep the following in mind while trading them.

Mishandling early assignment: Early assignment occurs when a holder exercises an option that you are the writer upon much early that you had anticipated, and at terms that are much less favorable than you had initially hoped. If this happens, it can be easy to become flustered and simply sell as requested, taking a loss in the process. Instead, it is important to consider all the possible options, including purchasing another option for the express purpose of selling it, to ensure that you mitigate the extra costs as completely as possible.

Ignoring the statistics behind options trading: One of the biggest mistakes that most newbie options traders make is that they forget the probability is a real thing. When you check a potential stock before purchasing an option, it's important to understand that the history of an option is important when deciding whether or not you should be investing in it, but so are the odds and probability surrounding whether or not a particular event is going to occur.

For example, a common strategy that investors use is to leverage their money by investing in cheap options so that this will help to prevent big losses on a stock that they actually own shares of. Of course, this is a good strategy, but nothing works one-hundred percent of the time. Make sure that if the rules of probability and simple ratios are telling you to stay away from a deal, you listen to the facts that are staring you in the face. Wishful thinking will come to bite you later on.

Being overzealous: Oftentimes when new options traders finally get their initial plan just right, they become overzealous and start committing to larger trades than they can realistically afford to recover from if things go poorly. It is important to take it slow when it comes to building your rate of return and never bet more than you can afford to lose. Regardless of how promising a specific trade might seem, there is not risk/reward level at which it is worth considering a loss that will take you out of the game completely for an extended period of time. Trade reasonably and trade regularly and you will see greater results in the long term guaranteed.

Not being adaptable: The successful options trades know when to follow their plans but they also know that no plan will be the right choice, even if early indicators say otherwise. There is a difference between making a point of sticking to a plan and following it blindly and knowing which is which one of the more important indicators of the separation is between options trading success and abject failure. This means it is important to be aware of when and where experimentation and new ideas are appropriate and when it is best to toe the line and gather more data in order to make a well-reasoned decision.

This also means having several different plans in your options trading tool box and not just resolutely sticking to the first one that brings you a modicum of success. This is crucial as there are certain plans that will only work in specific situations and knowing which to use when, in real time, will lead to significantly greater returns on a more reliable basis every single time.

Likewise, an adaptive options trader knows that market conditions can change unexpectedly and is prepared to respond accordingly. This means understanding when the time is right to go in a new direction, regardless of the potential risks that doing so might entail. Sometimes a good trader has to make a leap of faith, and a trader who is successful in the long term knows what signs to look for that indicate this type of scenario is occurring in real time. Unfortunately, this type of foresight cannot be taught, and instead must be found with experience.

As long as you keep the appropriate mindset regarding individual trades, any new strategy that is attempted will result in valuable data, if nothing else. It is important to understand that learning not to use a specific course of action a second time is always valuable, no matter the costs.

Ignoring the probability: Always remember that the historical data will not apply to the current trends in the market at all times which means you will always want to consider the probability as well as the odds that the market is going to behave the way it typically does. The odds are how likely the market is to behave as expected and the probability is the ratio of the likelihood of a given outcome. Understanding the probability of certain outcomes can make it easy to purchase the proper options to minimize losses related to holdings of specific underlying stocks. When purchasing cheap options, it is important to remember that they are always going to be cheap for a reason as price is determined by strike price of the underlying stock as well as the amount of time remaining for the option to regain its value, choose wisely otherwise you are doing little more than gambling and there are certainly better ways to gamble than via options trading.

Letting the opinions of other influence your trading: While every day trader is going to have opinions regarding the best way to trade this type of stock or when to use that indicator, the best day traders tend to avoid this advice like the plague and instead work out their own. The only thing you really need to focus on in order to make the right types of trades in the right timeframes is math and anything else is only going to get in the way. Keep in mind that you want to analyze and observe economic and political events not get caught up in them.

Not dealing with short options properly: While, in theory, it might seem like buying back short options at the last moment is the best choice, this practice is sure to hurt your more than help you in the long run. It may be tempting to hold onto profitable options in order to squeeze the maximum return out of each investment but you need to be aware that the potential for a reversal is always lurking in the shadows. Instead, a good rule of thumb is to buy back options that are currently at 80 percent of your ideal return or higher and let the extra take care of itself. While it may hurt to leave some potential profit on the table, it will improve your overall reliability, netting you a profit in the long run.

Not considering exotic options: An exotic option is one that has a basic structure that differs from either European or American options when it comes to the how and when of how the payout will be provided or how the option relates to the underlying asset in question. Additionally, the number of potential underlying assets is going to be much more varied and can include things like what the weather is like or how much rainfall a given area has experienced. Due to the customization options and the complexity of exotic options, they are only traded over-the-counter.

While they are undoubtedly more complex to get involved with, exotic options also offer up several additional advantages when compared to common options including:

- They are a better choice for those with very specific needs when it comes to risk management.

- They offer up a variety of unique risk dimensions when it comes to both management and trading.

- They offer a far larger range of potential investments that can more easily meet a diverse number of portfolio needs.

- They are often cheaper than traditional options.

They also have additional drawbacks, the biggest of which is that they cannot often be priced correctly using standard pricing formulas. This may work as a benefit instead of a drawback; however, depending on if the mispricing falls in the favor of the trader or the writer. It is also important to keep in mind that the amount of risk that is taken on with exotic options is always going to be greater than with other options due to the limited liquidity each type of exotic option is going to have available. While some types are going to have markets that are fairly active, others are only going to have limited interest. Some are even what are known as dual-party transactions which mean they have no underlying liquidity and are only traded when two amiable traders can be found.

Not keeping earnings and dividend dates in mind: It is important to keep an eye on any underlying assets that you are currently working with as those who are currently holding calls have the potential to be assigned early dividends, with greater dividends having an increased chance of this occurrence. As owning an option doesn't mean owning the underlying asset, if this happens to you then you won't be able to collect on your hard-earned money. Early assignment is largely a random occurrence which means that if you don't keep your ear to the ground it can be easy to get caught unaware and be unable to exercise the option before you miss the boat.

Along similar lines, you are going to also always want to be aware of when the earning season is going to take place for any of your underlying assets as it is likely going to increase the price of all of the contracts related to the underlying asset in question. Additionally, you will need to be caught up on current events as even the threat of influential news can be enough to cause a significant spike in volatility and premiums as well. In order to minimize the additional costs associated with trading during these periods, you are going to want to utilize a spread. Doing so will minimize the effect that inflation has on your bottom line.

Chasing bottoms and tops: There are certainly some strategies out there that are effective when used near the turning points of existing trends. These are in the minority, however, which means that picking bottoms and tops is, more often than not, a risky proposition. Unfortunately, it is an all too common mistake for traders to invest money into securities that are either too low or too high, gleefully ignoring the 2 percent rule as they do so. This impulse should be avoided like the plague and replaced with a focus on major inbound price moves instead. Sticking to one side of markets that are range-bound will lead to better long-term results at least 90 percent of the time.

Sticking with relative trends: If a trend is already well-defined in the market then it is entirely possible that it is going to continue long enough for you to make some money off of it but it is far from a guarantee. The market will naturally fluctuate up to 20 percent of its current average with very little warning, before settling back to the current standard. This means that if you recklessly jump onto a specific trend without doing the required homework you will frequently find yourself making a momentum play that is never going to go anywhere.

Before you make a move regarding a specific trend, there are three distinct timeframes you are going to want to consider first. If you are prone to trading in the short-term then you are going to want to keep an eye on the weekly hourly and daily charts. If you prefer holding onto trades for a longer period of time then daily, weekly and monthly charts are typically going to be more useful.

Chapter 7) Thinking like an expert trader

Know when to go off book: While sticking to your plan, even when your emotions are telling you to ignore it, is the mark of a successful trader, this in no way means that you must blindly follow your plan 100 percent of the time. You will, without a doubt, find yourself in a situation from time to time where your plan is going to be rendered completely useless by something outside of your control. You need to be aware enough of your plan's weaknesses, as well as changing market conditions, to know when following your predetermined course of action is going to lead to failure instead of success. Knowing when the situation really is changing, versus when your emotions are trying to hold sway is something that will come with practice, but even being aware of the disparity is a huge step in the right direction.

Avoid trades that are out of the money: While there are a few strategies out there that make it a point of picking up options that are currently out of the money, you can rest assured that they are most certainly the exception, not the rule. Remember, the options market is not like the traditional stock market which means that even if you are trading options based on underlying stocks buying low and selling high is just not a viable strategy. If a call has dropped out of the money, there is generally less than a 10 percent chance that it will return to acceptable levels before it expires which means that if you purchase these types of options what you are doing is little better than gambling, and you can find ways to gamble with odds in your favor of much higher than 10 percent.

Avoid hanging on too tightly to your starter strategy: The personalized trading strategy that you created in chapter four if you have been following along is an important step in trading properly, no two ways around it. That doesn't mean that it is the last strategy that you are ever going to need, however, far from it. Your core trading strategy is one that should always be constantly evolving as the circumstances surrounding your trading habits change and evolves as well. What's more, outside of your primary strategy you are going to want to eventually create additional plans that are more specifically tailored to various market states or specific strategies that are only useful in a narrow band of situations. Remember, the more prepared you are prior to starting a day's worth of trading, the greater your overall profit level is likely to be, it is as simple as that.

Utilize the spread: If you are not entirely risk averse, then when it comes to taking advantage of volatile trades the best thing to do is utilize a spread as a way of both safeguarding your existing investments and, at the same time, making a profit. To utilize a long spread you are going to want to generate a call and a put, both with the same underlying asset, expiration details, and share amounts but with two very different strike prices. The call will need to have a higher strike price and will mark the upper limit of your profits and the put will have a lower strike price that will mark the lower limit of your losses. When creating a spread it is important that you purchase both halves at the same time as doing it in fits and spurts can add extraneous variables to the formula that are difficult to adjust for properly.

Never proceed without knowing the mood of the market: While using a personalized trading plan is always the right choice, having one doesn't change the fact that it is extremely important to consider the mood of the market before moving forward with the day's trades. First and foremost, it is important to keep in mind that the collective will of all of the traders who are currently participating in the market is just as much as a force as anything that is more concrete, including market news. In fact, even if companies release good news to various outlets and the news are not quite as good as everyone was anticipating it to be then related prices can still decrease.

To get a good idea of what the current mood of the market is like, you are going to want to know the average daily numbers that are common for your market and be on the lookout for them to start dropping sharply. While a day or two of major fluctuation can be completely normal, anything longer than that is a sure sign that something is up. Additionally, you will always want to be aware of what the major players in your market are up to.

Never get started without a clear plan for entry and exit: While finding your first set of entry/exit points can be difficult without experience to guide you, it is extremely important that you have them locked down prior to starting trading, even if the stakes are relatively low. Unless you are extremely lucky, starting without a clear idea of the playing field is going to do little but lose your money. If you aren't sure about what limits you should set, start with a generalized pair of points and work to fine tune it from there.

More important than setting entry and exit points, however, is using them, even when there is still the appearance of money on the table. One of the biggest hurdles that new options traders need to get over is the idea that you need to wring every last cent out of each and every successful trade. The fact of the matter is that, as long as you have a profitable trading plan, and then there will always be more profitable trades in the future which mean that instead of worrying about a small extra profit you should be more concerned with protecting the profit that the trade has already netted you. While you may occasionally make some extra profit ignoring this advice, odds are you will lose far more than you gain as profits peak unexpectedly and begin dropping again before you can effectively pull the trigger. If you are still having a hard time with this concept, consider this: options trading are a marathon, not a sprint, slow and steady will always wins the race.

Never double down: When they are caught up in the heat of the moment, many new options traders will find themselves in a scenario where the best way to recoup a serious loss is to double down on the underlying stock in question at its newest, significantly lowered, price in an effort to make a profit under the assumption that things are going to turn around and then continue to do so to the point that everything is completely profitable once again. While it can be difficult to let an underlying stock that was once extremely profitable go, doubling down is rarely if ever going to be the correct decision. If you find yourself in a spot where you don't know if the trade you are about to make is actually going to be a good choice, all you need to do is ask yourself if you would make the same one if you were going into the situation blind, the answer should tell you all you need to know.

If you find yourself in a moment where doubling down seems like the right choice, you are going to need to have the strength to talk yourself back down off of that investing ledge and to cut your losses as thoroughly as possible given the current situation. The sooner you cut your losses and move on from the trade that ended poorly, the sooner you can start putting energy and investments into a trade that still has the potential to make you a profit.

Never take anything personally: It is human nature to build stories around, and therefore form relationships with, all manner of inanimate objects including individual stocks or currency pairs. This is why it is perfectly natural to feel a closer connection to particular trades, and possibly even consider throwing out your plan when one of them takes an unexpected dive. Thinking about and acting on are two very different things, however, which is why being aware of these tendencies are so important to avoid them at all costs.

This scenario happens just as frequently with trades moving in positive directions as it does negative, but the results are always going to be the same. Specifically, it can be extremely tempting to hang on to a given trade much longer than you might otherwise decide to simply because it is on a hot streak that shows no sign of stopping. In these instances, the better choice of action is to instead sell off half of your shares and then set a new target based on the updated information to ensure you are in a position to have your cake and eat it too.

Not taking your choice of broker seriously: With so many things to consider, it is easy to understand why many new option traders simply settle on the first broker that they find and go about their business from there. The fact of the matter is, however, that the broker you choose is going to be a huge part of your overall trading experience which means that the importance of choosing the right one should not be discounted if you are hoping for the best experience possible. This means that the first thing that you are going to want to do is to dig past the friendly exterior of their website and get to the meat and potatoes of what it is they truly offer. Remember, creating an eye-catching website is easy, filling it will legitimate information when you have ill intent is much more difficult.

First things first, this means looking into their history of customer service as a way of not only ensuring that they treat their customers in the right way, but also of checking to see that quality of service is where it needs to be as well. Remember, when you make a trade every second count which means that if you need to contact your broker for help with a trade you need to know that you are going to be speaking with a person who can solve your problem as quickly as possible. The best way to ensure the customer service is up to snuff is to give them a call and see how long it takes for them to get back to you. If you wait more than a single business day, take your business elsewhere as if they are this disinterested in a new client, consider what the service is going to be like when they already have you right where they want you.

With that out the way, the next thing you will need to consider is the fees that the broker is going to charge in exchange for their services. There is very little regulation when it comes to these fees which means it is definitely going to pay to shop around. In addition to fees, it is important to consider any account minimums that are required as well as any fees having to do with withdrawing funds from the account.

Find a Mentor: When you are looking to go from causal trader to someone who trades successfully on the regular, there is only so much you can learn by yourself before you need a truly objective eye to ensure you are proceeding appropriately. This person can either be someone you know in real life, or it can take the form of one or more people online. The point is you need to find another person or two who you can bounce ideas off of and whose experience you can benefit from. Options trading don't need to be a solitary activity; take advantage of any community you can find.

Knowledge is the key: Without some type of information which you can use to assess your trades, you are basically playing at the roulette table. Even poker players show up to the table with a game plan. They can adapt to the circumstances and learn to read other players. That way, they can tell the contenders from the pretenders. Options trading are no different. If you are unable to use the information that is out there to your advantage, then what you will end up with is a series of guesses which may or may not play out. Based purely on the law of averages you have a 50/50 chance of making money. That may not seem like bad odds, but a string of poor decisions will leave you in the poor house in no time.

So, it is crucial that you become familiar with the various analytics and tools out there which you can use to your advantage. Bear in mind that everyone is going to be looking at the same information. However, it is up to you to figure out what can, or might, happen before everyone else does. This implies really learning and studying the numbers so that you can detect patterns and see where trends are headed, or where trends may reverse. The perfect antidote to that is vision and foresight. Practice building scenarios. Try to imagine what could happen are trends continuing. Or, what would happen if trends reversed? What needs to happen in order for those trends to continue or reverse?

When you ask yourself such tough questions, your knowledge and understanding begin to expand. Your mind will suddenly be able to process greater amounts of information while you generate your own contingency plans based on the multiple what ifs. That may seem like a great deal of information to handle, but at the end of the day, any time spent in improving your trading acumen is certainly worth the effort.

Conclusion

Getting started in options trading can be an exciting time. It is a time where you get to work with the market and perhaps make some more money in the process. Most people start out with this, with the help of their broker, to make a little extra money on the side to help them pay bills, get a retirement plan, or to just have a little extra spending money. No matter the reason that you choose to get into options trading, if you make sure that you spend time learning about it and have a strategy in place for picking out the right options, you are going to see some results.

The last thing that we are going to discuss in this guidebook is some of the characteristics that need to be in place to help you be a successful options trader. There are a lot of people who get into options trading because they are excited or they want to make some extra money, but not all of them are going to see results. So, what makes some stand out above the rest? Let's take a look at some of the characteristics that you need to have so that you have a chance of becoming a successful options trader.

Have enough capital

The first thing that you should have is enough capital to get started. Capital is going to be the amount of money that is in your account and it will be used to pay for any transactions that you go through as well as any losses that you are dealing with as well. Many people who first get into options trading end up not having enough money to help them out. They will have to take out some trading time in order to send over money to help them get started, which is basically time wasted.

While some people like options trading because it doesn't require as much of a startup cost as the stock market and other trading options, you do need to make sure that you are keeping enough capital in there to handle your trades. The successful traders will make sure that they always have a good amount of capital in there so even if they end up with some bad trades, they have a bit of a cushion to fall back on.

Don't take the bigger risks

Traders who are successful in options trading are the ones who won't take as big of risks with their work. They don't see the point in taking a big gamble just for a tiny chance at seeing a big payday. They will spend their time working on trades that have high gain but low risk. Yes, this means that at times they are going to pass up some of the more thrilling opportunities that come their way, but this is because the risk is so high that they are not likely to ever see the payoff.

Some beginners have an issue with this because they want to see those big paydays right away. They may feel annoyed at the smaller payoffs and think that they need to go after the gold right from the beginning. But the best choice is to work with the small gains so that you only experience small losses as well. You will still make a good income over time because you won't see the losses.

Trade when the time is right

Since the successful traders are good at avoiding risks, they are very careful about when they enter and exit a trade and will only do so when they think that it is a good time. They have done their research and they have a good idea of the big picture, rather than always calling their brokers up to do some more trades for them.

Sometimes this does mean that they need to sit on the sidelines for a little bit, waiting around to see if the odds will ever be stacked in their favor. There are a few resources that they will use to help them figure out the perfect time to jump right in. For example, they like to take a look at the "Big Picture" article that is released each day by Investor's Business Daily. This article is great because it lets them know how the market is doing such as whether the market is going upwards if there is any pressure in the market, or even if the market is about to go down again.

They have their own plan

We have spent some time talking about the importance of having a plan and even outlined some of the things that you can consider when it is time to pick out a plan, such as the best strategies to use. But it is so important to get that plan in place if you want to be successful with options trading. A successful trader goes the extra mile; they not only have a plan in place, they write it down so they can keep track of all the thoughts in their head and revert back to that plan anytime they are questioning a decision.

There are a lot of things that you can consider writing down in your plan. You can write down your entrance and exit plan. You can decide on how much risk you would like to take in this market, the goals that you have overall, how the market is doing at the time, and even the strategies that you would like to use depending on how the market is doing.

In terms of all the specifics that you should include, a successful trader will make sure to include everything. This also includes a rundown of what will happen if the worst-case scenario hits and they end up losing money. They can write down how much they will lose if that scenario is a reality and when they will finally exit. This is a good way for them to reduce how much money they end up losing and to manage their risk at the same time. Yes, all traders want to do well with their options and only want to see profits, but there are times when the market doesn't always react the way that you want or that you will make a mistake and it is always a good idea to have a plan in place to keep you on track so you can minimize your losses.

There are a lot of different types of investments out there that you can choose to work with. Some are going to include taking over real estate and renting it out or selling it to others. Some will get into their own business and try to make money that way. And still, others will get into the stock market and hope they can make the right decisions. But one investment that is different from all the others is options trading.

This guidebook has taken some time to talk about options trading and all of the neat things that you are able to do with it. We talked a bit about what options are and some of the benefits of choosing to work with them instead of with some of the other investments out there. In addition, this guidebook moved onto some of the best overall strategies that you can use with options trading and what kind of market scenarios you encounter when using some of them.

As with any investment type, there is some risk involved when you get into options trading. The good news is that we spent some time talking about the most common mistakes to avoid and how to reduce the amount of risk that you take on inside this investment opportunity. Options investing are a tricky investment to choose to go with, but it provides a great return on investment and is often easier to get into compared to the stock market.

Swing Trading

A Simplified beginner's guide on swing trading, stock market, forex and options with strategies plan, risk and time management. Learn how to invest money, trade and swing a big profit!

[Henry Hill]

TABLE OF CONTENTS:

CHAPTER 4: THE 11 COMMANDMENTS OF SWING TRADING

1. MAKE SURE TO HAVE LONG STRENGTHS AND SHORT WEAKNESSES
2. THE OVERALL DIRECTION OF THE MARKET AND YOUR TRADE SHOULD BE ALIGNED
3. ALWAYS LOOK AT THE LONG-TERM CHARTS
4. DO YOUR BEST NOT TO ENTER NEAR THE END OF THE TRADE
5. TRACK A CONSISTENT GROUP OF STOCKS
6. ALWAYS HAVE A CLEAR PLAN
7. ALWAYS INTEGRATE FUNDAMENTALS INTO YOUR TECHNICAL ANALYSIS
8. MAKE SURE TO MASTER THE PSYCHOLOGICAL SIDE OF SWING TRADING
9. TRY PUTTING THE ODDS IN YOUR FAVOR
10. TRADE IN HARMONY WITH THE TREND TIME FRAMES
11. MAKE SURE TO USE MULTIPLE INDICATORS AND NOT CREATE ISOLATION

CHAPTER 5: PROFIT AND LOSS LEVELS

STOP LOSS LEVELS
A Gnat on an Elephant
Correct SL Levels
Position Sizing
TAKE PROFIT LEVELS
TP Levels
An Alternative

CHAPTER 6: SWING TRADING GUIDING PRINCIPLES

KEEP IT SIMPLE
TREAT YOUR SWING TRADING ACTIVITY LIKE A SERIOUS BUSINESS
DEVELOP A WORK PLAN
ACTIVELY MANAGE YOUR RISK TO REWARD RATIO; FOCUS ON THE ENTRY
MEASURE YOUR RESULTS AND ADJUST ACCORDINGLY

CHAPTER 7: SWING TRADING RULES

RISKS OF HOLDING A SECURITY
Earnings Reports

Introduction

Some people tend to confuse swing trading with other types of trading. It is important to know that each type of trading is different. For example, when you are a day trader, you will buy and sell stocks in one day. You do not hold stocks overnight. If you do decide to hold a stock overnight, you turn it into a swing trading stock. Swing traders tend to hold their stocks for a few days; however, they also have a limited time frame. While the average swing trader might hold on to stocks for a couple of weeks, some might hold on to stocks for as long as a couple of months. Typically, if a trade is held longer than this, it isn't considered a swing trade anymore. However, there are always exceptions to every rule.

Why Swing Trading Over Day Trading?

While you can take up any type of trading, many people feel that swing trading is better than day trading. Lately, day trading has become a popular topic because it can be completed within a few minutes to an hour or so. However, this is also one reason that people tend to turn away from day trading.

Other than the different time frames between day trading and swing trading, many people chose swing trading because they feel it is less demanding. There is a lot of truth to this as day traders often feel a bit more stress as they have to pay such close attention to the stocks in order to trade them in just the right moment, which can be within minutes, in order to make the best profit. While everyone has to focus on just the right moment to trade so they receive the best profit, day traders need to close out their stocks the same day they purchase them, otherwise they will most likely lose money.

Furthermore, day traders have to watch several screens throughout the day. Of course, much of this depends on how many stocks they take on. However, this tends to become very challenging, especially for beginners. When it comes to swing traders, they have to watch several screens closely, but not to the intensity of day traders.

Another reason people chose swing trading over day trading is that it's easier to be a part-time trader. While there are part-time day traders, many feel that it is a full-time job if you want to gain the best profits from the career.

When it comes to swing trading, you are given a few days and up to a couple of months to watch your stocks and find the best time to make your highest profit. Because of this, people don't feel as much pressure.

Swing traders also don't have to worry about making sure they have the greatest equipment and worry about all the algorithms that go into day trading. Instead, swing traders can get a platform and perform their own trades, once they learn, on a typical computer. Of course, you will still need to make sure that your computer is reliable and have the same high-speed internet that day traders need.

Stock Trends

Like with other types of trading, you will need to heavily focus on analysis in order to try to gain an idea of where the stock trend is heading next. For example, if you look at a stock's trend history for the last couple of months and noticed it has been in an upward trend, you might assume that this upward trend is going to continue. However, you will also need to look at other features in order to officially determine if this is the best stock for you. Thankfully, trends tend to repeat themselves which is why people can easily predict where the stock is going to go. However, this doesn't mean that trends don't quickly change.

There are times during an upward trend when you will see what traders call a pull-back. This is when the trend of the stock drops down but then rises back up later. Pull-backs also repeat. However, if they are successful, they will have higher lows and higher highs than the previous pull back.

This is a pattern that you will want to notice as a swing trader because, as long as the stock will work with your strategy and everything else matches up with your trading plan, it is the trend you want to find. The best time to buy one of these stocks is when is during a pull-back. This is when the stock will be at a low price, which means your profit will be greater, once the stock shoots up to a higher price and you can sell it at the right time.

Another type of trend that you have to understand as a trader is the downward trend. This trend is the opposite of the upward trend but still can give you a profit, if you understand when to buy and sell the stocks. The best time to buy the stock on a downward trend is when the stock is at a low point. Of course, you will want to sell the stock when it is on its way back up from the lowest point, a term which is known as pull-up.

While this might sound pretty simple, it can actually be a little harder to understand and find the best time to buy and sell. The biggest way you will find the best time to buy and sell the stock is through technical analysis, which I will discuss later in this book. The basis of technical analysis is you will be able to identify the patterns because you analyze the historical trend and information of the stock. Through technical analysis, you will receive tools that will help you isolate and identify the patterns.

How to Decide on the Right Stocks

One of the most difficult decisions you will run into as a swing trader, or any trader, is deciding what stocks are the best to trade. There are a lot of factors that go into this from the strategies you use to your lifestyle. Unfortunately, I cannot give you a guide that strictly tells you what stocks you should go out and take on. However, I will try to give you information that can help you make your own decision.

One of the key features to look at when you are choosing your stock is to find a stock that comes from a large capital company. These companies might be part of the blue-chip stocks, such as Amazon and Walmart. However, they don't have to be. In general, large capital companies tend to have at least $5 billion dollars. These stocks are generally the most sought-after stocks in the market, which help make them highly tradable. They are also known to give you a good profit because they have a long history of success.

The trend is another key feature that you want to pay attention to. You want to make sure that the stock has been going in the same direction for a few days, if not a few weeks. This will help you to note that, chances are, the stock will continue this trend. Of course, if you decide to take on the stock, you want to continue to closely watch the stock because you never truly know when the stock will switch directions and you can find yourself losing capital instead of gaining.

Ideas on Good Swing Trading Stocks

While I cannot tell you exactly what stocks to get, I can give you an idea, so you can at least start to look at some stocks that many swing traders put into their basket.

Netflix

Netflix is considered to be one of the top swing trade stocks for 2019. Of course, this stock has a higher price than most swing trade stocks, which is often harder for beginners to take advantage of. However, if you have enough finances to put into Netflix, many traders feel it is a good option. Furthermore, because of the successful history of Netflix, many people believe that the stock isn't going to see a huge downward trend anytime soon.

Amazon

Amazon is similar to Netflix. It is believed to be one of the biggest swing trading stocks for 2019 because of its successful history. Like Netflix, Amazon is also on the more expensive side, however is known to give great returns.

MKS Instruments

In 2019, most tech companies are some of the top stocks that people take on as swing traders, day traders, and investors. MKS Instruments is based out of Massachusetts and has been on an upward trend for a while.

Chapter 1: What Is Important to a Swing Trader?

Typically, positions will be held for less than a week when swing trading, with buy and sell decisions being taken purely on price movement and not company fundamentals. In fact, most swing traders use analytical tools to 'trawl' the market for potential tradable stocks.

Because of this trading profile, and the short time frame of position holding, it is right to assume that swing traders have no concern for what a company makes or sells, nor its balance sheet, profitability, market sector, state of the economy, etc. A long term investor, of course, would analyze all of these factors before making an investment decision.

There are only two factors which concern swing traders:

- Flows of funds in and out of a target stock

- Risk to capital and ease of trading the target stock

How Swing Traders Make Trading Decisions

With no reference to company fundamentals, it is clear that swing traders use other indicators as a basis for trading in and out of stocks: predominantly price and the way the price is moving initiates a buy or sell indication.

Swing traders rely on the theory of predictability in an unpredictable market, and some reference technical indicators such as Elliott Wave, lines of support and resistance, short and longer term moving averages, and Bollinger Bands. However, while all of these technical indicators form a basis for the concepts behind the foundation of swing trading, as we will see in this eBook, the way in which asset prices move and are influenced by trading psychology is what dictates the price moves on which swing traders thrive and profit.

The Idea of Predictability in an Unpredictable Market

Markets are unpredictable. No one can say with certainty in which direction a market will move, nor how far or how fast on any given day, week, month, or year. Outside factors create fear and greed which moves markets up and down, seemingly at will. However, what can be predicted to a far greater degree is the predictable nature of humans, and this includes investors.

When a stock is moving up, investors tend to want to buy. When it is moving down, investors tend to sell. This is the foundation of swing trading, and what makes swing trading a close cousin to momentum trading.

Swing Trading and the Psychology of the Crowd

This predictability of the crowd is what causes stocks to move up and down.

As a stock's price moves up, with buyers stepping in, this creates a situation where the increasing price encourages further buyers as traders and investors pile in, not wishing to miss out on the market move. This is the psychology of greed, fear, and hope, literally forcing investors to buy in reaction to what others are doing and in tandem with what others are doing.

However, each move will eventually run out of steam as those that bought stock early seek to realize profits and sell out. When this happens, the stock forms a peak and reverses direction. This causes greater numbers of investors to sell, providing momentum to the downside until the stock is deemed to have fallen far enough.

It is this action of the crowd which gives stocks lines of resistance and support, and which gives the swing trader one of their greatest trading opportunities – but only if trading discipline is maintained. Traders who fail to trade with discipline and follow their emotions will always lose money in the longer term.

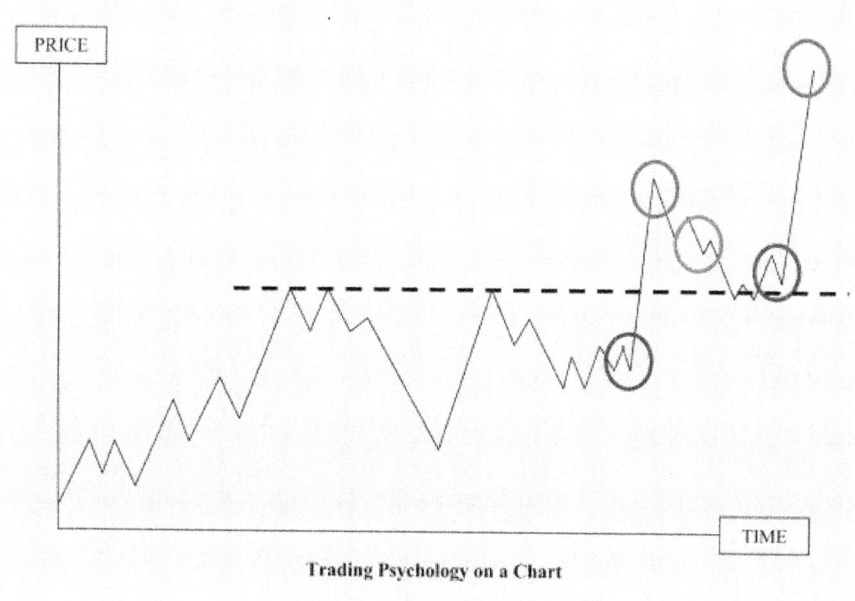

Trading Psychology on a Chart

Swing traders reference chart patterns to make their trade decisions, so it is worth looking at a chart to see how different types of traders act in markets which also helps to identify how psychology affects these different types of trader.

The **blue circle** is where a breakout trader would buy stock. They see the stock trading out of a recent range and hope that others come and buy the stock to produce upward momentum.

141

The green circle is where the new, ill-disciplined trader typically buys. He operates under the fear of missing more of a market move. This is where a breakout trader hopes to sell.

The orange circle is where momentum traders buy. In this case the momentum trader has seen the stock pull back and sells to profit from further selling. They would reverse their trade position when trading momentum reverses.

The **red circle** is the point at which a swing trader would buy. Most of the novice traders have already sold and cut their losses, and momentum traders may have begun to step in and take their profits.

Notice how also, the **black dotted line**, which was before a significant line of resistance (from which the price retreated) has now become a line of support, from which the stock will bounce.

Perhaps the strongest tools in the tool box of the swing trader are the **understanding of trading psychology** and **self-discipline**.

Having established the importance of price and trading psychology, we should point out that price is not merely a function of buying and selling but also is by determined by the strength of buying and selling interest. This is indicated by the volume of trade taking place in the market.

The Importance of Trading Volume to a Swing Trader

As we've discussed, a rising stock price tends to create buyers. This creates greater trading volume, which in turn increase stock price and brings more buyers into the market. Price momentum increases and the stock price rise more sharply.

In a falling market, more sellers come into the market which increases traded volume and the velocity of the price fall.

So, asset price trends are not only confirmed by increased volume, but also exaggerated by it.

Now let's look at how volume is also used as an indicator of an impending change in direction of price movement – remember, this is when, as a swing trader, you will want to make your move.

At some point in a rising market, traders will begin to believe the stock price has moved too far (and perhaps too fast). These traders will back away from committing new funds, with volume retreating also. So, a good indicator of impending price reversal in a rising market is when the stock price continues to trade higher but volume decreases.

The same can be said of falling markets, with one notable exception. Sometimes a stock price fall sees a large and final drop as holders become panicked and dump stock for fear of mounting losses. Such a fall often follows a period of steady trading volume in a falling market – this trading pattern is termed 'capitulation'.

Such an exaggerated spike in price decline and volume increase often precedes a period of consolidation, when trading volume reduces and markets trade range bound.

As with every rule, there is always an exception.

If a stock price has been trending either up or down in little volume, and the volume suddenly spikes higher this, too, is likely to precede a reversal of price trend.

Chapter 2: Swing Trading Mindset

Mindset is a topic that is grossly overlooked by most traders, even successful ones. A lot of you might feel this information is not necessary or is boring. You might feel your time is better spent studying indicators. You're free to do so of course. It's just that once you've lost money and learn your lessons, you'll find yourself right back here, if you're lucky and haven't blown your capital already. Ultimately, your mindset determines your results.

What is mindset though? Is it just how you view things? Is it something that is affected by the physical structure of your brain? This is what we look at in detail in this chapter.

We will begin by looking at the physical structure of your brain and how that affects the way you make decisions. This will help us better understand our internal beliefs and barriers we often put up, even when we desire something greatly. Comparing these beliefs to the nature of trading and what successful trading beliefs are will help you understand the gaps in your mind and how to get from here to there, so to speak.

So let's begin by taking a stroll down evolutionary road!

The Evolution of Your Brain

The human brain is an intricate system of complex processes. When one starts thinking of the brain, it's easy to meet yourself coming back the other way. Consider this: We don't fully understand our own brain. Thus, we can conclude that our own brain doesn't understand itself!

Such logical quandaries aside, looking at the evolution of the brain is an informative exercise since it gives us an insight into how our decision making evolved and where its weaknesses lie.

The Parts of Our Brain

Without going into great scientific detail, our brain can be divided into three major areas, in terms of evolution, namely: The reptilian brain, the limbic brain and the neocortex. Looking at the structure of the brain, we can see quite easily how each successive part builds on the previous one. At the bottom, near the brain stem we have the reptilian brain, followed by the limbic brain and on top of everything else sit the neocortex. This pretty much indicates how our brains evolved and how we went from being a base life form to an intelligent one (well, most of us anyway).

The reptilian brain is the oldest of the lot and is responsible for a bunch of vital functions such as regulating our heartbeat, breathing, etc. Despite it being a base version of the modern brain, its value is not to be discounted. It does have its drawbacks though. The reptilian brain tends to be impulsive and rather rigid. This is because over everything else, it values reliability. Indeed, looking over the functions it has to regulate, reliability is its buzzword so it should come as no surprise that this is prioritized.

Next, we have the limbic brain which evolved in the earliest versions of mammals. This is responsible for our emotions and contains an important organ called the Amygdala. The limbic brain regulates our emotional responses to events, classifying them as desirable or undesirable. While it is more evolved than the reptilian brain, the limbic brain also tends to be a bit impulsive and short-term focused. Think of any lower form of mammal you encounter in the world and this sort of behavior is made obvious.

Most animals have priorities that can be summed up in one word: Survival. The limbic brain does everything in its power to help you survive. Feeling hungry? It alerts you by sending signals to your stomach which your brain in turn decodes as hunger and if not attended to, will cause irritation. It is important to note that the limbic brain is not a creative one. Its priority is to simply ensure the worst doesn't happen to you and it is highly tuned to this, ever alert, to something life-threatening happening.

This is why you feel a sudden lurch when you're in a life-threatening situation, such as wandering by mistake in front of a speeding car. The limbic brain throws your body into overdrive which causes you to leap out of the way. The rate of your heartbeat is a measure of the kind of stress that is caused when this happens. Needless to say, this is a vital function but living constantly under the influence of this sort of brain is quite stressful and exhausting.

Evolution provided a solution to us in the form of the Neocortex (NC). This is the part of the brain which sits on top of everything and has a left and right hemisphere. The NC is the most rational part of our brain and is responsible for advanced thought and creation, like language, abstract concepts, etc. Pretty much everything we see in our world today is a result of it being created in the NC. More than anything else, it is this which gives human beings a close to unfair advantage over every other life form on this planet.

The NC is the part of your brain that urges you to take a step back and think things through. For example, imagine you're in a situation where you're hungry but need another 5 minutes, literally, to finish a piece of work after which you're done for the day. Your reptilian and limbic brain only sees the immediate hunger and presses you to find food immediately to satisfy it. Your NC though urges you to take a step

147

back and reason that spending 5 more minutes to complete this work is not going to kill you or even remotely threaten your survival. It's more desirable to bear the hunger for 5 more minutes and then enjoy your meal and the rest of your day in peace.

This ability to reason and think forward for long-term is what is completely missing from the lesser evolved portions of our brains. The NC doesn't have complete control over us, however. While it seems like a good idea to have a rational mind controlling us, the NC isn't particularly good at short-term, life-threatening situations (as yet). This is why our limbic and reptilian brains are essential.

Faced with an oncoming car or vehicle, our NC would take far too long to activate our body into the state it needs to be and is a pretty useless master of our survival mechanism. Back when our world was wilder and our lifestyles were a hunting-gathering one, the limbic brain was of utmost importance. The NC helped design weapons and discover fire but it was the limbic brain that warned us of predators and other threats nearby.

Our world today is far removed from that and the limbic brain doesn't play as important a role. The number of life-threatening situations we face on a daily basis is far less than what our earliest ancestors used to face. Comparing our societies today to even the Middle Ages, it is obvious how much more evolved and peaceful today's world is, the nightly news notwithstanding.

Here's the thing though: the limbic brain doesn't know all that. As far as it is concerned, it needs to keep you alive. The way it detects life-threatening situations is by looking for clues and reading your physical signs. If your hair is standing on end, or if you feel threatened at any moment, it jumps into action and activates a response which puts you under stress. Stress over a long period is harmful but is extremely useful in the short-term. It gives you additional energy and works as an energy boost, giving access to reserves of strength you didn't know you had.

When this happens, your NC is completely taken out of the loop and cannot help you. This is a great thing if you're down a dark alleyway and see someone approaching you with something tucked under their coat. What if you're sitting in front of a trading screen though and see yourself lose money you have worked so hard to gain? The limbic system doesn't know the difference between a dark alleyway and a sunlit trading room. It reads the cues and activates stress. Hence, you feel burned out and exhausted, frustrated, etc. There's nowhere for that energy to go and you just turn it inwards damaging yourself. This is why trading is especially challenging.

The stress response gets activated within you because the limbic brain is taking its cues from deep seated beliefs you have about money, the nature of trading, success, failure, how it relates to your life, etc. When an external event either contradicts a belief that is deep seated within you, you feel threatened and your limbic brain jumps into action.

Dogs are....

Dogs are often called Man's best friend. There are many though who have had unpleasant experiences with dogs growing up and are not very keen of them. Some of us are, indeed, outright afraid of them. Such people have a deep-seated belief "Dogs are vicious and will attack me."

Irrespective of what caused this belief, can you see how this impacts their world view? Let's say such a person is in a park a dog comes running to them, eager to play and be petted. What would this person's reaction be like? The minute they see the dog running towards them, this perfectly rational person's limbic brain senses the physical cues of a dog approaching, reads the belief about dogs being a threat and instantly senses a life-threatening situation.

Once in this state, with the NC shut off completely, the person misses all the cues of friendliness the dog is exhibiting. The dog is not growling or baring its teeth. It is bouncing along as it runs towards them and isn't running in a purposeful, taut manner. Its tail is wagging as it comes closer and it has been friendly towards all other people in the park. None of this matters once the limbic brain is in charge and the only thing flashing in the person's mind is "dog=threat." The person is incapable of processing anything else.

If you could somehow freeze time and sit next to this person and point out all the cues above, they would simply deny it. This isn't because they're stupid. It's because they literally cannot see these things. Their brain isn't allowing them to see these cues and process them. Instead of saying they're being stupid, a better way of framing this is by saying their "stupid brain" is in charge currently. This is how perfectly rational, intelligent beings can turn into stubborn, irrational people. Instantaneously.

The same thing happens when you sit in front of a trading screen and lose money on your trades. Suddenly, you perceive a threat since you're in "losing money=bad" mode and you cannot see what is literally right in front of you. You miss opportunities your NC would have picked up and you start questioning your strategy, yourself, your broker, etc. The worst part is all this feels completely normal to do. After all, it is your own brain telling you these things!

So what is the solution? Clearly brain surgery to remove your limbic brain is not an option since we are not evolved enough beings to be

150

able to discard it. Looking back at the dog scenario though, we can see how an internal belief is what led to this mess in the first place. If there was no belief that said "dogs=threat," we would never have perceived the dog as a threat. While changing a belief is not easy, it sure is the easiest option available.

Anatomy of a Belief

Beliefs are created within us, firstly, via experience. Something occurs in our lives which produces a deep emotional response and this gets seared onto our brains. A large majority of beliefs though are created when we were under the age of 5. It is estimated that a child at this age has already created over 90% of their beliefs!

This seems a bit unfair given how early this is in our lives. Our environment plays a huge part in forming our beliefs. We unconsciously model the people around us at this stage and adopt their behaviors and beliefs. Knowing all this, if you wish to be a trader, if your parents felt money was something that is bad and that being rich meant you had to be corrupt, how do you think your trading is going to go? Do you think you will ever be able to hold on to your gains? Wouldn't your belief be activated when you make some money, kicking your limbic brain into action, and cause you to do something boneheaded those results in you losing your gains?

Beliefs ultimately rule everything about our lives. The good news is they can be changed. This is why throughout this book, you've been impressed upon: Your mindset is what makes you money. Your mindset is simply a collection of all the things you believe. Change your mindset, change your results.

The first step to changing your beliefs is to start examining them. What are your beliefs about money? What does success mean to you?

Does your belief about money clash with your belief about success? These questions require serious thinking and you should take your time to really dig in and explore these answers. Hence, this is why beginner traders ought to spend 80% of their time working on their mindset.

While doing this, also ask yourself what it is you believe about trading and traders. Do you believe trading is a high energy activity? Do you believe the markets are random or somehow secretly ordered? Do you believe traders are a bunch of alpha male, bullying, swearing, and boy's locker room types? Ask yourself as many questions as you can and note down the answers.

The second step is to examine these beliefs vis-a-vis what it is you wish to achieve. For example, if you believe money is bad but wants to be rich, that's an obvious clash. Examine all your clashes and don't worry about trying to find a clash for every single belief. Sometimes, you don't know enough to realize there is a clash.

The third step is to observe your results. If your results are not in sync with what you desire, there is a clash you do not know about. Your existing clashes will also explain your current results but if they don't, this is the clearest indication that there's a block somewhere and you aren't aware of it as yet.

The final step is to learn and install beliefs that are in sync with what you want. If you want to be rich, money is good. If you want to be a successful trader, you need to learn the correct nature of the market and uninstall the wrong information you've been carrying around.

The way to install a new belief is via awareness and repetition. Any time you sense the incorrect belief raising its head, you need to counter it by rejecting it and repeating to yourself the belief you do wish to install. There are a number of great self-help books which will help you understand this process better. The concern of this book though, is to help you realize the true nature of the markets.

The Nature of the Market

Whichever market you choose to get involved in, be it the stock market or forex, etc., there are an innumerable number of traders involved. Over and above the traders, you have investors whose goals are very different to yours. These days, we also have government operating in the markets, via central banks. With these many different players all with differing objectives and goals, it is safe to say that the market is a random, chaotic beast.

An ordered environment gives us directions by itself. Think back to your days in school. How long did it take you to figure out the way school worked? You attended class, turned in your assignments, took an examination and once you passed that exam, you moved on to the next level. Do this twelve times and you're in an advanced school known as "college." Repeat the same process and after four or five years, you're done with schooling and begin the "job" phase of your life.

Jobs work much the same way except there's no examination and it isn't as ordered. However, the randomness is low. You show up to work, do a good job and you get paid. Simple. Somewhere along the way all this order starts getting boring and you look at the millions available in the market. You unconsciously apply the same method you've been using in your ordered environments till date, in the market. You think if you study up a bit, pass the examination that is your daily trading session, you'll get paid via profits. Sounds simple!

This is what causes people to chase high hit rate systems and a "secret key" to the markets since they intrinsically have been conditioned to think everything is ordered. The market, though, is not ordered. It is a supreme example of chaos.

So how does one navigate chaos successfully?

Probability and Chaos

On the surface, a chaotic environment appears completely random. This is indeed true for an environment which is perfectly chaotic. The markets, however, are not so. We can say this with conviction because everything that happens on your screen (which represents the market) is dictated by the underlying order flow.

Order flow is just interactions between sellers and buyers. There is literally no other activity taking place in the market. The average road when you're out driving is more chaotic and random than the market given the larger number of activities that are occurring on it. Aside from the drivers, you've got people crossing the road, car turning, vehicles changing direction, etc. In the market but contrast, there are just buyers and sellers. That's it.

As a result of this, following patterns of buying and selling and allying ourselves with them becomes a lucrative model of making money. This is why indicators work. All they're doing is summarizing order flow into an easily presentable format for you to decipher. There is a snag though. Given the different motivations of the buyers and sellers, it becomes difficult to sift through all the intentions present and choose the right bunch of orders we wish to follow. Thus, some noise is to be expected in our data.

This is where an understanding of probability helps us. You see, every pattern or indicator gives us the likelihood of something happening next. When applied as a system, this probability of being correct is our hit rate. Given our hit rate, we then figure out a good reward/risk ratio which enables us to make money. Let us look at this via an analogy.

Most readers of this book would have, undoubtedly, been to a casino. You may have even heard of the markets being compared to a casino and all traders as gamblers. Let's leave that aside for a moment. When you enter a casino as a gambler, you know the odds are squarely against you. Each game in the casino has certain odds attached to it. Let's say you play a game which has odds of 70% against you and 30% for you. In other words, you will lose 70% of the time and win 30%.

From a gambler's standpoint, this is a rubbish deal. Being gamblers, most people can't resist the thrill anyway and play this game. What is the casino's thinking about all this though? Let's say the game has a fixed bet and the payout is double your bet. Let's assume an even distribution and the results below.

Round	Result	Payout
1	L	-R
2	L	-R
3	W	2R
4	L	-R
5	L	-R
6	L	-R
7	W	2R
8	L	-R
9	L	-R

Table 2: Sample Payouts Over 10 Bets

The casino pays out double the bet amount on 3 separate hands. However, given the odds, they always make money over 10 hands because the probabilities play out.

In real life, the distribution is uneven. A player could conceivably win all 10 hands. So what does the casino do? Assuming there isn't any cheating going on, they simply encourage the player to bet more and play more. Why? **Because the odds have the best chance of playing out over a large number of hands.** This is why the more you play, the more gifts you receive in a casino. They're just making sure the odds line up in their favor.

We can draw some very interesting conclusions based on this:

1. THE CASINO DOES NOT CARE ABOUT THE RESULT OF ONE INDIVIDUAL HAND. EVEN IF THE PAYOUT IS A JACKPOT OF 10 MILLION OR 1 MILLION, THEY HAVE THE ODDS FIGURED OUT.

2. THEY WANT THE MAXIMUM NUMBER OF HANDS TO BE PLAYED. THE MORE THEIR CUSTOMERS PLAY, THE MORE THE MONEY THEY MAKE.

3. THE CASINO IS NOT RELYING ON LUCK. THEY'RE SIMPLY STEPPING ASIDE AND LETTING THE ODDS PLAY OUT.

4. THE GAMBLER IS THE ONE RELYING ON LUCK AND IS OVERLY INVESTED IN THE RESULT OF INDIVIDUAL HANDS.

5. THE GAMBLER IS THE ONE PLAYING FOR AN EMOTIONAL HIGH. THE CASINO IS THE RATIONAL PLAYER.

If it isn't obvious how this applies to your trading as yet, here goes: when trading, you want to be the casino, not the gambler. This is why you should not care about what the next trade does since it's the results over a large number of trades that matter.

This is why the common belief that being right about the market equals making money is wrong. You can be right about the market and still lose money if you don't have the math on your side (that is how much more are you making on your winners than your losers). This is why looking at just your hit rate doesn't make any sense.

Once you understand the way the market works that is via probabilities it becomes easy for you to remain in control of your emotions. You don't need to fight against your gambler's instinct because you are not engaging with the market as a gambler anymore. Your approach is a fully rational one.

Responsibility

Take a minute to answer this question: Who is most responsible for the result of your individual trade?

Those of you who have read enough self-help books would have answered: I am! Well, you are responsible for everything **except** the result. The result of an individual trade is completely out of your hands. Let's break this down some more.

Your trade will move into a profit on the basis of price moving a certain distance. What causes price to move? The order flow. What is the order flow? The buy and sell orders of other traders! So the next time you get disappointed or angry at the market after a loss, ask yourself: Who is most responsible for your trade's result? Who exactly are you getting angry with?

You are responsible for everything leading up to the result. This includes your preparation, your analysis, your execution, your in-trade management (if any) and your post trade management. These elements combine together to form your edge in the markets and determine your hit rate and reward/risk. The result of each individual trade? You have as much control over that as you do over the weather. Think of that the next time you lose your cool when you experience a loss.

Most traders make the mistake of doing this backwards. They act irresponsibly with regards to preparation ("I'll tough it out, it's all in the mind"), analysis ("Yeah this thing is going UP, never mind the signals!!"), execution ("I'll log this trade in the journal later. Let me look at how fast this is going to move NOW!!") And post trade execution ("YEAH, party time!!" or "@*%&X %!!!"). The only thing they do claim responsibility over is their trade results ("Yeah I made/didn't make money today"). Compare this to the actions of a gambler and you'll see how misguided this is.

Execution Flow

Most traders make the mistake of thinking of execution as merely looking at the signal their technical system gives them and entering or exiting a position. This is but a part of it. You see, your execution extends much beyond your market hours. Roughly speaking, we can divide execution into pre-trade, in-trade and post trade execution.

Pre-trade execution comprises of your preparation routine. Everything from physical to mental preparation, you checking in with yourself to make sure you're in a fit state and all the way up to trade to your pre-trade analysis. Your pre-trade analysis is determined by the technical system you choose for yourself.

Thus far we've covered candlestick patterns and four indicators you can use immediately to make money. You can use just one of these indicators or a combination of them to develop a system which makes the most sense to you. Too many beginners think developing the technical system is all there is to trading successfully. In reality, it is the smallest portion of the big picture and it really isn't very complicated.

Your in-trade execution begins with you observing a signal via your technical system and entering a trade. Placing your stop loss correctly, your take profit level and maintaining a stable mental state are all a part of in-trade execution. If you place your stop loss and take profit (SL and TP) correctly but become overly invested in the result of the trade as it moves either towards your SL or your TP, you're not executing correctly. This doesn't mean you terminate the trade but merely that you note this down in your journal.

Filling out your journal and saving the screenshots of your trade also form a part of your in-trade execution. Once either you're SL or TP is hit, you note down the result of the trade in your journal, save the screenshots and take stock of your mental state. This is the first step of your post trade execution.

Executing all these steps requires a lot of practice and concentration. Your day needs to be planned and you will need the utmost discipline to follow this. This is the reason why making money in the markets is so difficult. While you can get away with faulty execution on a few trades, ultimately, in the long run, the market will catch up to you. Money is made in the long run, not the short run and that is what counts.

This concludes our look at the mindset side of trading. Hopefully, this chapter has impressed upon you the singular importance this holds for your trading results.

We're almost at the point where we can build a successful swing trading system. Prior to that though, we need to look at one last fundamental aspect of trading: Stop Losses and Take Profits.

Chapter 3: Treat Swing Trading Like a Business

One of the most important pieces of information to receive as you start on your journey is that you will become more successful as a swing trader if you treat it as a career and not just a hobby. You don't have to work full-time in order to believe that swing trading is a profession to be taken seriously. Some traders decide to work part-time because this is best for their lifestyle. For example, a stay-at-home parent will often become too distracted to focus on trading the whole day. When you take on trading full-time, you will usually be in front of your computer during the hours the New York Stock Exchange is open, which is about 9:30 am to around 4:00 pm Eastern Time zone. This means, if you live in California, then you will start your day before 6:30.

Establish Your Business Plan

Because you should treat trading like a profession, it is important to follow a number of steps you would use when starting your own business. First, you will want to make sure you create a business or trading plan. This is a plan which will discuss all the details about your style as a trader. You will discuss your enter strategy, exit strategy, your pre-trading analysis, and your post-trading analysis.

What is a Business Plan?

Your business plan is going to be your comprehensive guide that will help you with your decisions as a swing trader. These are not only important because every business should have one but because they can help you make the best decision when you are faced with deciding if you should take on or sell a financial instrument. No matter how well you have researched swing trading or how long you have been a swing trader, when you are faced with a decision you can easily struggle to come up with a solution. This is when your trading plan will come in handy. You will focus on every aspect that goes with swing trading, including tips to help you focus on making the right decision and why.

It is important to evaluate your trading plan often. In fact, many traders state you should read through your trading plan during your pre-trading analysis. Other traders state that you should at least read through your plan and make any changes, if necessary, on a weekly basis. Whatever you decide to do, you want to make sure that you know your trading plan as well as you knows anything else in trading. Even though you will be reading the plan often, you still want to make sure you have memorized the plan as this will help you when you are faced with a difficult decision.

Why You Need a Trading Plan?

Your trading plan has several advantages. First, it will help you make decisions when you are focusing on a trade. While you might feel that these decisions should be easy, there is a lot of analyzing and details that go into making a decision to take on a financial instrument. This means that when you are faced with a decision that you need to make within a minute or two, you can often become stressed or worried about your decision. Of course, this isn't something you want to do when it comes to trading as then you might make the decision with your emotions, which definitely isn't something you want to do as a trader. If you find yourself in this position, you can turn to your trading plan. This plan will walk you through your decision, so you are less likely to make any mistakes.

Set Your Schedule and Stick to It

I talk about establishing your schedule; I am not just talking about how long you will sit in front of your computer when you are trading. There is a lot of information which goes into creating your schedule.

First, you will want to decide if you are going to become a part-time or full-time swing trader. This will let you know how much time to set aside for your trading career. For example, if you are part-time, you might think about focusing on trading a couple of days during the week or trade in the mornings. However, if you are a full-time trader, you will probably want to stay close to your computer during the hours the stock market is open. Below are the pieces of your schedule you should make sure to include no matter how often you trade during the week.

Pre-Trading Analysis

You will want to make sure to include time for your pre-trading analysis, which is a part of your trading plan. This analysis typically takes place before the stock market opens; however, some traders will use the first half hour as their analysis time. For instance, if you want to make sure your analysis is complete by the time the stock market opens, you will want to make sure you are done with this part of your day by 9:30 Eastern time. This could mean that you start your day at 5:45 am or 6:00 am as it is a good idea to have at least a half hour for your pre-trading analysis. However, many traders state that beginners should allow themselves a bit more time because they are still learning the whole trading system. Therefore, it could take them more time to analyze the changes that occurred in the foreign stock market or the United States stock market overnight. On top of this, they might take more time reading the news.

The Market

Of course, you will want to make sure that your schedule includes the on goings of the stock market. For example, you will want to note that from about 9:30 am to around 10:00 am, the market is in volatile mode. This means that there are a lot of changes occurring in the market which makes it unstable. When the market is unstable, you typically do not want to make and purchases or sales. Most people tend to just sit back and watch the market or spend their time reading the news or doing some research.

Another time to note about the stock market is that from about 11:15 am to around 2:00 pm is when the market seems to have the lowest amount of activity. Many traders refer to this time as the stock market's lunch time. Before 11:00 am, many traders will end their day as they are only part-time. However, those who are full-time might continue to research or look for stocks until their lunch time.

Starting around 2:30 pm, the stock market will begin to pick up again. When this happens, you will start to see activity and, if you are planning on making a sale or trade, you will most likely start looking into that. This activity continues until the stock market closes around 4:00 pm.

Post-Trading Analysis

Post-trading analysis is just as important as pre-trading analysis. You want to make sure to make time for this every day and it will occur after you have completed your day. During your post trade analysis, you will reflect on your day and you can do this through a trading journal or by taking screenshots of your charts for any trades you made that day.

If you use a trading journal, you will want to make sure to note every detail you feel is necessary about the day. This not only includes any financial instruments you bought or sold but also why. You will want to focus on why you made the decision, what strategy you used, what factors contributed to this decision, you will want to discuss if you were distracted, what device you used (computer, phone, etc.), your capital gain or loss, and anything else. It is important to write down as much as you feel you will need to so when you can get a sense of where your strengths and weaknesses are. On top of this, you will be able to get to know yourself as a trader.

If you decide to take screenshots of your charts, you will want to make sure to make notes within your charts. You will want to find a spot where you won't become distracted and can still read the chart easily. You will want to make the same type of notes you do in your trading journal. Of course, you could always take screenshots of charts and also keep a trading journal. How you do your analysis is up to you.

Take Your New Career Seriously but Not Too Seriously

Before you get into swing trading, whether you are going to focus on it halftime or full-time, you want to make sure that you are 100% committed to the career. It is very important that you don't feel like this is something you just want to try because you are bored or want to see if you can make some extra money every month. However, if you do feel this way, it is best to start up part-time and go from there.

At the same time, you need to make sure that you don't fall into the trap of taking your job too seriously. While this might sound odd, it can happen and has happened to many people within their jobs. Typically, when people start taking their job too seriously, they start to let it consume their life and there is very little professional and personal life balance. In fact, what happens is people tend to put all their time and energy into their job that they reach a state of exhaustion.

Becoming exhausted from trading can happen to anyone, and it is a fairly common trait, especially for beginners. Part of this reason is because they don't understand how demanding trading really is. Therefore, when they first get into the business, they have not dedicated enough time for what they wanted to do. Of course, this can be easily fixed by creating more time for trading or taking on less stocks. But, at the same time, they could reach a state of exhaustion before they realize they took on too much.

How to Tell When You're Heading Towards a Burn-Out?

Becoming burned-out from you job can happen to anyone. In fact, most people feel that they reach a stage of burnout at least once throughout their professional career. It is important to note that if you start to feel burnt-out, it is best to take a step back or a break. If you continue to work at the pace you are going and become too exhausted, you can easily start to cause other work-related problems. For example, you can start performing poorly. When it comes to swing trading, you might find yourself making more mistakes and unable to read and analyze charts that you used to be able to understand easily.

Many people reach a state of burn-out simply because they feel their job is too stressful. In fact, stress is the main factor of becoming burned-out. This is a common problem for many people in the trading community because, even swing trading, can be demanding.

There are many basic signs for a person who is starting to become burnt-out from their job.

1. You have lost your motivation for your job.

One of the biggest signs that you are nearing or becoming burnt-out is you has lost motivation for your job. This can happen to anyone and in any field, not just trading. In fact, you might have already felt this way in a previous job. When you lose motivation, you really begin to feel that you can't do the tasks that you once used to do. You might feel that you are too tired to perform the tasks (exhaustion is another sign of being burned-out). You might also feel that the tasks aren't worth your time or find yourself procrastinating.

2. You feel a lot of negative emotions.

Another sign that you are becoming burned-out is you feel more negatively towards your job than positively. You might find that you are easily irritated by your co-workers or even feel that you just want to be left alone. You might find yourself becoming easily frustrated at the simplest tasks you need to complete. Of course, you will want to remember that people generally feel a bit negative about parts of their job from time to time. If you find yourself feeling negatively occasionally, you might not be burnt-out. However, if you notice that you are more negative than you typically are, especially if you begin to become concerned over your mental health, then you are most likely burn-out.

3. Your job performance is suffering.

One of the biggest ways to notice that you are burnt-out is by looking at your previous job performance and comparing it to your current performance. If you found your performance is sloppier and you are not putting as much effort into your job duties, then you have most likely become burned-out.

4. Always thinking about work, even when you're not working.

While people usually think about the things they need to do at work when they are not on the clock, if you find yourself doing this often you could easily be at the burnt-out stage. In fact, part of the reason you might feel burned-out is because you think of your job when you should be focusing on other things to give yourself a better balance between work and home.

This is one downside when it comes to working from home. People who are used to working in an office and then start to work from home can often find themselves working longer hours or thinking about work more. One reason for this is because it's more convenient for them to get to their office as it might just be down the hall. Furthermore, if you are a trader, you might trade through your desktop, which you use throughout your day for various reasons. This is why it is important to make sure you have some type of work schedule that you stick to when you work from home.

5. Your mental health is starting to decline.

Your mental health is one of the most important factors of your life. It is just as important as your physical health. In fact, it's been proven through scientific studies that if you're struggling with your mental health, you can become sick more often. Because your health is so important, you have to make sure to keep your mental health as healthy as possible. In order to do this, you have to watch for any signs of feeling burned-out. Unfortunately, once your mental health start to decline you have felt burned-out for a while.

Once you start to notice yourself struggling with your mental health, you can quickly run into other concerns, such as anxiety and depression. You start to take less care of yourself. For example, you might feel that you don't have to eat healthy when you typically watch what you eat. You might also stop exercising as you just don't feel like it anymore. It is important to note that if you start to feel this way, you should take a break from your job as quickly as possible. Even taking a couple of days or a week off can help you feel better about yourself and set your motivation back on track.

Chapter 4: The 11 Commandments of Swing Trading

Some of the most experienced swing traders of 2019 like to focus on what has become known as the 11 commandments of swing trading. Popular trader, Melvin Pasternak, developed this list and discusses it after his trading classes.

1. Make Sure to Have Long Strengths and Short Weaknesses

There are two periods that you should be looking for when you are taking on a trade. The first period is known as bull and the second period is known as bear. You need to be able to identify these periods when you get into the market because this will let you know what the market conditions are like for that time.

When you look at the bull market condition, you are looking at an increasing market. The stock trends are on an upward trend, which they have been on for a good period of time. This proves that the levels of the economy are high and you should spend your time looking for longer trades.

When the market's condition is focused on bearishness, this means that the stocks are on a downward trend. The prices of stocks are dropping and many traders believe that this is the spiral that they will see in some stocks for a period of time. Bear conditions happen when the economy isn't doing very well. This is normally during points of economic recession and when unemployment is high. When you notice the bear conditions, you will want to focus on short trades as this will limit your risk of loss, especially if the downward trend continues.

2. The Overall Direction of the Market and Your Trade Should be Aligned

This is one reason research is important. You not only want to research when you are starting your swing trade profession, but you also want to continue your research. In fact, every day that you sit down in front of your desk, is a day that you will be doing research. One of these reasons is because you have to make sure to research and analyze every stock. This will help you determine whether you should purchase the stock or not.

When you are focusing on your research for a particular stock, one of the main focuses should be does the stock match the overall direction of the market? When it comes to the stock market, you will find that it's either on an upward or downward spiral. You will want to match your trade with this direction.

3. Always Look at the Long-Term Charts

One of the biggest mistakes that beginner traders often make is that they will only focus on the short-term charts when they are looking into a stock. Many experienced traders feel that this is the wrong course of action as you should have a better idea of what the trend of the stock has done over at least a six-month period. Of course, you can always go longer than six months.

You should start with the chart that will give you a couple of weeks. From there, you will want to make sure you go over the chart and notice every single detail. There is nothing that you should miss during the analysis of your chart. After you have looked at the first couple of weeks, then you can dive more into a long-term chart, such as the six-month chart. Again, follow the same microscopic process you did with the previous chart. Do your best not to miss anything. In fact, some traders will often create an excel spreadsheet where they can list everything they have to view in the chart and even write down information. This is a great piece of advice for any beginner.

4. Do Your Best Not to Enter Near the End of the Trade

Once you start to get into the stock market, you will notice a trend when it comes to traders. You will find that the stock market is busy within the first hour because there are so many traders who are buying new stocks for the day. You will then notice that the stock market begins to get quiet around the 11:00 hour because people are either holding on to their stocks or closed out for the day. However, about the last hour, which starts around 3:00 pm, you will notice the stock market picks up again as people, especially day traders, sell all their stocks and close out.

As a swing trader, you might not buy and sell stocks every day. Unlike day traders, you can hold your stocks for a few days to about a week or two. However, there are a few traders that are not allowed to do this as it would cause them too much loss.

Another reason people enter into trades earlier rather than later is because this can give you the most profit, especially if you find a stock that is hitting an upward trend. On top of this, you will have less risk to worry about if you enter a trade early. Doing your best to cut down on risk is always something traders focus on, even if they don't mind taking risks.

5. Track a Consistent Group of Stocks

Just like every trader is different, every stock is different. This is why it is important to not focus on jumping from one stock to the next. Instead, as you are learning the tricks and strategies of swing trading, you will want to start getting an idea of what kind of stocks you like.

Every stock has its own personality and once you catch on to that specific personality, trading will become easier if you stick to groups of stocks that are similar.

One reason for this is because you will most likely be able to use the same strategy for all of your stocks. This can help you when it comes to learning techniques and strategies. It is easier to stick to one strategy because there are so many tiny details about swing trading you need to remember, the human brain can only hold so much information.

Another reason for this is because this allows you to be able to manage a certain amount of stocks consistently. If you are a full-time swing trader, you will find this system will give you less stress, keep your focus, and increase confidence in your abilities. Of course, all this will help you keep your right state of mind as a trader.

6. Always Have a Clear Plan

Whenever you enter a trade, you will want to make sure that you have a clear plan of action. This plan will most likely be your trading plan; however, this is known to change from time to time as traders start to learn and grow with their profession. While this is great as it means you are becoming a more successful trader, you will also want to make sure that you continue to update and adjust your plan as you need to.

Before you enter any trade, it is best to go through your plan and make sure that it will work with that stock. If you find it won't, then you will need to either adjust your trading plan or choose a stock that will fit your trading plan better.

You will want to make sure that everything is including in this plan from your entry to your exit. You will want to make sure that you have all the key points and details down. On top of this, you will also want to make sure that you have a stop-loss strategy in place so you can quickly let go of that stock through a trade and walk away from losing a large amount of money. Remember, when you decide the stop-loss strategy is the best course of action, it will happen quickly. In fact, trading is a very faced-paced business, which is another reason making sure you always have a clear plan of action is a commandment.

7. Always Integrate Fundamentals into Your Technical Analysis

While I will discuss technical analysis later in this book, one of the 11 commandments of swing trading is to make sure that you integrate fundamentals into your analysis. If you have looked into day trading, you will know a bit about fundamentals and more about technical analysis. However, when it comes to swing trading, fundamentals becomes just as important as technical analysis. The main reason for this is because you hold your stocks longer than a few minutes to a few hours.

8. Make Sure to Master the Psychological side of Swing Trading

As you will see later in this book, there is a lot of psychology that goes into swing trading. In fact, psychology goes into any type of trading, but it is more crucial when it comes to swing traders. While part of this is about keeping the right mindset, the other part comes from the overall experience of swing trading. There are a lot of factors, such as making mistakes, learning, and losing that can affect your psyche throughout your day. For example, if you take a loss you might find that you feel like a failure after you have closed out your day. This can affect your personal life as well as your working life. It is extremely important to make sure that you have a healthy frame of mind and not just the right mindset when you are a trader.

9. Try Putting the Odds in Your Favor

Sometimes you will look at a trade and wonder if you will be able to make a profit on it. This is why it is important to use technical analysis with every trade. However, even if you feel that you might not be able to make a profit, this doesn't mean that you walk away from the trade. In fact, you can take this time to work on putting the odds in your favor. While this means you might end up risking a profit, trading is always full of risks. In fact, you will never be able to fully eliminate risks. Therefore, there are times where you have to take the leap and use certain techniques in order to try to work the trade into your favor.

One way to do this is by having a target price, which should always be a part of your target plan. This price will tell you when you should quickly turn to sell or trade the stock and when you should hold on to it for a bit longer. No matter what the market conditions arc, you always want to stick to your target price. Therefore, you want to make sure that you complete your technical analysis to the best of your abilities before you go forward with your trading plan.

Furthermore, it is important to not only assess the chart once but also to reassess the chart. This means that you don't just analyze the chart before you take on the trade as you will continue to look at the chart and see what the stock's trend is doing in real-time. This means that

175

you will notice the stock price increase and decreasing throughout the time you are analyzing.

10. Trade in Harmony with the Trend Time Frames

When it comes to the stock market, there are three types of trend time frames. The longest time frame is a year. The intermediate time frame is about three months. The shortest time frame is less than a month. When you are a swing trader, you will typically focus on the intermediate and short-term time frames. However, there are traders who have stated that they have looked at trends as far back as six months. Typically, swing traders don't have to focus on the longer time frame because they are considered to be short-term traders. At the same time, swing traders need to do more than just look at the short-term trend lines.

In fact, many expert swing traders will tell beginners that if they only focus on the short-term time frame, they are more likely to make mistakes. While you can always get a good sense of what the stock is doing with the short-term time frame, this can also limit you. The stock market is a very unpredictable place. This means that the further you look back, the better your idea will be about the type of trend that goes with the stock. The key is to heavily focus on the short-term trends and then do an analysis of the intermediate trends.

11. Make Sure to Use Multiple Indicators and Not Create Isolation

Sometimes traders will often feel that they only need to use one tool to give them an idea of what stock will give them a profitable trade and what stock won't. You should never do this. You always want to make sure that you use multiple tools and that these tools give you consistent results. For example, you might use a strategy, candlestick chart, volume, and other tools in order to find out that your trade will be profitable.

One of the reasons this is important is because it helps you limit your risks. The more tools you have that give you consistent results, the more likely you are to be able to make a profit.

Chapter 5: Profit and Loss Levels

Stop Loss and Take Profit levels are your exit points in the market. These are the levels which determine how much of a loss you take or how much money you make on the individual trade. Unfortunately, the way most trader's trade, they tend to morph these levels into Take Loss and Stop Profit levels.

Understanding the technical and mental side of these levels is essential to your performance, which is why we went over risk management and mindset prior to this, despite SL and TP being a technical subject. These levels are a snapshot of how trading works. Technical analysis combining with your mindset and risk management skill to ensure success. Let's take a deeper look at them.

Stop Loss Levels

As the name suggests, the stop loss level is that point on a chart beyond which you do not wish to be involved in the trade and would rather exit at a loss. Practically speaking, when you designate a stop loss level, your broker places an order at that level for you which close your position for a predetermined loss.

So in a long trade, your stop loss would be below your entry point. The stop loss order would be a sell order which closes your long position at a loss. In a short trade, your SL is above your entry point and the SL order is a buy order which closes your trade for a loss.

Most trading platforms provide easy options for you to place this order and it is essential that you do so. Beginners often fall into the trap of placing "mental" SLs because they feel their stops will be hunted by more experienced players. There is this erroneous belief that the bigger traders in the market push prices to a level where obvious stop losses ought to be, trigger those stop losses and then push the price back in the direction of a profit.

A Gnat on an Elephant

Let's get something straight. You as a retail trader are as relevant to the full-time professional trader as the events unfolding in Antarctica right now are for your breakfast tomorrow morning. Yes, there might be some sort of a butterfly effect thing that might happen, but the possibility is a remote one. This ridiculous belief that institutional and professional traders wake up every morning and using their multimillion-dollar infrastructure go looking to make money of the stop losses of the retail trader (who probably uses a discount platform) is beyond ridiculous.

Does it matter to you where an ant has decided to store its food? Do you wake up every morning telling yourself, "Today is the day I raid that squirrel's food stash"? Of course not! That is what precisely you are assuming though when you say your stop losses are being hunted by other traders and this is why you use "mental" ones. Yes, using mental stop losses is "mental" for a beginner trader. In more than one sense.

This myth has been perpetuated thanks to poor mindset on the part of unsuccessful traders. Rather than accept responsibility that they are determining poor stop loss levels, surely, it must be someone else's fault that they lose money! These traders cannot be blamed for this; it is out of their control! Take a moment to think about the beliefs these traders possess and how it contradicts the true nature of making money via trading.

Correct SL Levels

Placing stop losses is a skill that you will get better at as time goes on. You will probably have the majority of your SLs tripped before price goes in the original direction quite a lot in the beginning. Determining SL levels is a combination of understanding S/R, the volatility of the instrument and a gut feeling which comes with experience and errors.

The true definition of an SL is "the point beyond which if the price were to move your entry doesn't make sense anymore." This is a rather vague statement that doesn't help us when we're starting out, no matter how correct it is. Start off by placing your SL order under or over the closest key S/R levels to your entry point. Why key S/R level?

Well if you recall what constitutes a key level, you will recall why this level would act as a barrier for price. Key S/R levels are the best options for your SL levels in a balanced environment. In a highly imbalanced environment, you can use a more dynamic level like the 20 EMA to inform your stop less level. In other words, place it beyond the 20 EMA. If you're using a crossover strategy, you can place it below the crossover point as well (in appropriate environments).

The volatility of the instrument determines how far below or above you place the stop loss order. More volatile instrument requires greater breathing room than less volatile ones. When starting out, it is recommended you choose a slightly less volatile instrument. To get an idea of an instrument's volatility, observe how cleanly it respects key S/R levels when it retests them in different environments. Can you draw a relatively thin zone to mark the key level? Or is the zone wide? The wider it is, the more volatile the instrument. Take into account a large number of bars when determining this to avoid any recency bias (that is overvaluing the present).

Position Sizing

This is another area where beginners get tripped up. There's all sort of entry strategies out there involving pyramiding and scaling. It always pays to keep things as uncomplicated as possible. As such, leave the pyramiding, etc. to more experienced traders. Simply enter your full position size upfront.

How do you determine position size though? Well this is a relatively straightforward task and we'll use the example below:

Account size: 10,000 $

R: 0.25% or 25$

SL distance: 10 points

Position size= (R/SL) = 25/10= 2.5 units

The idea is the maximum loss you can sustain on this trade is the R amount. This is the simplest way to approach position sizing.

Take Profit Levels

Take profits can be approached in two different ways, unlike SLs where your only concern is determining the close key S/R level.

For beginners, a "set and forget" strategy is highly recommended. A set and forget strategy means you pick an SL, you pick your TP and then do nothing except observe the market as it moves towards either of those levels. You don't close out the trade at any time, and instead wait for one of those levels to be hit to exit the market.

TP Levels

Your TP level will simply be the place where, once price reaches it, you will make a pre-determined R multiple on the trade. When you have lots of data (at least 100 trades), you will know exactly which multiple makes you the most money and can calculate the level accordingly.

For the first 100, picking a 2R level is appropriate. Once you have enough data, you may realize that a 1.5R TP level increases your hit rate as well as your overall profit or maybe a 3R level decreases your hit rate but increases profits. Either way, you must understand, your first 100 trades are for the purposes of gathering data only. This is why it is crucial you keep your risk as low as possible.

These data gathering trades should not be on a live account as we'll see in the next chapter. For now though, let us look at how you calculate the TP price level. The calculation is the exact same formula as the SL one.

Account size: 10,000$

R: 0.25% or 25$

TP: 2R or 50$

Position Size: 2.5 units

TP distance from entry point= (TP/Position Size) = (50/2.5) = 20 points.

So in the above scenario, if you entered a long position at $100 and have placed your SL at 10 points, your positions size is 2.5 units, your SL sell order is placed at $90 and your TP sell order is placed at $120.

An Alternative

The set and forget is what you ought to start with in the beginning. Once you've placed over 200 or so trades, you can begin experimenting with your TP levels. You see, to make the most money possible, it is essential to let your winners run. To let them run, you will need to evaluate the upcoming S/R and determine whether price is likely to break through it or not.

This obviously requires a degree of emotional detachment from the result of your trade. If you've already made 2R on the trade, will you be strong enough to hold on for a further potential 5R? How would you react if it went up to 5R and then swerved back below 2R? Only you can answer this honestly and this is why it is recommended to stick to the set and forget method for at least 200 trades.

This concludes our look at the basics of SL and TP levels. Remember, once you've gathered data over 100 trades, you will need to analyze them to see what hit rate and R multiple makes you the most money. You might need to extend your TP level and reduce your hit rate or reduce your TP level and extend your hit rate. Ultimately, all that matters is which scenario maximizes your profit (not how many trades you were correct on or some such).

We're finally ready to put together everything we've learned into a full-fledged swing trading plan. The next chapter will delve into this and by the end of it; you will be ready to trade!

Chapter 6: Swing Trading Guiding Principles

Before I discuss various strategies that can be used to swing trade, let's look at the basic guiding principles that I build these strategies on. They are as follows:

- Keep it simple.

- Treat your swing trading activity like a serious business.

- Develop a work plan and stick with it.

- Actively manage your risk to reward ratio; focus on the entry.

- Measure your results and adjust accordingly.

Each of these principles is discussed in more detail below.

Keep it Simple

You may have heard of the term "paralysis by analysis". This happens when you analyze something to the point where you cannot make a decision. Some swing traders overcomplicate their analysis of a security by using multiple indicators that all have to line up for them to enter a trade. In real life, everything does not often line up perfectly and you have to go with what you feel is right.

I have thus far covered many different tools and indicators you can use to help you to make a decision. You do not need to use all of them to be a successful swing trader. Once you find 1 or 2 that work well for you, you should then stick with those. If you decide to use a few different tools that all need to align, it will likely mean that you are not going to be trading very often. That is not necessarily a bad thing though. It is better to sit on your hands and wait for a good trade versus jumping in and out of marginal trade setups and slowly lose your money. The only one who wins in that case is your broker, as they collect fees for all of your trades (the successful ones and the losing one's).

Find several indicators that work well for you and focus on using them. Don't trade often, but trade smart, by knowing why you are entering a trade and, most importantly, knowing your risk to reward ratio and exit price points. As you gain more experience in swing trading, you will be able to better recognize trades that are going to work out even if everything is not perfectly aligned.

Having said this, when you do happen to find a number of indicators that are all aligned with the trade you are considering taking, it can certainly provide some level of confidence that you have a potentially profitable trade.

Treat your Swing Trading Activity Like a Serious Business

Should you decide that swing trading is a right fit for your personality, and that it is able to fit into your life along with all of your other interests and responsibilities, then you need to treat this activity as a very serious business. It will require an investment of time and effort, which hopefully will lead to some very good rewards.

Have a designated area where you do your research and keep all of your records. You are essentially becoming a professional money manager for yourself, so you should keep your work organized at all times. Everything you do with your business should be oriented toward making sure you are a success. If you feel like a professional, then you are more apt to trade like one.

Develop a Work Plan

Have a work plan and stick with it. Your work plan should include checking the market at the open and before the close. During this time you should monitor your positions, set alerts and possibly enter orders at target levels that you think might get filled during the trading day.

I also recommend that you review your portfolio and market performance every night from Sunday to Thursday to ensure your assumptions about your positions and portfolio are still valid. On the weekend, you should try to do a more thorough review.

It is important to establish a work plan and keep it consistent. By keeping your work plan relatively consistent, you can measure your performance without introducing additional variables. Measuring your performance allows you to find areas to improve and make changes as you see fit.

I will discuss the routine of a swing trader in Chapter 14, which you can adopt or use as a guide to developing your own plan that works for you and your specific situation.

Actively Manage your Risk to Reward Ratio; Focus on the Entry

As a swing trader, your first and most important tool is your capital or cash. As I have said before, without cash you cannot be a trader. I have written at length already about the necessity of assessing the risk to reward ratio on every trade and also on how much capital you should put into each trade. Following your rules on these points will prevent you from quickly losing all of your capital. You will be wrong on your trades some of the time and you need to make sure you live to trade another day.

Just planning and knowing your stop-loss and profitable exits are not enough for swing trading. Your entry becomes the next important step in your trade. You have already determined your stop-loss point and your target price(s) for a profitable exit. However, you calculated the risk to reward ratio based on an assumed entry price point.

Let's assume you found a good setup during a scan in the evening after the market has closed. The security closed the day at $10.50 and you see an upside to $12.00 with support at $10.00 where you would stop out. Therefore, you have a potential $0.50 loss compared to a $1.50 gain to the upside. That is a 1 to 3 risk to reward ratio, which is very good, and you are ready to pull the trigger and place a buy order in the morning. The market opens the next morning and the security you are ready to buy opens up at $11.00. What do you do? The novice trader is already invested mentally in the trade so they buy. Unfortunately for them, their risk to reward is now 1 to 1 with the downside to $10.00 and upside to $12.00. This is no longer a good trade at that entry point.

The rational trader reassesses the situation. They may put a buy order in at $10.50, hoping to catch the entry they wanted on the security during the normal daily price gyrations in the market. This will give them the risk to reward ratio that they need to make a good swing trade. If they do not get a fill, then they need to reassess again, and maybe move on to finding another trade with a more appropriate risk to reward ratio.

The bottom line, do not get emotional and chase a trade. The "**fear of missing out**" can motivate you to make a bad trade and you should be aware of this when picking your entry price on a trade.

Measure your Results and Adjust Accordingly

As a trader, you must track your results to measure your performance. Nothing gets improved that does not get measured first. Every trader should use a tool to record the different aspects of each trade, from initial assessment through to the risk to reward expected, the entry point, and, finally, the exit. The tool can be a spreadsheet, it can be done on paper or it can be web-based. It does not matter how you do it as long as the process allows you to track the details of each trade as well as your performance.

Once you have your trades recorded in detail, you can go back at any time and review how the trade worked. You can compare your performance on using the different indicators, i.e., is one working particularly well versus the others that you use? Are you getting good entry points on your trades or do you need to exercise more patience? Are your exits working or are you consistently exiting a trade too early and not getting all of the money you could on a profitable trade? Are you respecting your stops?

Having all of this information to review will help you adjust your trading process and plan accordingly to maximize your performance without letting emotion enter into your decision-making.

Chapter 7: Swing Trading Rules

Before discussing specific strategies that can be used for swing trading, let's go over a few rules that I usually follow and why I have them. These are my general rules, which have evolved through experience and knowledge gained over the years. It is up to you to develop your own set of rules, which may include some or all of these.

The rules are based on 2 factors that I consider important in order for a trader to keep their capital and have a profitable business. These factors include the following:

- risk of holding a security

- over-the-counter stocks

Each of these factors is discussed in detail below.

Risks of Holding a Security

As a swing trader, under the right conditions you can see significant gains just by holding overnight or up to several weeks, which is what makes this type of trading attractive.

Earnings Reports

Even if a company reports good total revenue and profit numbers, there can still be some negative comments made on **"forward guidance"** for earnings that the market did not expect. One negative comment could easily send the price heading lower even if all of the other results were very good. This would be great if you were short the stock, but not good if you were long and hoping for a move higher after the report.

There are other ways to play earnings report events such as using **options** to limit risk and potential losses. Options strategies are more advanced and are not covered in this book.

Announcements about a Product or Service

Any positive or negative announcement about a product or service provided by the company has the potential to move the price significantly, either up or down. Pharmaceutical companies are a great example of this type of announcement. Events such as the results of a drug trial can cause a stock price to swing dramatically one way or the other depending on the outcome. If the results are negative - look out below – because small pharmaceutical companies have been known to lose 75% or more of their value overnight. If you happen to have a long position in the stock, you will have a substantial loss. Just like earnings reports, the problem with this situation is that the trader does not know which side to take prior to the announcement.

Other events, such as a product recall that would negatively impact your position, can also take you by surprise. Alternatively, you might be holding shares in a small company that wins a contract with a large company. Singular events like these are harder to predict and can be primarily managed by limiting how much of your portfolio is invested in any one position.

Secondary Offerings

Companies that need to raise money to sustain their operations while they develop a product or service often do secondary offerings. Announcements about an offering are usually done after normal trading hours and might come as a surprise to many holders of the stock. These offerings are often done when their stock price is moving higher, which would have led you to think you're "on a good roll" with your long position.

The amount of the gap down will depend on how far below the current market price of the stock the offering was completed at. For example, if a stock ends the trading day at $30.00 per share and the company announces a secondary offering at $23.00 that is probably going to be viewed by existing shareholders as very negative. Recent investors at around $30.00 are going to be really unhappy and selling will likely follow. If the secondary offering was done at $28.00 on the other hand, then that is not so bad because the new investors are paying much closer to the market price.

The offerings are not made public until they are completed and so there is no way to know when a company might do a secondary offering. This makes them hard to guard against as a swing trader. The best you can do is understand it is a risk and companies that burn a lot of cash with little current incoming revenue are the most susceptible to this risk.

Downgrades, Upgrades and Short Sellers Reports

Brokerage firms and analysts are constantly upgrading and downgrading companies and modifying their performance expectations. Some brokers have specialists that follow only one stock such as Apple. Other firms have specialists that research and report on a sector like semiconductors. A rating downgrade or upgrade by a brokerage research firm can cause a stock price to move one way or the other depending on the sentiment expressed in the report.

There are also a number of firms that specialize in looking for companies where they can make an argument that the business model is flawed or where there is the potential for fraud being committed.

These firms focus on finding companies to short and then release their arguments as to why they feel the company is overvalued. I recommend you watch "The China Hustle" (which is available on Netflix at the time of writing) if you have any doubts about how fraud can happen relatively easily in our regulated markets.

These analysts will normally release their reports outside of normal market trading hours, therefore, unfortunately for a swing trader, it is impossible to see these reports coming. Like many other unique events, the only way to protect yourself from a big loss is to practice your risk to reward strategies and limit how much of your total portfolio is invested in one position.

Other Announcements

Any other negative announcement such as a data breach, an SEC investigation, or a new lawsuit can hurt your position if you're long. A positive announcement such as the introduction of a new product, a partnership with another company, or the resolution of a lawsuit can negatively impact your account if you are short.

Unanticipated events are one of the challenges a swing trader faces and, as with all other unexpected occurrences, the best way to protect yourself from these is to practice your risk to reward plan. There is always the possibility that a singular event will work in your favor, such as being long a stock that announces a major partnership. You are there to capture the upside but you need to follow your trading plan and your risk to reward plan to protect your account on the downside.

Changes in Market Sentiment

Events and announcements can change market sentiment overnight. Regular reports such as the Institute of Supply Management's Manufacturing Purchasing Managers' Index (known as the PMI) are used as an indicator of the overall economic condition of the manufacturing sector. A release of an unexpected number can cause the overall market sentiment to become more positive or negative. With the PMI, a reading above 50 indicates that that particular sector of the economy is expanding, and a reading below 50 indicates it is generally contracting.

There are numerous other government and non-government reports regularly released such as housing starts, non-farm payroll numbers, inflation numbers, and Federal Reserve announcements, and each has the ability to impact overall market sentiment. A swing trader should be aware of these coming events and whether or not the market participants are putting a lot of weight on the release of an upcoming number. These events are easily accessible on a variety of websites including Estimate (under its Calendar tab).

Over-the-Counter or Penny Stocks

Over-the-counter trading happens off of the regular exchanges like the NYSE, NASDAQ and NYSE American (formerly known as AMEX). These transactions happen between dealers and can include stocks, bonds, currencies and other financial instruments. The stocks traded can include both company shares that are listed on recognized exchanges like the NYSE and stocks that do not have a recognized listing on an exchange. These unlisted stocks are primarily referred to as over-the-counter (OTC) equities.

These unlisted equities are traded through dealers because they are too small to get a regular listing on a recognized exchange and therefore they are unlikely to meet an exchange's requirements for listing. Unlike listed companies that are required to make regular filings with the SEC, OTC equities may not file as often or with as much detail, which means there could be limited information available about the company.

OTC equities may also trade in just a small number of shares per day. This limited trading activity means that there is a greater potential for share price manipulation by insiders and that it could be difficult to exit a trade once you have a position.

I avoid trading any OTC equities for the reasons listed above. I also try to avoid trading penny stocks (stocks under $1.00 per share), as they can also be more easily manipulated by insiders and are therefore less predictable. On occasion, I may consider a stock trading under $1.00 if there is a strong case for going long, but it would be a rare exception to my rule.

There is no need for a Retail trader to trade listed stocks OTC. If a stock is not listed on a regular exchange, then I do not trade those equities. This leads us to my next rule:

Rule #5: avoid trading over-the-counter (OTC) equities or stocks trading for under $1.00.

Chapter 8: The Art of Selling Short

One of the biggest pieces of advice you will hear from other traders is that you have to buy low and sell high if you want to make the best profit. This makes complete sense. Think about how retail markets work. Stores will often buy their stock at a lower price than what they sell them for. For example, the store owners might be able to purchase a notebook for $1.00 a piece, but when they put the notebook out on their shelves, they will most likely raise the price, which means you could be buying the notebooks for $1.50, which gives the store a 0.50 cent profit on each notebook they sell.

You want to think the same when you are trading stocks. You want to make sure that when you complete your trading plan for that particular stock that you set a stop-loss price as this will tell you how low you are willing to go. For example, if you decide that you don't want less than a dollar loss on a stock, you will set your stop-loss price at a dollar less than you paid for the stock. Of course, you hope that you will make a profit, which means that you will sell the stock at a higher price than what you paid for.

I have already discussed the difference between bull market and bear markets; however, to give you a bit of a review, a bull market occurs when the stock market is doing well and prices are rising. A bear market occurs when the stock market prices are dropping. So, when it comes to a bear market, you might ask why people trade as there isn't a way for them to make a profit. However, there is a way that traders can continue to make a profit when the stock market is seeing low numbers and this is through a technique called short selling.

How Short Selling Works

Unless you become a day trader, most traders will believe that they will hold on to their stock for a good period of time. Of course, when it comes to swing trading, you won't – or shouldn't – hold on to a stock for longer than a couple of months. With that stated, there are many beginning traders who feel that they are going to start trading and hold the stock for as long as possible as this will give them their best profit. If this is what you are thinking, you are looking more towards investing than trading.

The basic definition of short selling is when a trader takes on stock knowing that he or she is going to sell the stock after it has fallen in value. Of course, this is something that you are typically told not to do. However, there are many people who have used this position during bear markets and have found that it can be profitable. But, you are probably wondering how, if the price has lowered, the trader makes a profit from short selling. The truth of this trick is simple – the trader never actually takes ownership of the stock. Now your next question might be how a trader can sell a stock, and receive a profit, when he or she doesn't even own the stock. To look at this in a more basic way, let's look at it in two parts.

First, you have the part where the trader borrows the stock. This is usually done through a loan, which is similar to borrowing money from the bank. This means that the trader fully intends to buy the stock he sold back, which brings us to the second point. Because the stock prices continue to decline, the trader knows that he or she will be buying back the stock at a lower price than what they sold it for. Once they rebuy the stock, they send it back to the original owner, which closes out the loan, and the trader was able to make a bit of profit.

In order to start short selling, you will open a margin account through your broker. This account will use your profits in your account as collateral, just as a car is used as collateral for a vehicle loan. This means that if you are unable to repay your broker back in any way, your broker still receives the money as he or she can take it right out of your account. Furthermore, you need to note that you must be able to follow the 2:1 ratio when it comes to short selling. This means that your account must have at least 50% of what you are asking to borrow. For example, if you are asking to borrow $10,000 then you will have to have $5,000 in your account.

You need to be able to sell the stock to the first willing buyer. There isn't a huge time-frame for short selling. In fact, it tends to happen very quickly. Then, once the stock has sold, you have to go to the open market with that money and find a lower price for that stock. As you are doing this, it is important to remember that you have to buy back as many shares as you borrowed. Once you decide on your stocks, you will then inform your broker, who will make the transaction through your margin account. From there, your broker will receive his or her funds and you will receive the remaining profit.

The Risks of Short Selling

Of course, there are a lot of risk when it comes to short selling. The biggest risk is that you can never really tell the future. No matter how much you analyze charts or the general stock market conditions, such as if it's a bull or bear market, you will never be able to officially tell what a stock or the market is going to do. Because of this, one of your biggest risks is that you will have to buy back the stock at a higher price than what you sold it as. If this happens, you will take a loss instead of make the profit.

Another great risk when short selling is that you can get yourself into debt. Think of this – if you are unable to make a profit and you borrowed $20,000, this means you only have about $10,000 in your account. Therefore, not only will your broker take all the money in your account, but you still have to pay back the remaining $10,000.

Short selling is very strategic which can be risky, especially for a beginner. Short selling can seem like a very strange way to do things during an economic downturn. In fact, many beginners often question if short selling is even legal. Which it is, short selling is completely legal and is known to be a popular practice when the stock market is in bull conditions. However, because of its strategy and its risks, it can also be confusing for a beginner, even though you will be working with your broker.

Therefore, like with any other strategy, you want to make sure that you fully understand everything there is about short selling from the process to its risks before you decide to take on this technique during poor stock market conditions. While short selling occurs in a way that is meant to protect the trader's account, you also want to make sure that you understand that you can still bring yourself into debt if the process doesn't work as well as it should. You will also want to make sure that you go through the same trading plan, research, and following all your rules and guidelines before you decide to short sell. Understanding exactly what the stock market and the stock is doing will help limit your chance of a huge loss and, potentially, bringing yourself into debt.

Chapter 9: How to Start Trading

Now, it is time to move on and get to some of the basics about doing an actual swing trade. We are going to take a look at some of the steps that you need to take in order to enter the market, the types of positions that you can choose to take, and even how to take each of the positions that you choose. This will help you to get set up when it is time to do that first trade with this kind of trading strategy!

Choosing to Buy Long or Sell Short

The price of a stock is going to do one of three things at a given time. It will either go down, go up, or it will move sideways. When you enter into the market as a swing trader, you are expecting that the stock is going to either go up or it will go down. If you think that the stock will see an increase in its price, then they will purchase the stock. This move is going to be considered "going long" or having a "long position" in that stock. For example, if you are long 100 shares of Facebook Inc., it means that you purchased 100 shares of this company and you are making the prediction that you will be able to sell them at a higher price later on and earn a nice profit.

That one is pretty easy to understand, but what if you are looking at a stock and you expect that the price is going to decrease? When this situation occurs, you can choose to borrow shares and then later sell them with the expectation that you will purchase them back at a lower price and make a profit later on. At this point, you may be wondering how it is possible for you to sell shares that you don't own or that you don't hold in your own account?

This is pretty simple. Brokerages have a mechanism that will allow a trader to borrow the shares. When you end up selling shares that you don't actually own, it means that you are "going short" or "being short' on a stock. When a trader says that they are short on a stock, it means that they borrowed shares from the broker and then sold them with the expectations that the price will drop, and they will be able to replace those shares by purchasing them later at a lower price.

When you are setting up an account to trade, you will probably need to take the time to fill out some additional forms with the broker so that you can take this short position with a stock. You should also have an idea that this option can be riskier compared to just going long or purchasing a stock, so you must be actively there to manage the position.

Short selling can be an important tool for you as a swing trader because the prices of the stocks are usually going to drop much faster than they will go up. It is a good rule of thumb to say that stocks are going to fall three times faster than they rise. This is often because of the human psyche; the fear of loss is more powerful than the desire for a gain.

When the stock starts to move down, shareholders are going to fear that they will have to lose their profits or gains, and they move to sell that quickly. This selling activity is going to feed into more selling as shareholders continue to take the profits and traders start to shorten. This additional shorting activity adds to the downward pressure that is there on the price. This sends the price of the stock into a strong decline, which means that short sellers are able to make a good amount of profits while long traders and other investors are going to enter panic mode and may try to dump their shares to protect themselves.

Knowing this information can make it easier to do the trades that you want. It can help you to figure out which position you would like to enter based on how the market or that particular stock is doing at the time. This also shows you that it is possible to get into the market and make profits, no matter which direction you think the market is heading.

How to Enter a Trade

If you are brand new to trading, you are probably curious about how you would sell or purchase a security. Any time that the market is open, there are going to be two prices for any security that can be traded. There will be the bid price and the ask price. The bid price is what buying or purchasing traders are offering to pay for that stock right then. The ask price, on the other hand, is the price that traders want in order to sell that security.

You will quickly notice that the bid price is always going to be a bit lower simply because the buyers want to pay less, and the asking price is always going to be higher because sellers want more for their holdings. The difference between these two prices is known as the spread.

The spreads that are found will vary for each stock, and they can even change throughout the day. If a stock doesn't have a ton of buyers and sellers, then there could be a bigger spread. When there are more buyers and sellers, then the spread between these two prices will be much lower.

As a swing trader, when you are ready to enter into a position, you are going to have two choices. You can either go in or pay the price that the seller is asking for right away or you can place a bid that is at or below the bid price. Paying the asking price immediately can be beneficial because it ensures that the purchase transaction is completed or filled but may mean that you will pay more for it. When a trader places a bit at or below the current bid price, they may be able to make the purchase at a lower price. But, there is the risk that no seller will want to sell for the lower price, and the order may not get filled.

When you are ready to get started with a trade, you will simply need to pick out your trading platform (we will talk more about this in the next chapter), pick out a stock, and then decide whether you want to pay the asking price or wait and see if you can get it for the bid price. Then, you can enter into the trade and complete the rest of your strategy.

Investment and Margin Accounts

There are two types of accounts that you can choose to open in order to trade stocks. The two main options include the margin account and the investment account. With a margin account, you can borrow against the capital that you have placed in your account. The investment account, on the other hand, will allow you to buy up to the dollar value you hold in that account. You are not able to spend more than what you have put in that account at a time.

When you decide to open up a margin account, you may be able to borrow money from the investment or brokerage firm to help pay for some of your investment. This is a process that is known as buying on margin. This can provide you with some advantages of purchasing more shares that you would be able to afford if you just used the capital in your account, and it can help you leverage to get more profits with your money.

However, there is a catch with this one in the form of more risks. When you borrow the money to do your investments, there will come a point when you must pay the loan back. If you earn the profits that you think you will, it is easy to pay this back. But, if you lose out and make the wrong predictions, you are going to have to find other ways to pay the money back. Making investments with leverage can magnify the percentage losses on your money.

As a beginner, you should stick with a regular investment account. Trading on margin can increase the amount of risk that you are taking on in your trades. This may be tempting because it can increase your potential profits, but there is a lot more risk that comes with it as well. You will do much better going with an investment account instead. This way, you can just pull out the money that you are comfortable with rather than hoping that you make a good prediction in the beginning when you are learning.

Picking out a Broker

During this process, we also need to take some time to discuss picking out a broker. If you have already gotten into other forms of trading in the past, then you can simply work with the same broker that you already have. But, if you are getting into trading and this is the first one you have done before, then you will need to search to find the right broker for you.

There are many different brokers out there, and many of them can assist you with swing trading. The biggest thing that you will want to look at is the commissions and fees that each broker assesses against you. Since swing trading times are relatively short and you will enter into and out of trades within a few weeks at most with each trade, you want to make sure that the profits you make aren't eaten up by the commissions to your broker.

There are different methods that the broker can use to come up with their fees. Some will charge a fixed rate for the whole year. This often works well for long-term trades and probably won't be an option available to you since you will do more trades. The two options that you will most likely deal with include a fee for each trade or a fee based on how much profit you earn.

If you can, find a broker who will earn a fee based on your profits. This way, you are not charged a ton if you do a bunch of trades during that time. If you earn a good profit, you will have to pay a bit more because of the percentage. If you earn less on one of your trades, then you won't have to pay the broker as much as you did before.

Before you enter into any trade, make sure that you discuss the fees with your broker. They should be able to outline their fees and can discuss with you where your money will go when you work with them. This can help you to get a good idea of how much you will spend based on how much you earn, how many trades you decide to enter into, and more. Get the commissions and fees in writing, along with any other agreements that you and the broker and their firm agree to in order to protect you.

Picking out How Much You Want to Invest

Finally, before we move into talking about some of the different swing trading platforms that you can work with, we need to discuss some of the basics of about how much you are going to invest in your account. Since we have already discussed the importance of working with an investment account rather than trying to do the trading on margin, you will need to decide how much money you would like to put into your account.

First, talk with your brokerage firm and decide how much you need to put in to meet their requirements. Some brokerage firms will ask you to spend a certain amount or keep a certain amount in your accounts at all times in order to trade. If your chosen firm has that kind of requirement, then make sure that you put in at least that much. Putting in more is up to your discretion.

If there isn't a requirement for a minimum, it is best to start out by putting in an amount that you are comfortable losing. No one hopes to lose money on any of their trades. But, it does happen, especially when you are a beginner. Putting in just the amount that you would be willing to lose if something goes wrong can help to reduce the amount of risk that you are taking on.

Getting started with swing trading can be exciting. This is a fun type of trading that moves quickly and can help you to earn a good profit in a short amount of time but still doesn't require you to spend all day on the computer watching how the trade is going. By following some of the tips above, you will be all prepared to take on some of your first trades with this strategy.

Chapter 10: The Basics of Swing Trading Platforms

Before you are able to start trading, whether you decide to do the trading full-time or part-time, there are a few tools that you will need to make the trading easier. First, you must make sure that you open an account and that you do it with a broker. Your broker will then be able to supply you with an online order execution platform. You will need to take the time to learn how to use it, but you will find that most of them are easy to learn to use.

Fortunately, there are many brokers and stock trading platform options available that make it easy for you to do your trades online. But, the choices that you have with brokerages will often depend on the country that you are living in at the time. If you don't already have your own trading account that is active, you should do a search online in order to find reviews of the brokers available in your area. Some of the things that you will need to consider when picking out a broker include the type of account, the commissions and fees that the broker charges, and the platforms and tools that they offer. Let's take a look at some of the factors now.

Type of Account

The first decision that you must make is whether you want to open an investment account or a margin account. Margin accounts do allow you to borrow against the equity that is present in the account. This is great for allowing you to make bigger investments with the money that you have. This is going to require some additional paperwork, and not every brokerage account will offer this option. If you want to trade with a margin account, you need to search around to find a company that will do this with you.

If you want to work with an investment account, you will have many more options when it comes to the brokers that you want to use. This also includes less risk for your trades and can help you make smarter investment decisions. But, no matter which account you choose to work with, make sure to research your options and then find the broker who will work the best for you.

Commissions and Fees

The costs to trading are usually going to be right at the top of mind for an investor when it comes to them purchasing and selling stocks. If you do several of these trades during the day, you will find that the costs add up quickly. Since you are a swing trader and will be doing quite a few of these trades, you want to make sure that you get the best deals when it comes to the commission that you pay.

Being able to compare the commissions for each broker can be confusing. Some are going to offer a flat fee for each trade, and this can range between $5 and $35 depending on what you are doing and the company you choose and how many trades you do each month. Sometimes, you will be able to get a discount based on doing a minimum number of trades for the month.

There are also some brokers who are able to charge a fee based on the number of shares that you purchase or sell, and there will be a minimum charge that you will see. For example, they may charge $0.005 per share, but you have to do a $1.00 minimum for your trades. If you purchased 1,000 shares, you would pay $5 in commission, and then, there are some brokerages that charge an activity fee or other fees based on the services and tools that you can take advantage of.

Platforms and Tools

The trading platforms that you can use are going to be different based on the brokerage that you choose. Some are going to offer different amounts and levels of services depending on how much you will pay. To do swing trading, you will want a platform that offers real-time quotes and a straightforward order process that does the trades right away to keep you up to date and to ensure that you don't miss out on the prices that you want.

It is also ideal if you are able to pick out a platform that can give you real-time charting, one that can give you at least a bit of help with technical analysis, and one that can provide you with information such as research reports, analysts' ratings, and financial data. These features may vary based on the strategy that you want to use.

Some of the things that you should look for when it comes to picking out the brokerage and the platform that you want to use include:

- **Research:** There are some platforms out there that will provide some reports that are exclusive to their subscribers. Much of the research that you will need, though, is available for free online. This is a nice feature if it is offered, but not one that you should base your decision from.

- **Investment offerings:** Some brokers will differ on the funds and securities that they will allow you to trade with them. Most are going to have a good range to work with. If you have a particular security you are interested in, go ahead and search for that with every brokerage you are considering.

- **Education:** Some brokerages will offer you tutorials and other educational options for how to do the trading and how to use the platform. This can make things easier when you are first getting started.

- **Mobile access:** This is another one of those nice things to have and can be useful if you happen to be on the go a lot and still want to be able to monitor your trades. It is definitely a positive if a brokerage you are looking at provides this service.

- **Scanning tools:** When you are looking for a platform, you want to have options that scan for the best purchasing opportunities. You don't necessarily need a real-time scanner if you choose to go a different way, but it can be helpful. There are also some great free online scanning tools that you can implement as well if you choose.

- **Alerts:** The brokerage that you choose should provide an alert service. This is something that will send an email or a text to you when events occur. For example, if you are waiting for a good entry price for a stock, you could set up the account to send you an alert about this, so you can act quickly when needed, without missing out on a great opportunity.

Getting started with your first trades in swing trading doesn't need to be difficult. Sometimes, the most important thing is to pick out which brokerage and platform you want to work with, figuring out what fees they like to charge, and then putting your money into the account. From there, you can decide on the strategy you want to work with and start out with your first trades!

Chapter 11: How to Assess the Risks of Each Trade

No matter how many safeguards you put in place with your trading, you will find that there is going to be some risks, and since you are working with swing trading, you will find that there are even more risks with this kind of trading than with some of the other options due to the smaller time frame for the trading. Being able to manage your risks in an effective manner can make a big difference in how successful all of your trades will be. There are four main things that you can do to help you limit your risks and protect your capital, and they include:

- Learn how to properly assess the risk and the reward of each trade

- Set up your stops and your targets

- Manage the dollar size of each trade

- Maintain a journal that has all of your trading activities to help measure your performance and find ways to improve it in the future

Assessing the Risk and the Reward for Each Trade

The first thing that you need to focus on with each of your trades is how to manage your risk. The objective here is not to buy and sell stocks; it is to make a profit in the stock market. Your broker is the only winner if you just go in and randomly buy and sell stocks in the market without any thought of how you are going to do this. Your job as a trader is to learn how to manage both your risk and your account.

Whenever you click on the buy or the sell button, you will expose your money to the risk of loss. Figuring out how to limit this a little bit can make a big difference how much you can earn.

A trader who is unsuccessful will likely look at an entry and then only think about the profit they will make on that trade. But, a trader who is successful is always going to consider the upside and the downside with any trade they choose. So, they are going to think about how much of a risk they are going to have if they take a loss. It is all about comparing the amount of risk that you are going to take to the reward that you are hoping to get from that trade.

To help you get a good trade setup, you should expect to get at least two times the reward when you compare to the risk that you plan to take. If you can get this number higher up, the reward is even better. If you use this strategy with your trading, you will find that you can be successful, even when you end up being wrong a few times.

Let's take a look at a good setup for this kind of trading and how we are able to assess what the risk will be when it is compared to the reward. On February 11th, a trader is looking at the chart of ETF XBI and notices that there is a nice setup for them to purchase some shares or for them to go long. The basic principles of why this would be a good trade will be discussed a bit later.

While looking at the charts for this trade, the trader would determine that, if they went long on XBI at $87.50 a share, they would risk about $1.00 a share. At around the $86.50 level, the low close of a recent price move, the swing trader would consider the trade a failure, and they would then sell the position for a loss if this did happen.

For the reward, they are hoping that the XBI stock is going to reach $91.00 for each share or the prior area of resistance. This can help them earn $3.50 a share for this one. This means that, in this scenario, the risk is $1.00 a share, but the reward is a potential $3.50 a share. This ends up being a very good risk to reward ratio. If the reward only ended up being $0.75 a share, then it is best to look for another option since the risk is too high for that trade.

Setting Your Stops and Targets

Now that we have a little better idea of the concept of risk to reward, the next thing that we need to take a look at is how to put all of this in action. The stop loss is very important no matter what kind of trading you work with, but it becomes even more important when you are working with swing trading and you want to preserve your capital. As a successful trader, or someone who is hoping to become successful, you need to see this stop loss as your best friend.

Any trading system or strategy will end up with losses at some point. A trader who is successful will accept these losses, and then, they will be able to walk away from a trade that didn't make them a profit. Once you have gone through and done a complete assessment of a trade, and you have figured out that the potential reward is at least 2 times the risks; you will then push the right buttons to complete the trade.

Once the trade is started, your capital is now going to be at risk, and the best way to protect it is to set the stop loss price. This stop point is going to be the price level where you determine that the trade is going against your predictions and you want to make sure that you don't lose too much. The place you put this stop loss is going to depend on the trading strategy that you choose to go with, but it basically will help you go with a small loss rather than the potential big loss that could happen.

The stop loss is a good way to keep your ego and your emotions out of the game. You have to learn as a trader that the market is right, even if it is going against the predictions that you make. You can't control the market; you can only try to predict where it will go. If you are sitting there rationalizing the trade or looking for some justification on why the market isn't moving the way that you want it to, then emotions have gotten in the way and you are in trouble.

Manage the Size of the Trade

The next thing that we need to take a look at is how to manage and control how much of your available capital you are going to invest in one particular trade. Even with a great strategy and a lot of planning, there are going to be times when you have winning trades and times when you will have losing trades. This is why it is important to never overcommit your capital on one trade or you may work yourself out of the market.

Many experienced traders will use a rule of thumb that says that, for one trade, you should not risk more than two percent of your capital. This means that if you put $20,000 in your account, then you shouldn't risk more than $400 on the trade. Let's look at an example of how this would work.

Let's assume that you want to work with a stock that is trading at $10 for each share. You are looking at the price, and it seems like the movements are going to go higher. You want to enter here because it looks like the price is going to head up to $10.75, where it will then find some price resistance. There is also some price support at $9.75, which means that you won't lose a lot of money on the trade either. This helps you to figure out how much reward to risk ratio you are dealing with, and in this case, you are going to find that the reward is three times as high as the risk.

Once you figure this out, the next thing to consider is how much you should purchase the stock. In other words, how much money should you put into the trade? Going with the same example where you have $20,000 total capital, you shouldn't risk more than $400.00. With a stop loss placed at $0.25 per share below the entry of $10.00, you wouldn't want to purchase more than 1600 shares. With this method, if you do get stopped out, you will only lose $400 at most on that trade.

Of course, you don't want to end up losing anything on the trade if you can help it. You want to make a prediction that the cost will go up and you can enjoy a nice profit in the process. But, this is a good way to protect yourself and limit the risk to your investment. If you went through and didn't put in a stop loss or you invested more than the two percent, you would end up losing a ton of money if you made a lot of investments.

Maintaining a Trading Journal

The final thing that you should consider doing is maintaining a trading journal that will talk about the different trades that you have done. You can do this online or keep a paper copy nearby. When you are done with one trade, make sure to write down what happened during that trade, what strategy you used, what was going on in the market, how much you spent, and more.

This is a step that a lot of people like to skip, but it can really help you out later on. The more details that you can add to it, the better it is. If you ever get stuck with one of your trades or you aren't sure how to handle one situation or another, you can refer back to this journal and see what advice it has. You may be surprised that, after a particularly hard situation in a different trade, you can look back in this journal and find the answers that you need.

Chapter 12: The Biggest Rules to Follow in Swing Trading

Swing trading can take some time to master. It is easier to work with compared to working with day trading, but it is much harder and requires a lot of patience and time commitment compared to working with some of the longer-term investments that you can choose. Despite this extra work, there is the potential for you to make a big profit with limited risk if you follow the right rules. This chapter will take some time to look at some of the rules that you need to see success when it comes to swing trading.

Align the trade with the market

When you are trying to figure out what trades to do, you always need to take a look at what the market is doing. The market is not going to behave in the manner that you would like, so you need to learn how the market is about to behave and then pick your trades to go with that.

The overall direction the market will take will be measured through the S&P 500. These trends will provide you with some context for making your short-term trades. Remember that short-term trades will be a bit different than you will find with long-term trends and look at how the market will behave in the next few weeks is more important than worrying about how the market will do over the next few years.

However, you also do need to pay some attention to the trends that happen over the long-term with swing trading. These trends will often show up again and again for a particular stock and take a look at them can help to increase your profit potential. Yes, it is important to take a look at the short-term and see what is going on with the market to see if anything is about to change and then trade along with that trend. The more you can look at the charts, both long-term and short-term the more you will be able to make good decisions on your trades.

Go short weakness and long strength

You should not avoid or fight off the tape once you figure out what the overall trend is. You need to look at the charts to find long trades that will work during periods of bullishness. And then when you are dealing with periods of bearishness, you need to find the right short trades. These trends will help you to get the results that you would like when it comes to successful swing trading.

Enter at the beginning rather than the end

One mistake that some beginners will make is that they will try and enter the trend near the end of it, rather than catching the trend at the beginning. This will limit some of the money that you can make if you wait too long to enter into a trend. Of course, it is much better to get into the market at some time for the trend, before it goes down because you will be able to make some money, but the earlier you can get into the trend, the more money you can make.

When looking at the charts, it is important to look for early signs of the change. The earlier you can see these new trends, the less risk you will take with swing trading and the bigger the profits you will make. This means that you have to be active. Trends can go quickly and if you are not careful about what is going on in the market, and you are not looking at the market averages, you will end up missing out on some trends and will miss out on some money, or even lose money.

Looking at the overall market averages on your charts will help out with this. When you look at the market averages, you will sometimes see that the stocks have been oversold or overbought. When this has happened, it means that it is likely they will turn around again soon. If the trend looks like it is about to reverse, you can jump in, get the stock for a good price, and sell it over the next few weeks when things start to go back up.

You need to get some of your own indicators in place to figure out when these trends are about to happen. The Volatility Index, the Put/Call Ratio, and the Arms Index are good tools. You will be able to see, through these methods, when the market is testing a major zone of resistance and support, and it can help you to predict what will happen in the future.

On the other hand, looking at moving average crossovers and trend lines will make you fall behind. These are just going to confirm that a trend is happening and by the time you see them and join in on a trade, it may be too late to make any money. These tools can help you determine if you have made a good decision along the way, but if you are relying solely on them, you will miss out.

Never trade on one technical concept

With swing trading, things will change on a frequent basis. You need to work with trading quickly, picking up one trade and then selling it within a few weeks. You do not get the benefit of staying with the market for a very long time, or you are missing out on the profits you can make. Relying on just one technical concept will lead you to a lot of trouble along the way.

In most cases, the highly profitable trades will occur when you can find at least two (but more is much better) technical tools send you the same message. There are times when several of your tools will show the same indicators, and this means that the stock will rise or fall sharply in the near future. This is great news for you. The more indicators that show the same information, the more likely that the trend is about to occur and that you will make a large profit in the process.

However, there are times when one indicator will show that a trend is about to occur. If you only look at that one indicator, you may find out after entering the trade that it is wrong. You want to have at least a few indicators in place to help you make your decisions. The best opportunities for swing trading will show up in at least a few indicators, and when you can get three or more of these to show up with the same message over a two or three day period, this will increase your profitability.

Enter the trade with a good plan

There are a lot of different strategies and plans that you can go with. Many of them can be successful when it comes to swing trading, but you do need to pick out a good one and stick with it. One of the worst things that a beginner can do is get started with a strategy, see that it is maybe not doing as well as they had hoped, and then skipping over to a new strategy right in the middle of their trade. This is setting yourself up for failure, and you are more likely to lose money with this method than any other.

It is fine to switch out the types of strategies that you want to use if you find one is not the best for you. But you must make sure that you pick out a strategy and use it for the whole time of your trade. Even if the trade is not going the way that you would like, stick with the strategy. This will limit your risks, and you will learn more from the experience in the long run. If a strategy is not the right one for you, simply switch to a different one the next time.

Try to work the odds

You are not able to make the market work the way that you would like. The market will behave however it would like. There are a lot of different people who are in the market, and the swing trading will only take place over a few days. You need to learn how to work with the market, rather than trying to influence it.

It is never a good idea to risk a dollar just so you can make a dime. You have to pick out smart trades, trades that will lower your risk as much as possible while making your high profits. There will be some trades that may promise a lot of money if you try them, but the risk is so high that you are likely to lose all of your investment plus more without making anything.

The best trades that you can do are ones that will provide you with a strong profit if you make the right types of decisions, but where you can limit your losses as much as possible if you are wrong. The profits may not be as big as some of the trades that you can make, but it ensures that you will not lose out on all your investment either.

Learn to control the emotions a little bit

The most important thing that you can do when you get into swing trading is learning how to keep your emotions out of the game. This is important no matter which investment you choose, but it is especially important when you are working with some of these short-term investments. Once your emotions get into the mix, it is a lot harder to make smart decisions and smart trades that will lead to profits.

If you let your emotions get into the mix, you are likely to make poor trading decisions. You will make decisions that will lead you to lose money. You will stay in the market too long, hoping to earn more money, or hoping that you can recover some of your losses. Basically, when you start letting the emotions get into the mix, you are risking your money, and you will end up losing out on all your hard work.

For those who are not able to think through their decisions critically, who are not able to keep their emotions out of the trades that they will do, it is much better to just stay out of the market completely. Swing trading needs some fast decision making and the help of a lot of research. If you are not able to do this without all the emotions, you will fail in the long run.

Do your trading with a consistent group of stocks

When you first get started with day trading, it is pretty easy to jump around between stocks. You may find on that looks good and then want to jump to another once the trade is all done. There is nothing wrong with following the action, but it is always best to have your core stocks that you track on a regular basis and learn how they work.

Having a few regular stocks is a great way to see regular success with swing trading. These regular stocks will allow you to learn about the market better and can save a lot of time researching. You will have time to learn how the stocks work and understand how they have performed in the past and are likely to perform in the future. It takes some of the work out of it all when you can stick with a few core stocks over the long term.

Of course, there is nothing wrong going with a new stock on occasion if you see some big trends that are coming up. This can be a great way to increase your profit, especially if you have been in the market for some time. But chasing after those new stocks can take up a lot of work. Learn as much about your core stocks as possible and you will save a lot of work, reduce your risk, and increase your profits.

Everyone will spend time working with different methods and strategies when it comes to swing trading. And even with different methods, it is possible to see many people make a profit. If you follow some of these rules and learn how to pick the right strategy, you will see some great results when it comes to swing trading.

Chapter 13: Forex Swing Trading with Elliott Wave

While assessing the forex market for swing trade opportunities the attention is put on foreseeing directional changes or continuations for a given currency pair. For this, we depend on technical analysis.

In technical analysis, similarly as in fundamental analysis, there are slacking pointers and driving markers. A standout amongst the most solid apparatuses used to foresee forex market swings is Elliott Wave analysis. Elliott Wave analysis can be utilized to distinguish patterns and countertrends, pattern continuation or weariness and to assess the potential value focuses on a trend.

You can apply Elliott Wave analysis to both long and short position swing trade setups for your currency pairs.

Elliott Wave hypothesis is named after Ralph Nelson Elliott, who reasoned that the markets moved in a monotonous example of waves. He credited this activity to the mass psychology of the market.

Elliott presumed that the market's development was an immediate aftereffect of the mass psychology of the time and that the stock market is a fractal. A fractal is an item that is comparable fit as a fiddle, yet at various scales. An incredible case of a fractal in nature is a stalk of broccoli. The stalk and the individual branches appear to be identical; simply the branches are littler in scale.

Fractals happen to shape as per Fibonacci proportions. Is this an occurrence?

Elliott qualities this mass mental move to the human characteristic of crowding. Even though Elliott's speculations depended on stock market value developments, it has been connected to assessing Presidential endorsement appraisals and design patterns changes too.

The end, the market value activities are not the reason for financial development or back off, yet the impression of the mass psychology of speculators. If the disposition of the contributing open is playful, at that point a bull market results. This is counter to what most individual see, that because there is a bull market the state of mind of the contributing open is energetic.

Elliott Wave designs pursue an arrangement that the markets climb in a progression of 3 waves and down in a sequence of 2 waves. This three-wave drive and two waves restorative arrangement structure the establishment of the 5 Wave motivation design (the inverse is valid in a downtrend).

The Elliott Wave Counts are as per the following;

> Wave 1 - Short Covering
> Wave 2 - Pullback from Short Covering
> Wave 3 - Major Rally Phase
> Wave 4 - Institution Pause in the Rally
> Wave 5 - Retail Buying

Wave 1 is typically the weakest of the drive waves. It is a concise rally dependent on the short covering of the bears from a past move down. At the point when Wave 1 is finished, the currency pair auctions, making Wave 2.

Wave 2 closes when the market neglects to make new lows. You regularly observe prevailing inversions designs structure toward the finish of this wave flagging the being of the rally stage or Wave 3.

Wave 3 is the longest and most grounded of the drive waves. This stable sign currency is purchasing or selling toward the pattern. This pattern begins typically gradually, however will in general quicken as it breaks to new highs over the highest point of Wave 1.

Like any pattern, particularly a solid pattern an amendment will happen. Traders will start to take profits, and the currency pair will backtrack. This flags the start of Wave 4.

Again, the currency pair will rally introducing the Wave 5 rally. Wave 5 is commonly upheld by the retail traders and not institutional purchasers (the group) and will, in general, come up short on the energy produced in the Wave 3 rally. This makes dissimilarity that can be effectively estimated on any technical oscillator. After the currency pair breaks to new highs over the past Wave 3 high, the Rally loses steam and changes pattern.

This pattern change can result in either another 5 Wave motivation design or a restorative in nature.

Since we know what the Elliott Wave analysis is, how might a currency trade utilizing this analysis resemble, similarly for instance?

Hope to Wave 5 as the most dependably tradable drive wave. The trade sets up as pursues. Search for the Elliott Oscillator to pull back somewhere in the range of 90% and 140% of the Wave 3 high on a day by day diagram. This pullback ought to relate to a 38%-62% Fibonacci retracement from the Wave 2 augmentation. This flag is the most grounded when the Fibonacci retracement is between 38% - half.

Like any technical analysis device, you never need to utilize a pointer as an independent analysis device. A trigger and an affirming marker are required also.

Search for a trigger in light examples, for example, Harami, Tweezers or Harami cross. There is an assortment of programming bundles on the market that perform Elliott Wave checks and have other section flag pointers too.

Draw a relapse channel on the Wave 4 retracement and search for a break above or underneath the channel as affirmation to enter the trade.

Spot stops at the high of the Wave 1 advance, just underneath the 38% Fibonacci retracement level or where your individual exchanging plan directs. Trail your stops once the currency pair has progressed past the Wave 3 high. Search for inversion light examples like doji, hammers, meteorites or balancing keeps an eye on for signs that the wave is going to end or slow down. A commonplace value target is 127% retracement of the Wave 4 low.

This is only a look at how Elliott Wave analysis can be conveyed to upgrade your forex swing trade assessments. Look more into the Elliott Wave hypothesis and different systems as devices for expanding your forex swing trade opportunities.

Chapter 14: How to Analyze Stock Charts and How Do These Charts Work?

For many of the strategies that we are going to discuss in this guidebook, you will need to be able to go through and analyze stock charts. These charts can provide you with a lot of information on how the market and an individual security are doing at that time, and you can use them to make smart decisions about the way that you trade. This chapter is going to take some time to show you the different parts of these stock charts and teach you how to read them for your own swing trades.

Identify the Trend Line

When you look at a stock chart, you will notice a line that goes up and down for the stock. This is going to show where the stock is and where it has been over a certain period of time that you are looking like. While this one is pretty simple, we need to point out a few things to help you see what this line is about.

First, understand that all stocks, even ones that are strong and doing well, take huge dives and huge climbs throughout their lifespan. It is important to realize that this is normal and you shouldn't work on your emotions because this could lead you away from some great stocks that are only having a temporary downturn for a little time. You shouldn't react to huge gains or large drops. The trend line should lead you to dig a bit further into the stock.

Realize that, sometimes, a downturn in the stock isn't always a bad thing. For example, Apple had really great stock growth from 2009 to 2012, but from 2012 to 2013, there was a big decrease. Does this mean that the company was failing? No, there was just some different things going on in the company that led to a lower perception of them and made it harder for them to make as big of profits. Steve Jobs retired during that time, and Apple Inc. tried to expand into other markets where it was just too expensive to compete.

These things were easy for the company to overcome as they made some changes afterward. Good investors who dug a little bit deeper and saw these temporary issues may have jumped on the stock during that time when it was at a low price and then saw it grow and give them a lot of profit as time went on and Apple was able to recover.

Look for the Resistance and Support Lines

Once you have had some time to take a look at the trend line, it is time to look for the lines of resistance and support. These are the levels where a stock is going to stay between within a given period of time.

The level of support is a price that the stock is unlikely to drop below unless some big news happens to come out and causes the sock to go even lower. Then, there is the level of resistance, which is the level that the stock is unlikely to go above, at least for a little period of time.

Knowing these two points can help you to make some important decisions when it comes to your trades. It can also help you determine your risk to reward ratio when you are deciding whether to enter into a trade or not. Even if the stock or security ends up staying within that range, these levels can make it easier for you to get profits from your trades.

If you are watching the news or paying attention to the market, you will learn how to spot when a breakout is going to occur. This is when the price of that security will go either below the support line or above the resistance line. You want to watch out for those and pay attention to them to help you make the right decisions for your trade.

Of course, there can be some times when these numbers are going to change and the lines won't' stay the same. If a major change occurs or a big news announcement is made with the company, then these two lines can change. In addition, the resistance and support levels are not going to stay the same forever. If you want the stock for a longer period of time, you will see that these two lines are going to move as the stock prices change as well.

Since you are working with swing trading, you are only looking at a small area of time, so the resistance and support lines are probably going to be a good thing to watch out for. You should be able to see that the stock stays within that range for at least a few days, and you can certainly purchase when the stock price gets to the support level and then sell when the stock gets close to, at, or above the resistance levels.

Know When the Dividend and Stock Splits Occur

When you are looking at the charts for these stocks, you will be able to see if, as well as when, the company was able to issue a dividend. You can also check if there was ever a stock split.

A dividend is going to occur when the company or the board of directors more likely decide to hand out some of its earnings to the shareholders. This is only going to happen if the company earned enough profits to cover all its debts and obligations and then still has some leftover. If you own these stocks, you will earn a bit of the profit. Some companies are going to issue dividends, and some don't. Some people want to earn dividends on the investment and will search out these kinds of companies. But, as a swing trader, you won't hold the position long enough for it to really matter, so you don't need to look for these.

There is also a time when there may be a stock split. This is a move that is done strategically by the board of directors of the company where they decide to issue out more shares of stock to the public. For example, one year, Apple did a seven to one stock split. This means that, for every share of stock that you owned before the split, you now have seven of them. If you owned 100 shares before the split, you would now own 700.

When this happens, the value of the company isn't going to change, but the price of the share might. Companies will often do this if they find that their price isn't in line with competitors so that they are able to attract some of the smaller investors to come into the company since the share of the price is going to decrease.

When this kind of split occurs, you will find that it shows in the stock chart as well. Many times, when this kind of split happens, there are going to be more people who are willing to invest. It is usually going to be a good company that does a stock split, and more people are willing to come on board because the share price goes down. This increases the demand and can help increase the overall share price that is there. Knowing this can be important when you take a look at the stocks that you want to invest in.

Understanding the Trading Volumes Historically for a Security

When you look at the very bottom of a chart, you may see that there are a lot of small, vertical lines. These are going to be the trend of the volumes at which the stock is traded. These volumes are good to know, but they definitely shouldn't be the only determining factor when you are trying to decide whether to purchase a stock or not. Usually, these volumes are going to increase when there is any major news, whether good or bad, about a company.

When you notice that the volumes are increasing, you will also notice that this can cause a shift in the price of the stock, and this shift is going to happen quickly. It is important to remember, though, that it is not a good idea to assume that there is a correlation between the stock price and its trading volume. However, it is good to know what the volumes have been in the past and what they are doing now before you make any decisions.

Knowing the history of a particular stock can be a great way to figure out whether it is going to in the same way as it did in the past and whether it is a good idea for you to enter into the market or stay away from it for now. In some cases, the stock may go against its historical values because there is some big news released about the company at that time. This means that historical data isn't the only thing that you should take a look at when working on your trades. You need to spend some time digging deeper to figure out what is the best trade, but the historical data can certainly give you a good starting point and can add to your research as well.

These are some of the basics to help you out when reading your own stock charts. Each industry and each stock and security will have their own charts, so learning how to read them early on can be a great asset. Once you have taken the time to master these techniques, you should be able to analyze the historical activity of a stock at a high level.

Chapter 15: The Top Mistakes That Beginners Make

As a beginner, there are a lot of things that you need to learn to do well with swing trading. Learning all the strategies, learning how to read the charts and making smart decisions when it comes to picking out stocks to work with can be a challenge. As you are getting used to the whole process, it can take some time and effort, and you are likely to make some mistakes along the way.

These mistakes are pretty normal when you are a beginner, but no beginner wants to deal with them. They want to be able to make as much money as possible, without losing a lot of money as they start to learn how things work. This chapter focuses on some of the top mistakes that a lot of beginners make and some of the things that you can do to avoid these common mistakes.

Let the emotions get in the way

One mistake that almost all beginners will make is that they let their emotions get in the way of their decision making. They see that they are about to lose out on a trade or they see that the profits will keep reaching a higher value, and they want to stay in the market longer, despite what all their research and their strategy told them before. This will end up disastrous and is one of the leading reasons that beginners lose so much money and end up having to stop at day trading.

You need to learn how to keep the emotions out of the game. If you are a highly emotional person, swing trading is not going to be the best option for you to try out because things can change in an instant. The good news is that there are a few techniques that you can use to help keep the emotions out of the game so you can reduce your risk and increase your chances of profit.

First, make sure that you use stop points and that you stick with them. These stop points will ensure that you enter and exit the trade at the right times to either limit your losses or to help limit the risk that you have while gaining a profit. They aren't always full proof, but if you stick with them, you are less likely to have issues later on. Picking a good strategy, asking for advice, and really doing your research before you begin are all good ways to ensure you can keep the emotions out of your trading.

Forget to use stop points

The stop points will be so important when you start out as a swing trader. These points will tell you when to get out of the market, whether the market is going up or down and can reduce your risk. You need to have a stop loss point, which is the point you will get out of the market if you lose so much money, and you need a stop profit point, which is where you will get out of the market once you earn a certain profit.

Both of these are important to ensure you cut down on your risk and that you make as much money as possible in the process. For the stop loss point, you are figuring out how much money you are comfortable with losing in the market. Once the market goes down to this point, you need to get out. It is highly likely that the market will keep going down and if you don't get out at your stop loss point, you will potentially lose a lot of money in the process. This takes the emotions out of the game. You simply see that the stop point was reached and cut your losses until the next trade.

You also need to have a stop point for the profits that you want to earn. This may seem silly because you want to earn as much profit as you possibly can with each trade. But emotions can come into play here again too. Without the stop point, you may end up staying in the market too long, and make some costly mistakes. The market can turn around just as quickly as it went up, and if you are still in the market, you may lose all your earnings instead of gaining anything.

For this stop point, figure out what you can realistically make on the trade. Where do you think the market for your stock will go over the next few days based on the trend that you are setting? Put the stop point there and then as soon as the market reaches that point, you will take your earnings and withdraw from the market.

Putting in more money than you can afford to lose

With any investment that you work with, you need to be careful about the losses that you are dealing with. If you take on too much risk, you will end up losing all your money and never getting a chance to give it another try. Coming up with a good risk to reward ratio will help to limit your losses, but you also must make sure that you never put in more than you are willing to lose.

A good place to start is to put some savings behind for your swing trades. Never use money that you would need for rent, food, and other necessities. The second you do this, you bring the emotions into the game, and you are more likely to lose it all. Starting a savings account right now with the money you can use for swing trading allows you to have a little cushion without having to eat up all the money you need for other things.

When you are using the extra money, rather than money that you really need elsewhere, you are ensuring that you will spend it wisely.

You won't stay in a trade too long in the hopes of recovering that money. No one wants to lose money along the way when they are trading, but it is much easier to cut your losses when it was just a little savings rather than if that money was your rent payment for the month.

Not understanding your strategy

If you do not understand the strategy that you are using, it can be impossible for you to get results when you get started with swing trading. Your strategy will outline exactly how you will behave in each trade situation. It will tell you how to look at the charts, how to pick out the stocks, when to enter the market, and when to exit the market. Each strategy has the potential to be successful, but you need to understand the strategy and use it properly.

When you get started in swing trading, it is always best to start with a simple strategy. Yes, there are some more complex ones that may sound fun, but since you are already learning about the market and how it works, why add in more complications with a hard strategy. There are a lot of great strategies that are simple, and some even designed for the beginner, that will make you just as much money as the more complex strategies, without all the work.

Picking a strategy is really important when it comes to doing well in swing trading. Before you pick out one, make sure to read through them all and fully understand what you will need to do to make it successful. You want one that is effective and easy to follow, as well as one that you will not want to switch out of in the middle of the trade. There is nothing wrong with trying out different strategies to see which one you like the best in between your trades, but if you switch strategies while in the same trade, you are setting yourself up for failure.

Not having the right tools

As a trader, you need to have some of your own tools in place if you would like to get started with swing trading. This can be a very difficult method when it comes to investing, and without the right tools, you will miss out on some important information that can help you see trends and make smart decisions along the way.

The first place to go for some tools is to talk to your broker. Often the broker will have a variety of unique tools that they can give to you as part of their fees. If you don't know how to use some of these tools, make sure to ask questions and learn how to make it all work or you will miss out.

You can also bring in some of your own tools to the game as well. Find charts about the market, look online, and ask questions. Remember, the best way to notice a trend is when the same information starts to show up on more than one chart or tool so always strive to have as many of these tools available as possible.

Following others rather than learning your own way

When you first get started, it can be tempting to find a mentor or a group and then just follow along exactly with what they do each time. This is really tempting if you see that they are making a lot of money and you want to join and make that money as well. But in the long run, no one knows the trading style that you like, and there are times when even an advanced mentor will get things wrong.

Instead of following along blindly with what someone else tell you, it is better to learn your own way. There is nothing wrong with talking to a mentor and others who have been in the market for some time, but you need to learn your own methods, your own strategies, and how you want to behave in the market. This will help you to stay on track with your trades and will ensure that you don't get misled by others who may not have your best interests at heart.

Not cutting your losses

Even the best swing traders will make mistakes at times. They will misread the market, they will try out a new strategy that doesn't work for them, or the market just doesn't behave in the manner that they had hoped. And when this happens, the trader will lose out on their money. As a beginner, it is more likely that you will earn a loss at some point. The important thing is to learn how to cut your losses, rather than staying too long in the market.

Some beginners will see that they are losing money on one of their trades and so they will try to regain that money. Even with the market going down, and no signs of reversal, they will stay in the market and hope that things will reverse. This is dangerous because it results in you staying in the market way too long and you will lose out on way too much money in the process.

Instead of sticking with a market that is not working in your favor, it is much better to learn how to cut your losses. Pick out an amount that you are comfortable with losing if the market does not go the way that you would like, put a stop point there, and then withdraw from the market as soon as you reach that point. This will help you to limit your losses and can give you more opportunities to try another trade in the future.

Using vengeance trading

Vengeance trading is one of the worst things you can do as a new trader. It forces you to make unsafe trading decisions in the hopes of earning some of your money back after a loss. Unfortunately, since you are only thinking about earning your money back, and not about the decisions that will help you to limit your risks as a trader, you will end up losing a lot of money in the process.

It can be hard if you lose a lot of money on one of your trades. Everyone who gets into swing trading drams about making a lot of money and doing well with this investment. However, as a beginner, there will be times when you make mistakes or the market doesn't behave the way that you would like and you will lose some money in the process.

If you lose money and then start becoming desperate to make that money back right away, you have let your emotions get in the way. While it is normal to want to lose as little as possible with swing trading, you need to focus on picking a good strategy and learning how to read the market next time, rather than worrying about how to earn your money back. If you make smart decisions with swing trading, you will earn all the money back and more, but if you get stuck in vengeance trading, you will end up losing all your money in the process.

As a beginner, there is a lot to learn when it comes to swing trading. Swing trading can take some time and energy, and it is not as easy as you may think when you first get started. But if you learn how to get rid of some of these mistakes and you pick a good strategy to help you out, you are sure to see some great results in no time.

Conclusion

Congratulations on making it this far! You deserve some applause because this is a very dense book and its true value is apparent only upon repeated reading. The main cause for this is new traders entering the markets with the wrong expectations.

Not only do you have to master your strategy, you must, crucially, master yourself. You need to know yourself inside and out if you are to succeed in this endeavor. You need to put in a lot of work examining your beliefs about money, success and what it is you want in life. Remember, if there's a block in any of this, you will not be successful in trading no matter how good your technical skill is.

Take the time to practice first then get on a demo platform and only when you consistently make money on demo, go live. Many traders get impatient with this process and push forward as fast as possible. The specter of time is one of the biggest reasons for this. Most people reason that they need to become successful traders in the shortest time possible or they want to be like that other trader who became a millionaire within a year and so on.

Letting go of time limits is one of the first things you need to do. Simply accept it will take however long it has to take and you will eventually get there. Think of it this way. If you need to get to another town for an important engagement, will you worry about how long it takes to get there? Beyond the initial planning phase, probably not. You'll simply travel to the place and during your journey, you simply deal with whatever comes. You don't sit there wishing you get there a day earlier or an hour earlier etc. You might wish for it but it isn't your overriding concern. You just accept that you arrive whenever it is you arrive.

Treat trading in the same manner and stick to the path prescribed in this book. As your skill progresses, you will find suitable tasks to take on to enhance and satisfy your new skill level. Above all else, maintain a balanced, calm mindset and let it guide you forward.

Day Trading

A beginner's guide on how to trade, living in the market and make money with day trading investing in stocks, forex, and options with the best futures and strategies for a trader in 2019

[Henry Hill]

TABLE OF CONTENTS:

CHAPTER 6) COMMON MISTAKE WITH DAY TRADING

CHAPTER 7) ADVICE FOR BEGINNERS

CONCLUSION

Introduction

Broadly defined as buying and selling the same security in a single day, day trading is most common in both the forex and stock markets. Armed with a large amount of data, and an even larger bank roll, the best day traders take advantage of high amounts of leverage as well as strategies for success that come to fruition in the short term to make large sums from price movements that are otherwise relatively minor.

The process of day trading can be broken down into 5 steps that will always be the same regardless of the specifics of the trade that is being made. First, you will need to locate an underlying stock that you are interested in trading based on research done ahead of time. Next, you will need to determine if it aligns with your personalized trading plan. Then, assuming you are still interested in making the trade, you will take a position based on the current trend of the market before buying or selling once a specific type of movement occurs. Finally, you will repeat this process roughly 100 times a day.

Day trading can be as exciting as it is confusing for new traders, who are often attracted to the market because of the alluring potential for success it holds. After all, a job with unlimited income potential, flexible hours and the ability to be your own boss can sound alluring to just about everyone. The hard part, of course, comes from connecting the dots and determining the right path to take to reach this goal. What follows are answers to many common questions that day traders have when they are first getting started.

Is day trading just another type of gambling: While gambling and day trading do share a number of similarities, assuming the gambler is going about things in a professional way, there is one major difference that many people overlook when they claim that they are more or less one in the same? The reasons that they are not one in the same can best be illustrated by comparing trading to starting a business. While it is certainly true that there are countless traders out there who make a few trades, lose their shirts, and never trade again, if you look at those who go about things in a professional way, the odds are about the same as starting a small business, about 50 percent of which fail within five years.

Nevertheless, starting a small business isn't considered gambling, though it certainly is for the types of folks who think they have a great idea and go out right away and order a million pairs of mittens for cats who make too much noise when they walk. This is, of course, very different from someone who comes up with an idea for a niche of people they are a part of that meets a need that they know to be underserved.

All new ventures have some level of risk associated with them, and those that are successful are undertaken by those who do everything they can to mitigate the potential for risk. This same logic is put to good use by those who are successful at trading. While it is certainly possible that a trade that is very likely to go your way will unexpectedly take a turn for the worse, good traders follow plans which mean they know how they are going to act before they even begin for the day.

Gambling is based on the idea of throwing preparation to the wind and trusting in your luck to make everything work out in the end. While this is certainly how some people practice day trading, the percentage that is successful in doing so is quite small. Likewise, if you take the time to educate yourself, analyze your process and research your trades before you make them, you may not always be successful, but you certainly aren't gambling.

What's the first thing I should focus on as a new trader?

The first step towards becoming a successful trader is education, no two ways about it. You need to not only learn everything you can about your chosen markets, but you also need to learn how to successfully analyze underlying assets so you can determine which ones to track. Then, even once you know what you are doing and have assets you favor, you still need to learn how to determine the best entry and exit points possible if you hope to reliably make any money in the process.

The good news is that there are plenty of places you can go (besides this eBook) to learn the basics, most of which are completely free. A quick online search will provide you with countless blogs, forums, and YouTube videos all designed to help you get started as quickly and effectively as possible. If you are more interested in getting all of your information in one place, however, then you may be interested in a paid course instead, these will walk you through the entire process step by step, which is perfect for those who aren't quite sure what assets they are really interested in following.

How much money do I need to get started?

The short answer is the more money you can get started with the better. If you are looking to get started with the bare minimum possible, however, then you are going to want to ensure that you have at least $5,000 set aside expressly for trading purposes. This way you will be able to pay the commissions on your trades without worrying about if it is going to break you and also provide you with a little wiggle room as you will inevitably take some losses while you are getting used to the process.

While many sources recommend starting with a demo account or using one to practice new potential strategies the truth of the matter is that trading with fake money negates an important aspect of the real process, namely, learning to deal with the added stress that comes with putting your money on the line and taking your chances as a result. Keeping the right mindset, even when the going gets rough, is a key part of being a successful trader and a plan that works in a demo account might suddenly fall apart if you can't keep it together when the money is on the line.

While you do need $25,000 in your day trading account to trade without restrictions in most instances, that doesn't mean this, is the amount you need to start trading. Instead, when you are first starting out you will be limited to three instances of buying and selling within a five-day period. While this may seem restrictive at first, it is important to understand that it is in place for your own good. What's more, early on if you can find more than three worthwhile trades per week then you should consider yourself incredibly lucky.

Can I only trade part of the time?

Not only can you trade part-time, but it is also recommended that you do so exclusively until you take your starting trading capital and increase it to the point where any and all restrictions are removed from your trading account. While you certainly won't get rich in this way, you will join the ranks of a vast majority of day-traders who either work other full-time jobs or just enjoy the thrill of picking stocks with money on the line.

In order to be successful while trading part-time, all you need to do is to tailor your strategy around your schedule. For example, you can't realistically expect to be able to successfully make momentum trades if you know you have to be at your full-time job first thing in the

246

morning. However, as long as you consider your availability first, you can typically align your schedule with market hours somewhere.

The amount of time that you have available to devote to trading will also directly reflect on the amount of money you are able to earn while doing so. While, theoretically, day trading offers infinite potential for profit, it is unlikely that you are going to reach those heights anytime soon. Likewise, there is nothing guaranteed when it comes to day trading, this isn't a passive income stream and it isn't a way to get rich quick. In fact, focusing on the monetary side of things right from the start is only going to distract you from what you should be focusing on to start, potentially causing you to lose money. Instead, early on you should focus on making a successful plan and sticking with it; if you do that money will follow naturally.

Which broker is right for me?

Generally speaking, if you are first starting out then there is nothing wrong with going to a discount online broker like ETRADE or one of their competitors. From these brokers, you can expect a flat commission rate per trade as well as the trading tools you will need to properly get started while still keeping your costs as low as possible.

As you start to grow your account and develop more of a sense of the things you need and, more importantly, don't need from a trading account you will then want to look into something more specifically tailored to the type of trader you are becoming. Even if you don't ultimately end up making any changes, it is still important to reevaluate your trading platform after about six months as you never know when you will be able to find more competitive rates or better access to tools or education you can use to take your burgeoning trading career to new heights.

Chapter 1) Main tool and charts

Technical analysis

In order to properly understand technical analysis the most important thing you need to keep in mind is that the action the price has taken to get to the current point is likely going to repeat itself in the future which makes it a reliable way to predict future movement based on what is happening at the moment. As the forex market is always on five days a week, this means there will always be plenty of information to sift through when it comes to finding the relevant information that can help you determine how a

This fact makes it easy to use the tools of technical analysis including trends, charts, and indicators to generate a reasonably successful trade percentage. While some of the ways that it works are more complicated than others, in its most basic form technical analysis is all about the study of supply and demand and it uses its findings to determine the type of trend, if any, that is affecting the market at the moment. This can prove crucial to forex trading success in the long-term as the tools at your disposal will become even more useful as you have your own historical data to sample as well.

Assumptions of technical analysis

Technical analysis is about more than simply measuring the intrinsic value of a given currency, it is about using all of the tools at your disposal to see the patterns that have the greatest potential to generate a profit in the future. In order to do so, the entire process assumes that three key facts are true. First, the market is always going to discount everything if given enough time. Second, prices are always going to move in accordance with connected trends. Third, history is bound to repeat itself eventually.

The market is bound to discount everything eventually: While those who are proponents of only fundamental analysis might decry technical analysis for its heavy focus on the current price of the currency to the exclusion of all else, the fact of the matter is that it is able to do so because the current price of the currency in question is a true reflection of everything that has affected the price up to this point which means looking at the price is like looking at everything affecting the currency all in one place. All of this is then taken into account along with the broader economic climate as well as the current phase to determine when a valuable opportunity comes along.

Prices will always move in line with trends: Assuming the price of the currency in question is moving based on an established trend makes it possible to determine trends from past currency performance to apply to currency movement that is yet to come. Generally speaking, if a currency has experienced a specific trend in the past, it is more than three times as likely to experience that same trend again in the future when compared to either an entirely new trend or the opposite trend forming in its place. In order for technical analysis to work correctly, this is assumed to always be the case.

History will eventually repeat itself: If technical analysis is already assuming that prices follow the same trends time and again, then it is natural to also assume that history is bound to repeat itself in the currency market when given enough time. This can be chalked up to the fact that those who interact with the market are likely to always respond the same way to similar market movement. This is often what are plotted using chart patterns in an effort to determine these trends at their start when they can be capitalized on to the greatest degree possible. While some of these charts have been used for more than a century, they are still relevant today because traders are always going to react the same when it comes to both supply and demand.

Technical indicators

As the name implies, technical indicators are used in options trading as a way to determine trends as well as potential turning points in the price of underlying stocks. When used correctly, they can accurately predict movement cycles as well as determine when the most profitable time to buy or sell is going to be.

Technical indicators are typically calculated based on the price pattern of a derivative or stock. Relevant data includes closing price, opening price, lows, highs and volume. Indicators typically take the data regarding a stock's price from the past few periods depending on the charts the analyst favors and use it to generate a trend that will show what has been happening with a specific stock as well as what is likely to happen next.

There are two primary types of technical indicators, leading and lagging. Lagging indicators are used to determine if a new trend if forming or if the underlying stock is currently moving within an expected range through the use of existing data. If the lagging indicator points to a strong trend, then there is a better than 50 percent chances the trend will continue moving forward. Unfortunately, they are not especially useful when it comes to determining pullbacks or rally points that may appear in the future.

Alternately, leading indicators tend to come into play when traders need to predict a likely future price point when it is currently unclear if the current price is going to crash or rally. They tend to manifest as momentum indicators which help to determine the strength of the movement of the current trend which will help to determine if the trend is going to continue or reverse. As no trend will continue forever, the momentum indicator will allow you to determine how long of a timeframe your options should be in to ensure that you get out before the disruption begins.

Leading indicators are also useful if you find yourself needing to determine if the price of a specific stock has reached a point where it is unsustainable as this means a slowdown in the price is forthcoming. As overbought or oversold stocks experience a pullback when a slowdown occurs, knowing when this type of movement is coming can thus be supremely useful for several different trading strategies.

Candlestick charts

Candlestick trading starts with a price bar, which is a visual representation of the movement that a particular stock has taken over a preset amount of time that can be either weekly, daily, hourly, every 30 minutes or every 5 minutes.

When it comes to creating a price bar that is truly accurate you will want to collect a few different pieces of information. First, you will want to consider the price the stock in question started the day at, the next is the amount that it peaked at; you will also want to know its overall low point, and finally, the closing price. When you plug this information into the platform that you are using you will see that the data is ultimately plotted so that it looks like a box that has been struck through with a line. The points of that line equate to the low and high price while the outer bottom and uppermost edges of the box signify the closing as well as the opening price. Stocks that ended higher than they started are colored in one color and stocks that ended lower than they started are then colored in using a separate color.

Candlestick formation: This box that has been created is commonly called a candlestick and it does more than just provide you with details of what has happened in the past, it can also make it easier for you to determine what is likely going to happen in the future.

Range: The range of the candlestick is the visual representation of the current level of volatility the market is experiencing. The greater the current volatility level, the less reliable you can expect your chosen underlying assets to be when compared to their historical averages. You can then determine the volatility of the market by looking to the size of the line in relation to the overall size of the box. If the volatility is currently high, the box will be large, and the line will be relatively small. If the current volatility is low, the opposite will be the case.

Split line: Once you have a firm grasp on the range as well as the body you will then want to move your attention to the top half of the line. This line portion then caps at the highpoint for the price for the day while at the same time indicating the point where the supply once more began exceeding demand, thus resulting in an overall decrease in price. This also means that the top point of the line can be thought of as the maximum amount of pressure that that the underlying stock experienced in the chosen timeframe. The lower half of the bar, meanwhile, will detail the same specifics except regarding the low for the day and the point that demand began to exceed supply.

Dual price bars: Once you decide to add a second price bar to the analysis that you are doing, you will then be able to use the dual price bars as a cornerstone that provides you with a reasonable idea of the level of movement the price is experiencing in a more practical sense than if you were looking at a single bar. The second bar will also allow you to more easily determine if what you found in the first bar is a fluke or something that is actually actionable enough to make a move on before it's too late. Eventually, you will you will likely find this exceptionally useful if you need to determine if a bar is actually wide or is, in fact, average or other forms of comparison as well. This will allow you to understand the price action in a way that is more specific, and thus more effective than it would often otherwise be.

Hook reversal: A hook reversal is a candlestick pattern that materializes on the shorter timeframe charts. They can appear both on downtrends and uptrends and are useful when it comes to predicting a reversal in the current trend. This pattern appears as a candlestick with a higher low as well as a lower high when compared to the candlestick of the previous day. This is a somewhat unique pattern as the size difference between the body of the first and second bar is quite small when compared to other engulfing patterns.

When this pattern is found as part of an uptrend then the open will typically be near the previous high while the low will be near the previous low. This pattern is typically associated with other harami positions because the body of the second candle is formed inside the body of the first candle.

Abandoned baby: This is another candlestick pattern that is useful when it comes to determining the potential for a reversal in the current trend. This pattern is formed by a trio of candlesticks with several distinctive characteristics. The first bar is going to be a red candlestick that is large and visible within a previously defined downtrend. The second bar will have an open equal to its close that gaps beneath the close of the first bar. The final bar is going to be a white candlestick that is large and opens higher than the second bar. This bar also represents changing trader sentiment.

This is a somewhat rare pattern but is reliable when it comes to predicting a change in the dominant downtrend. The accuracy of the signal is then further enhanced when combined with additional technical indicators including RSI and MACD.

Bearish abandoned baby: This candlestick pattern is useful when it comes to signaling a reversal in an existing uptrend. It is also a trio pattern and the first part is a white candlestick that is large and found within a previously defined uptrend. The second bar is the same as that found in the bullish abandoned baby. The final bar is a red candle that is large and will open beneath the second bar. It is also useful when it comes to determining the current trader sentiment.

Pinocchio strategy: The Pinocchio strategy is an ideal strategy to use when, during the course of technical analysis, you come across a candle bar that contains both a small body and an abnormally long wick. Also known as a pin bar, this type of bar is much like the puppet it is named after in that the longer the wick grows, the more likely it is that the bar is providing you with inaccurate information.

When you are dealing with an extremely long wick then you can safely assume that the price of the underlying asset has moved about as far as it is ever going to move in a specific direction and that it is sure to turn back the other direction sooner rather than later. When you come across this type of bar then you know that it is time to start trading against the majority as things are likely to change, and soon. Once the wick starts to decrease in size you are then going to want to set a prediction on a call and when it starts to increase again you will want to change that prediction to a put.

Chart patterns to know

Once you have found a few underlying stocks that you feel are likely to move in the direction you are hoping for, the next step is to double check this fact before you get your hopes up. To do so, you are going to want to review the relative candlestick charts and try and determine the correct entry point based on the point where the first pullback occurred. While many traders will simply buy in at the point where the pullback occurs, this then creates an additional volume spike which pushes the prices even higher. As such, finding the best entry point, in real time, is the key to long-term success.

Flag and pennant: Both the flag and the pennant pattern are useful when it comes to showing retracement or other short-term deviations from the trend. When a retracement occurs this means that no breakout will follow suit at either the support or resistance level, but this won't matter as much because it proves the currency you are watching is doing something more complicated than simply following the existing trend. The lack of a breakout also means that this trend is only going to last for a relatively brief period of time.

You will know you are looking at a pennant as its support and resistance lines converge in such a way that they come to a point. A flag is more or less the same except that the resistance and support lines from the flag will be parallel with one another. After you know how to spot them, you will typically see both flags and pennants in the middle of trends that are currently in their primary phase. They tend to last up to 14 days before being absorbed back into the main trend. Both flags, as well as pennants, are most commonly associated with falling volume.

Utilizing a flag pattern is as easy as following through on the steps outlined here:

1. First, you are going to want to determine the point that the trend line that indicates low level support connects to the lower wicks of the initial candles that you are looking at. You will then want to determine the point that the upper trend line reaches the tops of those same candles. You will know these lines are correct if they are more or less parallel.

2. From there you are going to want to find the point where the movement of the price starts to get closer to the relevant of the two possible trend lines. After the session ends you would then want to determine an entry point that is 5 pips above this high point.

3. Never proceed without a stop loss, it is important to always remember that there is no method of trading that is full-proof enough that it warrants being careless in the market. Apply stop losses and apply them judiciously. You are going to want to place a stop loss order that is roughly two thirds of the way beneath the high that was recorded. This is important as it is possible for the trend to turn back in the other direction if the previous positive movement was a fake out and not actually the indication of a true trend.

4. If you are looking for a short term stance, then a flag can often be an indicator of a short term explosion which means you may be able to capture nearly 100 pips of profit in short order. On the other hand, you would also be right to hold out longer depending on what you expect the overall amount of profits to be.

Head and shoulders: Indicators that show the strength of the trend in question arc extremely useful and the head and shoulders formation where three peaks all appear within the same price chart window is one of the most reliable. You will generally see this type of pattern outlining a bearish trend that is likely to continue in the direction it is currently traveling. The main peak, the head, will be better defined than the shoulder peaks and each connects to the same price. This price is referred to as the neckline and if it hits the right shoulder then the price is almost always on the decline.

This formation often occurs when a large percentage of sellers decide to hold out for one last positive push before selling only to have the trend change out from under them, causing the price to fall and the head and shoulders to appear. If the opposite occurs then you are looking at a reverse head and shoulders which is a strong sign that the price is likely about to increase instead.

The inverse head-and-shoulders pattern is the exact opposite of the head-and-shoulders top, as it signals that the security is set to make an upward move. Often coming at the end of a downtrend, the inverse head and shoulders is considered to be a reversal pattern, as the security typically heads higher after the completion of the pattern.

In both instances, the price dipping below the neckline signals the true reversal of the trend in question which means the crypto currency will now be moving in the opposite direction. This breakout point is often the ideal point to go either short or long depending. It is important to keep in mind, however, that the crypto currency is unlikely to continue smoothly in the direction the pattern suggests. As such, you will want to keep an eye out for what is called a throwback move. This type of scenario can pop up when the price breaks through the neckline to set a new high or low before then moving back to the neckline.

When it comes to the head and shoulders pattern, you are going to want to also keep an eye on volume as it is often used at the point of the breakout as a means of helping to confirm the pattern. In this scenario, you are going to want to keep in mind that the bigger the volume of the movement, the better. For a top, if the price breaks above the neckline moving south, then it is best to look for points where this occurs during a large increase in volume as this indicates a rush to sell. Likewise, it shows that the underlying supply and demand of the market is moving in the way that the pattern predicted it would.

Volume is also useful as a secondary indictor during the formation of the pattern, even before the breakout occurs to determine the likely strength of the forthcoming movement. With a top, the left shoulder should show heavy volume when it hits the peak. Meanwhile, low volume should then drop the left shoulder almost to the neckline. Likewise, the run towards the peak in the head should also indicate lighter volume when compared to the peak that is formed from the left shoulder.

Cup with handle formation: The cup with handle formation typically tends to appear when a security reaches peak prices and then falls sharply for an extended period of time. Eventually, however, the security rebounds and the time is right to buy. This is an indicator of a trend on the rise and you should be sure to take advantage of any cup with handle formations that you see come into existence.

The handle will form on the cup when those who purchased the security at the previous high water mark and couldn't wait any longer begin to sell which makes new investors interested who then begin to buy as well. This type of formation does not typically form quickly, and indeed, has been known to take a year or more to become visible. Ideally, you would want to take advantage of this trend right when the handle is beginning to form. If you see a cup with handle forming it is still important to consider any day to day patterns that it is forming around as these are still likely to determine more of the overall effectiveness of buying at any individual point.

Scalping

In the world of options trading, the term scalping denotes the process of skimming for minute profits regular by entering and exiting positions several times each day. The process involves trading the basis of real-time analysis. The main aim of scalping is to maximize profit by getting into a position and staying with it for a very short timeframe and closing it for little profit. There are very many trades placed throughout the day, and most of the traders use a system that is based on a number of signals generated from technical analysis. The chart tools are made up of multiple signals that create the decision to buy or sell when they point in a similar direction. A scalper normally looks for large numbers of trade for small profits each time.

Many scalp traders look to make about five or ten pips in every trade they act on. To get worthwhile profits, they repeat the process throughout the day many times. Keeping in mind that one standard lot pip has a value of about $10, if the trader makes five pips of profit, then he has made $70 at a go. If option traders did such a trade ten times a day, then they will have made a profit of $700.

However, we all have to agree that scalping is not for every trader. It requires a person with the right temperament. A scalping trader has to love sitting in front of a computer for the better part of the day, and by better, we mean a lot of time. Again, a scalp trader must enjoy paying intense attention to the charts; otherwise, he/she might never see the opportunities. One cannot afford to miss the ball when trying to catch a move as small as five pips in a go.

A trader might have the capacity and appropriate temperament to sit and watch the moves all night and day and not even feel tired, but that is not all it requires. Scalp trading requires one to be very frisky and have the ability to react even without analyzing each and every move. You do not have enough time to think and over think. It is about pulling the trigger on impulse. This is very important for traders because they need to cut positions even if they move against the expectation by several pips.

Sometimes traders confuse market making and scalping. The two have a lot of similarities, but the market maker buys a position and immediately seeks to offset the position and capture the bid-ask spread. It is of the necessity that one understands the main difference between a scalper and a market maker. A scalp trader pays the spread price while the maker earns it. This means that once a maker sells on the 'ask' and consequently buys on the bid, he/she gain a pip or two automatically as a profit for market making. However, the scalper will buy on ask and consequently sells on the bid.

The scalper and the market maker seek to enter and exit the market as fast as possible, but the risks of a maker are lower than those of a scalper. Makers like Scalpers because they make many trades in a day, therefore, paying more spread to the benefit of the maker. The more that scalper trades, the more the maker earns.

A system used for scalping can either be manual or automatic. In the manual system, the trader sits and looks for indicators and decides whether to buy or sell. Automated systems are software that requires the trader to inform it of the signs it should look for, interpret, and trade. Scalping utilizes technical analysis, and the timely nature of the analysis makes traders prefer real-time charts as the tool of the trade.

Technical analysis is thought of as the most viable strategy for stock trading because of the size and liquidity of the market. One can also assume that scalping is the most viable strategy for a retail trade. Note that normally, a scalp trader is required to deposit a large number of funds in the account in order handle the size of leverage that the trader must apply to make the small and short trades worthwhile.

They highlight of scalp trading involves the lightning-like trades happening on the market. This strategy is risky and short term. The profits can be high, but other strategies are safer and look at the long term. The main advantage of the scalping strategy is that the trader does not need to wait for too long before a trade closes. The small timeframe reduces the chances of reversal that might damage a trading position.

Beginner traders often use this strategy because it requires little knowledge about the market. One does not need to understand the established theories if he/she is using the scalping strategy. Scalping is very helpful for traders who do not like to wait long for a position to close. The holding time is very little.

Many brokers disagree with scalping strategy and even some trading platforms prohibit the practice because; while in longer positions one can lose in a position without affecting others, in scalping, one loss can easily obliterate all the gains from other successful trades. A good trade can have a 1:1 risk/ reward ratio or less. Secondly, the profits generated by scalping are very minute; therefore it takes a very long time for a trader to reach his/her financial goal. A yield of five pips on one trade is not enough for most traders. Other traders simplify believe that scalping is less profitable and it is better to hold a long position.

In order to prepare for scalp trading, one should have a reliable and good access to the market makers. The platform should allow for speedy buying and selling. In a market as highly liquid, execution of transactions can simply take place in nanoseconds.

The platform: A scalp broker should be very familiar with the platform that the broker is offering. Different brokers offer different benefits. Therefore, the trader should at least open a practice account and interact with the services one on one. Scalping is very fast; therefore a platform should not have room for errors. The disadvantage of having a platform with no rooms for error is that once a button is hit, there is no turning back. This means that if a trader hits a buy button while he/she intended to hit the sell button, then he/she better hope that he/she gets luck otherwise he/she is guaranteed of a loss. Such mistakes cannot be afforded in the scalp trading practice because they will lead to losses. As such, one should do a lot of practice before placing real money on the account.

Guaranteed Executions: Scalpers need to be able to execute the trades at the time they wish, under the levels they want. As such, the traders should ensure that they understand the terms of trading lay down by the broker because some of them limit their levels to only those times when markets are slow. Other brokers might not offer an execution guarantee.

Slippage refers to the situations when an order is placed at a level a few pips away from the intended level. Scalpers rely on very little profit in each trade. Therefore, they cannot afford slippages as a cost above the spread. As such, the trader should ensure that the order will be and can be executed as soon as it is requested.

Scalping safely: Scalping is very interesting so long as one is winning but as soon as he/she starts to lose, the fun gets lost. In most cases, traders using scalp strategy eat up their capital to a large extent before that can admit that the trial was a failure. Naturally, human beings want to feel better and smarter than the market. However, the market is just it, and all that people can do is study and follow the hints. So far there is no perfect strategy to beat the market. If a trader wants to scalp, some rules might protect them.

Firstly, the trader should trade small. The opportunities for scalping are normally very tempting for the trader to take a big position for quick money. Now that is a highway to ruins. It is better to keep the trades small and also create room for loss and exiting without clearing out all the capital.

Secondly, a scalp trader should minimize risk through the use of stops. Scalping can easily go against the expectation. Because of its short timeframe, it does not use a risk-reward ratio under normal circumstances. Therefore a trader should set a stop loss and leave it alone. If a trader gets stopped out, he /she should accept the loss.

Chapter 2) Understanding Futures

As its name suggests, Futures is a market which mainly focuses on future prices. A buyer and a seller agree to buy or sell a particular amount of a commodity or security at a later date. Day traders benefit from the intraday price fluctuations between the duration of the contract during the day. Futures require less capital than stocks, but more capital than Forex. With about 3,500 dollars you can trade in Futures, where you can get Futures contracts such as S & P Emini. Different contracts give rise to different official market hours. The trick for a day trader is to keep tabs on the particular contract's official hours to know the right time to exit a market.

Also, specific day trading platforms have different requirements for Futures trading, and this should be an important factor for consideration.

Binary Options: Although less popular, this is perhaps the simplest market in which a trader knows in advance the timing and the returns of a successful position. This sector is seemingly booming, and regulations are changing. Remember that laws surrounding a market are a major consideration when you're thinking of getting into trading. Another factor to consider while trading in this market is if the asset you are trading will rise or drop in value. Understanding these dynamics is not difficult, considering the potential outcome is known beforehand. Binary options offer a unique day trading experience and can even contribute to traders' portfolio of the day.

Crypto currencies: Crypto currencies have become the talk of the day when it comes to trading. It is a market that has attracted many investors and became a great source of finances in the recent past, with the most popular currencies being Bit coin and Ethereum. There are minimal entry barriers, and the market is relatively easy to trade, even for beginners.

Commodities: This market simply entails the trading of foodstuffs, minerals, and even oil.

Risk in Day Trading

Risk management is among the fundamental lessons learned in trading. You must learn how to manage your money because, after all, it is not worth it to trade if you'll run broke after your first month in the venture. The most successful traders are those who know how to manage the different types of risks prevalent in day trading, with the greatest being the financial risk.

Financial risk: As the mother of all risks in day trading, traders must be careful about the volatility of the market prices, in which fluctuations can make one lose terribly. It is hard to benefit when a market moves in the negative direction by a large margin. Furthermore, there are few opportunities being preyed upon by too many traders. In cases such as this, it's always best to be careful whenever entering trading, and also entering a position on a particular day. Especially for newbies, it is recommended that they do not place huge amounts of cash into a single trade since this can discourage them from going on. Market information is paramount in avoiding financial risk.

Capital risk: There are various upfront costs associated with trading, including the software, infrastructure, and news services. There are other ongoing expenses in every platform, including commissions or ECN, interests, charting packages, as well as communication charges. You don't want to indulge in a venture where you will lose all the money you've invested. Also, you don't want to engage in a platform where all you'll be doing is paying for the ongoing expenses without really getting the value for your money.

Mental risk: Trading is perhaps the most addictive form of gambling, and with a trader's intelligence being enhanced day by day, they are much more likely to get addicted. One might wonder, why not be on their trading spot all the time and earn a lot of cash, provided they are good at it? It may look interesting, and you may be tempted to think that it is good for you, but in the long run, being addicted to trading exposes you to adverse mental risk. After all, the main aim of day trading is for you to have the financial freedom to do other things. If you do not take time off, when will you ever enjoy your money? Remember that too much work without play always makes one a dull person. You should control how much trading you do in a day, or how much space trading occupies in your mind. Do not invest in a venture that will give you financial freedom but a lifetime of mental bondage.

Types of orders in Day Trading

While placing a trade order seems as simple as clicking a "buy" or a "sell" button when it's time to do so, executing orders requires maximum attention to the various types of orders and knowing exactly what to do every time you are in the market. Each of the order serves a significant purpose.

The following is a checklist of trade orders that you should pay attention to in order to avoid slipping and losing:

Market order: This is perhaps the simplest in the trading market. It has a buying and a selling option. Usually, the trader has no control over the buying or selling price of the market order. The market gives you the prevailing price, and that is what you get. It is preferable at times when traders are in need of entering or exiting positions, but can be dangerous since you may buy at the ask price and sell at the bid price, or experience a large negative difference. The ask price is the one that sellers that are willing to sell to you have, and the bid price is the one that the willing buyers place.

Limit order: Likewise, there is a buy and sell limit order. It is a directive to purchase or give away a position at a specific price, different from the current price in the market. It gives allowance to the traders to trade at a preferable price, be it buying or selling. A buy limit order, for instance, allows a buyer to set a limit beyond which they can't buy shares. For instance, if the current price of a stock is 10 dollars, a trader may choose to set a limit of 8 dollars, and only when the price of the willing sellers hits 8 or below can the trader execute the order. A sell limit order, on the other hand, allows the trader to set a limit below which they can't sell an order to prevent them from making losses. A limit order is more preferable to market order when the trader has a lot of time to wait for the order, but the market order is considered more efficient just when the trader wants to execute orders quickly.

Stop order: This is a buy or sells order which is designed to help prevent losses for the investor. It is generally considered useful for long positions, but can also serve as stop-losses for short positions. A buy stop order, for instance, is one that is placed above the prevailing market price; hence, the order is executed at or above that stop price. Once the stop is reached, a buy stop order becomes more or less like the market order since the trader is given any price, and now they can stop before the prices move too contrary to their expectations. A sell stop order can be leveraged to exit a long trading position. Orders are filled when the price is at or below the stop point. Upon reaching the sell stop, the order is executed at the amount buyers are willing to give, just like in a market order, preventing impending losses when the prices are moving against the trader.

The major limitation with stop orders is that one cannot be sure of the buying or selling price they will receive. For that reason, there is the stop-limit order as described below.

Stop-limit order: This directive is almost comparable with the one above (stop), only that it has a boundary which prevents it from acting like the market order once the stop is reached. Clearly, it has the features of both the stop and the limit order. In this order, the trader sets two price points, the stop, and the limit price. It begins as a stop order, but upon reaching the stop, it turns into a limiting value directive. It gives the trader a degree of security to exit the positions if they suspect any impending losses and also allows them to set the price at which they prefer to buy or sell stocks.

Trailing stop order: This order has many similarities with the stop order, only that the stop order has a specific price that it targets for the order to be executed, while the trailing stop order allows a trader to set their preferred change in the prevailing prices. Traders use it to exit short positions, even though it is generally considered appropriate for long positions.

Essential Tools

Infrastructure: Day trading is just like any other profession that requires infrastructure to enable it to run. Technology has made trading easy because traders have access to most of the equipment they need, which includes computers or laptops, modems, routers, mobile phone with internet connectivity, and great communication capability. Also, traders need some specialized software to keep tabs on every activity going on in the market all day long.

The active traders who have made day trading their full-time job acquire Electronic Communication Networks (ECN) such as Select Net and Instinet to keep up with all the market activities. Having this software exempts traders from having to pay a fee for every trade to the brokers since they can solely access all information concerning their position. These ECNs are normally free but to join and use any, membership must be approved. They prefer this to get ECN capabilities to monitor the market. Alternatively, some traders, especially those who trade occasionally, use online brokerage accounts, whose major drawback is that it incurs more costs.

Such infrastructure requires some dollars every month. However, it is important to note that using the brokerage approach incurs you more costs and exposes you to the risk of getting delayed information. Yet in day trading, it is the little expense details that determine the difference between success and failure in becoming profitable.

Capital

The principles of day trading are applicable for all markets, including stock, commodities, and options, but the capital requirements vary for each market. As mentioned, and even as a basic rule of nature, you need capital for you to engage in trade. Hence, if you are thinking of starting up, you must set aside capital to start and be a reasonable risk taker, lest you lose it all. Be sure to have your initial capital outlay get you somewhere concerning your trading goals.

Some of the capital requirements reflect in commissions for the Direct Access Brokers. Commissions are computed on the basis of the volume of shares being traded. Whenever getting in and out of a position, you have to consider the corresponding commission charges. Some brokers ask for high commissions, while others are considered cheaper.

Other costs are incurred in the spread, which refers to the difference between the prices at which quick buyers get securities and the prices at which quick sellers sell their securities. Essentially, a trader must have the capital to be able to take bids. Also, as discussed in the infrastructure section above, all traders need market information, and they must be able to pay for it to access.

Information

Information is perhaps the single most significant tool that you need in day trading. Remember that you are relying on every slight price movement for you to make a move.

Whilst you are not really concerned with the intrinsic value of the companies whose stock you are trading on, you are definitely concerned with how these stocks interplay with others in the market.

Using special software, internet connectivity, and computers, day traders are able to perform technical analysis and compare historical price movements with the current to make a decision. They need to access charts and to also know how to interpret those chartings to their benefit.

Time commitment

As earlier mentioned, day trading is one of the trading options that can easily become a full-time job. To benefit from this trading, you have to be sure that you can commit up to 10 hours per day in the market, either trading or preparing to trade. You definitely need to maintain your focus on the market conditions to identify any short-term opportunities. You must research for the most recent news and ongoing news stories, including regulations and earnings reports that can potentially impact your profitability.

The right personality

Personality matters a lot when it comes to day trading. As mentioned earlier, a day trader is assured of benefiting in the long run if they are disciplined, consistent with their efforts, patient, and even tough-minded. Day trading is not for the faint-hearted. One has to be ready to embrace any results and move on to try what the next day has to offer. Also, one has to realize that profits do not come by the first time of trading. It takes time and effort to accumulate experience and trade like a pro.

A day in the life of a Day Trader: What traders normally do every day

Just like in any other business, mistakes keep happening in day trading. These include errors as simple as clicking on the wrong tab, say buy instead of sell, or placing a wrong position. Other errors come forth when the trader is bombarded with information surrounding the trade, which further causes panic. In this connection, it is paramount to have a proper schedule for pre, during, and post-trade to minimize the chances of errors. Active day traders begin their day following a plan that they intend to maintain for the whole day. Although every trade is different, the following is a checklist of what should be in your daily plan:

Pre-trade:

Check the economic calendar

Any big events in the economy can potentially affect your trade because the economy influences the prices in the market. The wise traders avoid being in trade at the time surrounding high impact economic events since anything can happen. The market typically opens at 9:30 a.m. ET. Hence, a wise trader catches up with any events that happened overnight or are coming up in the day that could affect their trade before this time. To see economic events, check the DailyFX economic calendar for Forex trade, Bloomberg for stocks, and the Yahoo! Finance earnings Calendar for individual company stocks to ensure the company has no major announcements or significant earning changes in that day. Since most of the traders participate in Forex and Futures markets, which are "around-the-clock" markets, traders can expect price rises before the market fully opens at 9:30 a.m. ET.

Launching the workstation

After checking and taking note of what the analysts have to say, day traders then head on to their workstation and launch the platform. A wise trader checks if the platform is working seamlessly by ensuring that quotes are streaming in smoothly from the brokers. Since there is interplay of various technological devices and software involved here, traders spend a few moments checking that everything is functioning properly.

Be sure to trade in the correct account

It is possible for a day trader to have a great trading day and realize in the evening that they have been trading in a simulated account instead of the real account with real capital. A beginner especially should be very cautious, since most will have the simulated account. Also, for a market such as Futures, be sure to trade with the highest volume contract and check to see the ones whose deadlines are over.

Note down significant texts

It is good to note down any scheduled high impact news releases as a constant reminder. In fact, you should include it in your chart at the approximate time it is bound to happen. It is entirely human nature to become too indulged in trade and end up forgetting such significant events.

Checking strategies

Check the automated orders such as stop orders and stop limit orders to ensure they are set correctly, since failure to do this may give you some of the most unwanted results. If you are using a robot to trade, ensure that all settings are correct to avoid mishaps. You already know by now that even if you are trading manually, you can have some automated orders as well; hence, this is a necessary step.

Check to position

This is especially a critical step for traders who use default position size. Errors could include an extra zero added to or removed from the actual position, which leads to a messed up trading session. Also, note your account balance to ensure that your market entry point and any stop order that you may set are well covered. Also, be sure that when positioning, you do it correctly to minimize the potential risk. Keep in mind the most amount of risk that you want to take in a particular day.

Self-reminder

It is good to set a few moments to go through the situations under which you've made mistakes in the past. This helps you to avoid committing the mistakes again if such situations arise again

Scanning the market for potential opportunities

When you are all set, everything is working properly, and you are mentally prepared to handle the day, hover over the market to identify the potential opportunities to trade. You can use the technical indicators option on the chart in your market for easy establishment of what's happening. Some traders have acquired market scanning software which identifies positions which meet their targets.

Conducting this assessment guides you on how to enter the market and start trading. In days with a high volatility tendency, you would expect a higher profit margin than when the volatility is stringent.

Early trading: The first few minutes of trading are technically volatile, so you want to give the market some time to balance and avoid being rudely stopped out of a position you may set. Traders then practice the waiting game at this moment until intuition can tell them to go ahead, based on their plans, experience, and observation of prevailing market price movement. In very short holding periods, which also means less profit expected, timing must be carefully done to jump in and trade during any opportunity. Remember that seconds make a huge difference in trading.

Now, this is the time you submit orders to the market, either in the state of market price orders or stop limit orders or any other depending on your goals. Whilst some traders prefer to enter simultaneous positions, others prefer to wait until one position closes to enter another.

In the time towards lunch is when traders become extra vigilant to check if their positions have reached the target, since the period after lunch is normally less eventful. High volatility and volume of trade gradually diminish towards midday. Essentially, therefore, the successful day traders are highly active during the morning and late-morning sessions.

Second wind: This represents the period after lunch to the time the market closes at 4 p.m. ET. Institutional traders come back from lunch hour and activity resumes, allowing traders a chance to look out for some more opportunities.

Traders continue monitoring their positions taken in the morning phase and now since they all have to close before 4pm. They are very alert to jump into any opportunity once their targets are reached before the close of the market. Also, traders rarely enter a position past their own limit time; say 3 or 3:30 p.m., to allow time for exiting properly without exposing themselves to losing risks.

As 4pm draws nearer, traders close the remaining positions and cancel orders that have not been filled. Leaving any open orders can cause huge losses, since they may automatically get filled without the notice of the traders.

This is just another day at the office, where you leave having broken even, experienced a loss, or gained a profit. To the successful and enthusiastic traders, the results of the day do not really matter. They look forward to what happens tomorrow and the accumulated events over time.

Post-market time: After closing the markets, traders review their day's activities, noting down what went well and what didn't, what worked and what failed, and their mistakes during the day. This helps them to note what can be improved for the sake of tomorrow. The more organized traders maintain a journal where they note down every trade and all its details, including whether it was a success or a loss. It is important to note that a journal provides a good framework for a trader hoping to elevate their trading efforts. It is also a good motivator to actually see that you have made some wins, and you can surely win again. Traders also go through financial news to get a review of the day's activity and plan for the next day. Finally, the trader shuts down their workstation and gets time off to rejuvenate and refresh for the next day.

Ideally, most of the time of a day trader's day is spent studying and seeking to understand the market and enhance their skills using simulations. Almost all traders had experienced a time when they traded for $1000 when they actually meant to trade for $100, but all this is part of a trader's development. A proper daily schedule that is well followed is what leads to success eventually for a beginner.

Formulating achievable goals and understanding common constraints

Having learned what day trading entails and the daily activities of a trader, you would think that perhaps pulling out an excel sheet and listing how much money you need to make each day to reach your goals is the way to go. In fact, this is the case for most traders. They cannot be blamed, because our society has taught us from our childhood that when you grow up, you work for a fixed amount of time for a particular amount of pay. However, one of the greatest lessons you learn as a trader is that the trading market does not really care about your daily or weekly or even monthly targets.

Day trading is complex, and setting a subjective goal does not really work. That said, I think that attempting to make profits, since this is the ultimate goal of every trader, without clear goals is like starting a journey without knowing the destination. Therefore, despite the complexity, you have to make (realistic) goals as a trader.

The first thing you should get off your mind is the employee's perception of work, where you think you ought to earn a certain amount after working for a certain amount of time. This mentality will have you placing trades even when conditions are not favorable as you try to get ahold of targets. This will frustrate you.

Second, when setting the goal per trade, try as much as possible to be realistic by matching your targets with the market conditions. Remember that setting realistic goals increases your chances of winning, and it is often the small wins that motivate you to keep going.

Also, relate your fixed goals per trade to the amount of risk that you have taken. For instance, setting a profit goal of about 30,000 dollars if you risked about 10,000 dollars is pretty reasonable. Over time and through a chain of trades, you are likely to get 3 times your capital investment and lower losses. Remember that you must account for losses. Since it is not good to over-focus on the negative side, the losses, it is good to consider them in your goal.

Also, relate your goal to the amount of volatility in the market. Volatility describes the number of price fluctuations in the market. High volatility translates into an equally big profit or loss margin. In low volatility conditions, the profit margin is likely to be low, and so is the loss margin. If you are sure of your strategy, timing, and position, you can set a higher goal in higher volatility, only you ought to be keen on the price movements.

Your goal should relate to the strategy that you are using and the platform. Every platform has different rules and techniques for trading. Based on the platform you operate on, you should be able to set a reasonable goal. If you aren't careful, you might set unreasonable targets that your brokerage platform may not produce.

Another tip to consider when setting trading goals is your mental status. Psychological issues inhibit clear thinking and prevent one from executing their technical trading strategy properly.

What differentiates between amateur traders and veteran consistent traders when it comes to making goals per trade is the factors considered when setting a target. Take it as a rule of thumb to refrain from looking for a quick fix, but instead work through your journey the right way. It is recommended that you use a simulation program to help guide you on how to set reasonable goals for each trade (Abdolmohammadi & Sultan, 2002). By observing your various outcomes from the strategies used in the simulation account, you are able to determine the potential amount of profit you can make from a trade. Also, be sure to use the simulation strategy in a demo account to be sure about your decisions.

Maintain a journal where you record your goals in the past, say, 2 months, against what you actually achieved. If you notice an improvement trend in your results, know that you are on the right track and that you need to implement the efforts you have been using consistently. Day trading is technically meant to be more risk-averse compared to other forms of trading since stops and profits are discovered in short, quick spans. Success in day trading goals depends on the ability of a single trader to execute orders sensibly when chances arise. You should strive as much as you can to focus on the process and not the results, to learn the plan that works for you and has probably worked for your mentors, and to be careful in analyzing the prevailing market conditions.

Keeping your emotions under control in day trading

Trading can be such a hugely emotional experience. One moment you are gaining, the next you are losing terribly. Day trading is fast paced, and there are many different kinds of orders to execute. If one is not careful, they may end up making their trading decisions based on emotions and not facts. Yet this is among the most detrimental things you can do in day trading. Also, the lack of a balance in emotions makes you become frustrated and quit sooner.

Humans are not by any means technical calculators, and sometimes our moves often become misplaced. Yet day trading has been proven to be a large cash machine if well utilized. The aspect of attracting profitability and sustaining the course requires a stable steering wheel, which is why you should be sure to leave emotions far from the trading station. It means being able to maximize your gains, minimize losses, and maintain mental fortitude to have strategies for both ways. The emotionally stable traders are always strategic, disciplined, and motivated, and they aren't simply gambling while in the market. They make conscious decisions to be as rational as possible. Gambling is what most people do while in trading, where they make decisions based on their emotions and cross their fingers instead of relying on their brain.

That said, emotional times will arise, be it in moments of victory or moments of losses. Your emotions will become involved at times. However, it is by being able to silence the inner monologue that you will attain stability on the ground. Doing so will not only earn you a sense of satisfaction in your job, but it will also mean that you are on track to getting higher profits. Rely on analytics alone and not feelings!

Factors to be considered when beginning to trade

There are various crucial factors for consideration for a beginner as they begin to trade. These include choosing platforms, strategies, and styles.

To identify the best platform for you to trade in, you should seek to understand the necessary conditions needed for you to succeed. For instance, Light speed is the platform with the highest potential to customize, Trade Station has the best tools for trading, and Interactive Brokers has the fairest costs for traders to maximize gains.

The most essential attribute of a day trading platform is the speed through which searching for information and the implementation of orders are done. Also, a good platform is one which offers a standard fee that does not change after a month or two. There are platforms which are made seemingly attractive by the promos, and it is easy for a trader to fall for the usually appealing promos which fade in a short while and leave traders frustrated. Also, a good platform should be able to access stocks from various places in the world and not be limited to just one country. If you opt for one that does not have further options, you are limiting your chances to benefit. Further, a good platform should be easy to use and easy to integrate with the services you are using.

Also, when choosing the ideal broker, you need to consider the speed of execution, in which you're sure the platform you settle for does not restrict you from getting the price you want when you need it. Cost minimization is also paramount for a day trader since you will most definitely be entering various positions and you need the lowest possible commission rates and fees. Furthermore, be sure that your broker is properly regulated and they are legally obliged to care for your finances. Your broker also needs to be able to offer you support whenever you require it since you can be sure of needing assistance from time to time. Thus, the platform needs to have strong customer support. Your ideal leverage and margins should also be present in the chosen platform. As explored in **the various days trading platforms** section above, you should carefully choose that which suits your overall plan, and which maximizes your utility.

You ought to keep in mind that in the trading market, there is nothing that comes for free. In fact, you might want to assume that a platform with lower trading costs translates into less quality, fewer tools, ease of use, and mobile phone unfriendliness. In any case, you should be able to have around or more than $25,000 to assume a normal trading pattern.

Also, factors to be considered when selecting the style of trading that suits you include the amount of time that you can devote to trading, your risk forbearance levels, your level of experience, the size of your account, and your personality. Are you really patient? Are you a fast learner? Are you generally tough-minded? All these are factors for consideration which allow you to have a positive trading experience, and help you benefit from trading greatly.

Day Trading Stocks

A successful trade is always going to be built on a measured approach. To ensure this is the case you are going to want to begin by choosing the type of stocks that align with your goals as well as your temperament. Furthermore, you are going to want to take any external knowledge you might have into account when choosing the right stocks to focus on. As an example, if you were previously in the medical field then stocks based on pharmaceutical companies might be a good choice. Regardless, it is important to always take the following three main aspects of every trade into account before you make any decisions.

Timeframe: First and foremost, you are always going to want to trade in a timeframe that you are comfortable with. Doing otherwise will simply lead to scenarios where you are not at your best because you are impatient or just plain nervous. If you are still trying to improve your overall trade percentage you will likely want to stick to the 5-minute charts until you can be truly comfortable dealing with the potential for risk that holding stocks overnight can cause. You will also need to consider if you prefer micromanaging trades all day every day or prefer doing all of your research over the weekend to pursue weekly trades come Monday morning. Micromanaging trades leads to short-term gains while weekly trades produce long-term gains.

Trading tactics: When it comes to choosing a methodology to use while trading, it is important to focus on what works for you instead of bouncing around based on what is popular in the moment. It is important to remember that every trader is going to have good days and bad days and if you can find a methodology that is successful at least 60 percent of the time then you are well on your way to success. Switching your tactics constantly is only going to skew your stats so you won't be able to determine the true cause of either your successes or your failures. What's worse, changing constantly will make it difficult for you to learn the intricacies of the methodologies you use meaning they will be less effective in even more scenarios.

Strategies to try

Fade: A fade is a trading strategy based on taking a contrarian approach to the current trend. This is a high-risk strategy that has the potential for high short term gains when it works out in your favor. The reasoning behind this is that once the initial surge or spike in price has occurred then the resulting retracement or pullback will be able to generate a profit. To know you are on the right path when it comes to one of these strategies, you will want to look for a gap between the price and the trend line; this means the price is heading more in the direction of the trend and away from the trend line.

The right time to fade a breakout is when you have reason to believe that the breakout from either the resistance or support level is false which means it is unlikely to continue for much longer. You would then want to put this strategy into play when you have reason to believe that this breakout is going to be substantial.

Most fade breakout trades tend to fail because the minority who chose to fade the breakout is frequently compromised by the major players in the market who want the current trend to continue. Remember, in order to sell something, you need to have a buyer and if everyone is currently buying above the resistance level or selling below the support level then the number of buyers for what you are proposing is going to be relatively slim. There is a reason that this is a high-risk strategy.

Blade runner strategy: The Blade runner forex trading strategy is a type of price action strategy that utilizes price action in order to find successful entries. It also uses round numbers, resistance and support levels, candlesticks and pivot points in order to ensure its results are as accurate as possible. While it is not always going to be necessary to utilize off-chart indicators, you will also want to include your favorites if you hope to have an additional confirmation before you make your final decision. Fibonacci levels are also an option in this scenario.

Generally speaking, the best course of action is going to bc to use a 20 EMA on-chart indicator or the midline of the traditional 20 Bollinger Band because either of these will properly support the strategy. Alternately, you can also use both together to further confirm that what you are seeing is correct. The results from doing so can then be traded with any currency pair along with any timeframe, though the five-minute chart is likely going to generate the best results.

While you can use this strategy successfully at any point throughout the day, there are certain times that are going to be more productive than others. For example, the early hours of the Asian session tend to generate a reasonable amount of breakout while also supplying a retest that is reliable enough to warrant entry while its later hours are typically quite slow. When it comes to the European session opens the prices are often quite volatile which makes finding an entry point a risky proposition, once things settle down it is then easier to get a few reliable entries if you are lucky.

The Blade runner strategy got its name from the fact that the 20 EMA functions as the knife edge that divides the price. If the price ends up being higher than the EMA while at the same time respecting it and retesting the EMA then it is likely going to fall on the long side. If the price is below the EMA, while still resting and respecting, then it is likely going to end up being on the short side.

Ichimoku Cloud Pattern Trading

This more insightful view, coupled with the fact that it is a very visual system in general, makes it easy for traders to quickly separate potential trades with a low probability of success from those that are more likely to work out in the end.

When translated, its name means equilibrium chart at a glance, which not only describes the system accurately but also outlines how it is used. The Ichimoku cloud pattern uses five separate components or lines, not individually, but rather all together to make it as easy to see the big picture when it comes to price action as possible. As such, a quick glance at the Ichimoku chart should be enough to provide you with everything you need to know when it comes to the strength and momentum of a given trend as well as the sentiment behind it.

Price action is typically gauged based on the perspective of whether it is in equilibrium or not with the market as a whole. The Ichimoku chart works on the assumption that the market is a direct reflection of human behavior which moves through its own states of equilibrium. Each of its 5 components then provides their own reflection of this equilibrium.

The Ichimoku chart is made up of 5 different indicator lines, a brief summary of each and how it is calculated is outlined below:

Tenkan Sen: This is the turning line and it is determined by adding together the lowest low and the highest high, and then dividing the result by 2 for the previous 9 periods.

Chikou Span: This is the lagging line and it is calculated by taking the current closing price and then time-shifting it backwards 26 periods.

Kijun Sen: This is known as the standard line and it is found by looking at the previous nine periods and adding together the highest high and the lowest low before dividing by 2 for each period.

Senkou Span A: This is known as the initial leading line and it can be found by adding together the kijun sen and the tenkan sen before dividing by 2 and then finally shifting the resulting amount forward 26 periods.

Senkou Span B: This is known as the second leading line and it is found by looking at the previous 52 periods and adding together the highest high and the lowest low before dividing by 2 for each period and then shifting the result forward 26 periods.

Settings: When it comes to the Ichimoku chart, each line has either one or two different settings based on the number of periods you are looking at the moment. The number 26 is pulled from the number of days in the standard Japanese business month, 9 comes from the number of days in a week and a half (minus Sunday) and 52 represents two months. While these numbers obviously don't line up with the crypto currency trading timeframe, they are still effective and thus should not be changed.

Tenkan sen: When the tenkan sen is similar to the 9-period simple moving average at first blush, it is actually a very different beast entirely as it actually measures the lowest low and highest high of the average price for the previous nine periods. Using the average pricing extremes over this period of time make it possible to provide a better overall measure of equilibrium as opposed to using the average of the closing price for the same period of time.

The tenkan sen is also able to generate periods of flattening, while a simple moving average does not. This is due to the fact that it uses multiple averages as opposed to a single moving average. This means that when the price is ranging the tenkan san will generate a clearer midpoint from its range because it is naturally flatter. When it is completely flat it is indicating that the previous nine periods were largely devoid of a strong trend.

First Hour Trading

While you might picture yourself as a full time trader spending every minute that the market is open glued to your multiple monitors, in reality, the market is only going to trend throughout the entire day some 20 percent of the time. This means that, despite what you may think, most of the time the market is actually quite dull. The only time that this is not the case is when a large volume of sharp moves happen which is the first hour of every day.

The First 5 Minutes: Many traders prefer the 5-minute chart as in this amount of time you get plenty of volume and price spikes as the gap between the close of the previous day and this morning's opening becomes apparent. What's more, if you are on top of the news from the day you can likely get an idea of where the market will be going which means you won't be starting the day blind. It is important to understand that this period is also the most volatile with an unstable range and few clear boundaries. Even with a system in place, the idea that a candlestick will play out as expected is still a gamble in this stage rather than a sure thing. If you are looking to get serious about your trading, then you should watch the first 5 minutes and not interact with it except in extremely favorable circumstances.

9:30 to 9:50: While many traders will wait for a completed 30 minutes before looking into ranges, it is statistically more likely that around 10 am, any false market movement will occur, leaving the 9:50 time frame in a strong relational position. This time period also provides you with the opportunity to get into the market while those who check the 15 minute charts are looking for their second candlestick and the strict 30 minute traders are waiting for their first candlestick to finish.

After completing 9:30 to 9:50, you will want to take the time to determine the low and high values for the morning. This will provide you with the clear indicators you need to determine boundaries that can indicate opportunities to take advantage of potential breakouts or primary trends. This will also allow you to set yourself up for any sharp reversal you expect to appear.

Between 9:50 and 10:10: This is the time period where you are going to want to make a bigger move based on the results from the first 20-minute period. This is the period of time when you are going to want to enter all of your trades for the day if you are trading the first hour as if you wait until 10:15 am, or later, then you will be severely hampering your ability to make a profit even if you make all the right decisions up until this point.

Between 10:10 and 10:30: During the final 20 minutes of the cycle, you are going to want to let the stock smoothly follow the trends that you noticed early on. While this might not seem like much, the reality is that if you got in at 9:50 am, then 10:30 am is 40 minutes which can make for a lot of time for movement during the early part of the day. You will be able to realistically wait until as late as 11:00 am if things are really moving well, though at the first sign of slowdown you are typically better off getting out. It is important to never just let your morning trades run on cruise control as you never know when things might switch directions, destroying your profits in the process. Remember, the odds that things will continue moving in your favor enough to make a real difference once things have slowed for the day are much lower than the state of the market changing and costing you money instead.

Despite the fact that if things are going well you won't have much to do during this period, it is important to never approach it in a manner that can be described as lackadaisical. You never know when the moment that things start moving the other direction is going to arrive which means you need to be ready and waiting for it when it does. It is important to have a clear exit point in mind going into this time frame and to never get greedy. The levels of movement that you will be working with in this instance are going to be incredibly small which means that if you so much as get up to use the restroom without closing out then you risk ruining all of your hard work. Don't throw it all away now, remain laser focused until you have finished the day's work.

Chapter 3) Day trading pros and cons

While the above makes day trading sound relatively straightforward, the truth of the matter is that it has a variety of pros and cons that means it is not for everyone. Take a look at the following list to determine if there isn't another type of trading that is better suited to your goals.

- **Pros**

  - Large profit margins: For those who do it right, day trading can be a very profitable career path with profits that are greater and more reliable than just about any other type of securities trading.
  - Work for yourself: Many of the most successful day traders are self-employed which means they don't have to answer to anyone, they can make their own hours and set their own profit goals.
  - Always exciting: Dealing with the shortest market timeframes means that day traders typically see more action than any other type of security trader. You will have the opportunity to pit your wits against the market as well as your competition each and every day. Those who are natural thrill seekers will also appreciate the adrenaline rush that comes from rapid-fire trading and pulling a big win from the grip of defeat.
  - No degree required: As opposed to many other financial jobs, a perfectly successful day trader can be completely self-taught. As long as you are willing to put in the time

and energy to learn the skills you need, you can be a success with no expensive courses or degree required. Everything you need to learn can be found, for free, online.

- Tax write off: As self-employed individuals, day traders can write off plenty of their expenses when it comes time to pay taxes. Hardware, software, even home office space can all be written off by those who work from home.

- **Cons**

- High commission costs: Due to the fact that they make so many trades each day, day traders need to be careful of which brokerage they use as commission costs can easily eat into profits if they aren't careful.

- Extreme loss potential: Statistically, day trading is the most difficult type of securities trading to make a profit from on a reliable basis. A vast majority of day traders see nothing but losses for at least the first month they start day trading on a regular basis and more than 60 percent wash out before they ever turn a profit.

- High barrier to entry: Freelance day traders are typically competing against a wide variety of professional organizations that have a trade capital reserve of millions of dollars. This means that in order to have a chance of entering the market successfully they need to have a sizeable bankroll on hand, as taking out loans to fund your day trading dreams is never recommended. Additionally, you are going to need to factor in hardware and software costs as well as commissions, brokerage fees, live price quotes and more which will all add up much more quickly than with other types of trading due to the high volume of trades that are made on a regular basis. Outside of the financial concerns, many brokerages will not allow you to day trade until you have proven yourself competent at trading on a smaller scale beforehand.

- Self-employed: While there are certainly benefits to being your own boss, there are also plenty of drawbacks as well. This includes a lack of a retirement plan as well as health insurance, no assurance of a steady paycheck or a corporate infrastructure to help you out in any way. Additionally, you will need to keep in mind the relative isolation that comes with working by yourself with no one to lend a hand when you need it or to prevent you from browsing social media instead of working. Additionally, you will likely need to give up your steady paycheck before you start making reliable money day trading so that you can focus on it completely and get to where you need to be.

Knowing what leads to follow

Premarket movers: If the market hasn't opened yet, then the price of a given stock is always going to be subject to change. Nevertheless, it is still going to be an excellent place to start when it comes to deciding if a given stock is going to be worth trading on a certain day. The first thing you will need to be on the lookout for is those with a greater than average amount of volatility for the previous 30 days before checking to determine if the price at close lower or higher than average as well.

Social media: These days, there are just as many social media groups dedicated to the ins and outs of the markets as there are more official sources, and many of them manage to get the early scoop on the comings and goings of the market quite frequently. This, in turn, will make it easier for you to determine how the market is likely going to move before it has a chance to get started which will make it easier for you to get in on the ground floor of beneficial changes.

Earnings Calendar: A surefire way to see an increase in volatility is when earnings are reported. You are never going to want to jump on an assumed trend before they are released but shortly thereafter the trade gates will be thrown wide open.

Characteristics of a successful trader

Proper expectations: When it comes to honing your trader's mindset, perhaps the most important thing you can do is understand the results you are likely to experience. Having realistic expectations will allow you to respond appropriately both in times of failure as well as success. Specifically, this means you are going to want to banish thoughts of major success in a short period of time. This, in turn, will make it easier for you to prevent negative thoughts from creeping in throughout the day and causing you to take risks you otherwise would not take.

Additionally, it is important to be aware of what your emotional triggers while trading are likely to be. As everyone's triggers are different, the best way to understand your own is to keep a trading journal. In this journal, you are going to want to keep track of all of your trades, both successful and unsuccessful. You are going to want to note the date of each trade, the specifics surrounding it, the emotions you felt at the time, whether or not it was successful and why.

This exercise will not only help you to be aware of the emotions you are likely to experience in the future, it will help you understand why they appear in the first place. Emotions are the enemy of good trades and the best way to outpace your enemy is to know them inside and out.

For many traders, the strongest emotional triggers occur because they believe that correctly executing on a plan should lead to success 100 percent of the time. This stems from a misunderstanding of what considering a plan successful actually means. When it comes to options trading, a successful plan is one that hovers around a 60 percent success rate. This means that the plan is extremely likely to turn a profit in the long run but a full 40 percent of the time it is used it will end in failure.

Early riser: While trading in New York doesn't begin until 9:30 am, the most successful traders use the early morning hours to catch up on the international markets so they have a broader idea of what the day is likely to bring. Having a strong macro view is crucial to taking advantage of micro changes. The Western economy is strongly influenced by global markets and understanding one makes it easier to predict the other.

Dedicated: Common wisdom says that in order to truly master something complex, such as day trading, you need to put in 10,000 hours of practice time. This equates to 8 hours a day, for roughly 3.5 years. This is to say that becoming an expert day trader is more akin to a marathon, not a race. While it is true that some people, such as those discussed in chapter 3, were able to see huge windfalls in short periods of time, they are without a doubt the exception, not the rule and most people need countless hours of experience to understand when the perfect time to reap the greatest rewards really is.

Lifelong learner: The best day traders aren't the ones that are confident they've heard and seen it all before, they are the ones that understand that new and improved techniques are always coming along. Being constantly on the lookout for the newest advances in theory and strategy is what separates the true pros from the rank and file amateurs who will never be able to trade full time. The markets change every single day which means that even analysis from 7 days ago can be hopelessly out of date. Don't curtail your earnings potential make the choice to maximize it every day; remember, if you want to earn, you have to learn.

Patient: Once you have determined an ideal trade, you must be able to wait for the perfect moment when the price reaches your predetermined exit or entry point. You must follow your predetermined system and if the market doesn't reach your numbers you have to have the patience to move on to the next ideal trade. Chasing potential gains by altering your exit or entry points on the fly will rarely lead to success, it is best to wait for the ideal time to buy or sell instead.

Objective: It is important to approach each trade from a completely objective free standpoint. Regardless of any external factors, the best trades are those that are made based on a reliable system; it is as simple as that. If you listen to external sources, then you are letting other systems dictate your movements instead of your own. Evaluate each trade on its own merits and trust yourself to make the right decision.

Trading Discipline: As a new trader it can be tempting to pursue certain trades just because they "feel right." This, in turn, leads to a scattershot approach which will hurt your success in the long run. When it comes to making trades stick with these hard and fast rules.

- Focus on absolute truth: The only truth any asset has is its price in the moment. Don't get attached to trades good or bad, attachment will keep you from selling when all the signs point to sell.
- Follow the logic: If you choose an asset based on a proven strategy which says it is a good choice, you made the right choice even if the trade goes poorly. It is important to have a strategy and execute on it every time regardless of individual results (assuming it is a sound strategy, to begin with). Eventually, the odds will even out in your favor.
- Always know the odds: Prior to every trade, it is important to determine the level of risk versus the potential reward. Everyone's percentages are different depending on personal circumstance, know your risk/reward levels and never exceed them.
- Doing nothing can be the right choice: It can be easy to get into the habit of trading every day even if your current trades are still performing at acceptable levels. If it isn't broken, don't worry about fixing it.

- Let go of greed and fear: While trading, the two emotions you will encounter most are fear and greed. You will be afraid to make a trade and you will lose money because you waited. You will be greedy and hold on to something for too long and in so doing lose money. The sooner you learn that raw data is all you can trust when it comes to trading effectively the better.
- There are no shortcuts to success: There is no surefire system or program that will guarantee results, you can only improve as a trader by trading regularly, keep a tally on your results, seeing where you need to improve and working to improve in those areas. It is called practice, and it does make perfect.

The Benefits of Day Trading

There are traders who recommend against getting into day trading. They worry that day trading is too risky, too fast-paced, and that it is too hard to actually make any money with this form of trading. There are actually a lot of benefits that come from day trading as long as you know how to read the charts and how to do an accurate trade. Some of the benefits that you can get from day trading include the following:

- Day trading can eliminate some of your overnight risks. Depending on how the market does, there can be fluctuations that go between five and ten percent. The stock that is making a higher low and a higher high, and which even closed that day at a new high, has the ability to open up the next day at a low level. In one night, if things don't go right, you could wipe out all of your profit. And this all happens when you are sleeping! This doesn't happen with day trading because all of the trades happen and finish in one day. Political developments, disasters, and news are not going to disturb you. You can finish the trade and then go to bed without worries.

- You can use leverage.

Many brokers will offer you several times more than your capital margin. This provides you with more opportunities to control more investment than is available. If you are careful with your trading, this is a good way to multiply the profits that you can make. Leveraging is not usually recommended for beginners because it could result in you losing a ton of money as well but it is something to consider.

- Gives you a better chance to learn about the market.

Because you are doing a lot of trades each day, this is a great way to help you test out some trading patterns and learn more about the market.

- It can be done at home.

You can technically do day trading from home around your own time. You would just enter and exit the trades around your other obligations. Or, if you get good enough at this type of trading, you would just work this when you want to and can get all the profits in your free time.

- The satisfaction of the different challenges.

Many traders find that the continuous changes in the market can give them a feeling of accomplishment. It is an adrenaline surge that they enjoy and that keeps them working on this kind of market.

The Negatives of Day Trading

While many traders are able to make a good income with day trading, it is not the best for every trader. Some traders may want to work more with a long-term option. They may be interested in something that has a little less risk. Or maybe they aren't interested in being hooked to the computer and worrying about all the little shifts that occur in the market and how it affects their current trade. Some of the disadvantages that show up for some traders who are considering day trading include:

- During market hours, this trading takes a lot of intense focus.

If you have a lot of trouble focusing for a long period of time, or there are obligations that make it hard for you to do this, day trading can be frustrating. Day trading includes a lot of staying on your toes to figure out when the best setups are going to come along.

- You may miss out on some overnight gaps.

As many professional traders will tell you, there is a lot of money being left on the table when it comes to those overnight gaps.

- The market may move a lot but that doesn't mean your trade will move.

This happens often when we talk about day trading. This depends on how often the market makes a big move and then you either have a loss or barely break even. As a new trader, this may not make much sense, but it does matter with day trader.

- The market hours aren't the best for everyone.

Those who live on the east coast may have no problem with the hours but if you live in any of the other time zones, it can sometimes be difficult and inconvenient to trade in the U.S. markets. Some like this time difference though because they can get up early in the morning and get some good deals. Either way, you will have to watch the market and make the times work for wherever you are.

- There are a lot of opportunities for the trader to over trade.

Overtrading, either taking too many opportunities than you can handle or trading too big, is often something that happens with day trading. If you lack some self-discipline, remember there are always other trading methods to go with. The extra buying power that comes with this method of trading can give you a loose leash. If you have a lot of issues with staying disciplined, the temptation to overtrade could lead to your demise and a lot of lost money.

- You may spend too much on trading costs and commissions.

This can end up costing you a lot of money if you are not careful. Any time that you shorten up the timeframe you are working with which can come up with day trading, those commissions can sometimes cause issues.

- You will need more software than other forms of trading.

A good day trader will have some charting software, a scanner, and a broker to help them evaluate all the different choices that they can pick from. You can do day trading without this but it becomes a lot harder when you do.

Day trading can be a great way for you to make money but there are some situations where it is not the best option for you. Explore how day trading works and some of the positives and negatives before determining if it is the right trading method for you.

The Basics of Day Trading in Futures

Many people think of day trading as working with stocks. While this is one option you can choose, some people like to work with other options, such as futures. Futures can be effective because there isn't going to be a restriction on shorting when you work in this market.

First, let's look at what futures are. Futures are going to be financial contracts that will obligate a buyer to purchase their asset or a seller to sell their asset. This can be a physical commodity or a financial instrument. They differ from options, that is, you have to buy and sell these if you enter the contract, while an option will let you choose if you want to buy or sell. The contracts for these futures will detail the quality and the quality of the asset you are purchasing, and you simply need to set up the time limit of these to be for one day, rather than over a few weeks or months, or even years, to make it day trading.

While a day trading strategy for futures will often have many components and can be analyzed for how profitable it is in may ways, it is often going to be ranked based on the win rate, or the reward to risk ratio. The win rate is how many trades won based off all the trades that you did. So if you win 55 out of 100 trades, your win rate is 55 percent. As a day trader, having a win rate above 50 percent is pretty good. You can also work with the reward to risk ratio. This helps you determine how much risk you have to take to get a certain profit.

Since you are required to purchase or sell the future based on the contract you pick, it is important to pick a day that has a lot of volatility. This ensures that the price has time to go the direction that you want before you have to sell off. If the market isn't moving much, you may have to sell before you can make a good profit, or purchase when the price is too high.

Day trading with the Forex market

Another market that you can consider using when it comes to a day trading strategy is to trade in the Forex market. The forex market is a global decentralized market that allows traders to invest in currencies. This includes all the aspects of buying, selling, or even exchanging currencies at a determined price. In terms of the volume of trading, it is the largest market in the world. The main participants in this market will be international banks. But some individual investors choose to get into the market and make money as well.

Trading in the forex market is a great way to take advantage of changes in one economy over another. You will find that it is very similar to trading stocks and other options, but with day trading, you will really need to pay attention to the market and watch when the price of one currency goes up or down. Some of the basic guidelines that you can follow when you choose to day trade with forex will include:

- Trade just when the US and London markets are open. You may only want to trade for a few hours a day, usually when the two markets open. This helps you to not get worn out and make mistakes.

- When you trade, work with the one minute charts. This helps you to keep up with the small changes.

- Only trade in the same direction of the trend. You won't be in the market long enough to worry about anything else.

- Wait for a pullback. This pullback needs to stall out at some point or show some signs that the price is starting to move back in the trending direction. This must happen before it reaches a major prior swing low.

- When you see a pullback, your price needs to consolidate, which means that it must move sideways for at least two bars. Then you can purchase a breakout that is above the high price of this consolidation. This can take some patience because it may not stall the whole way and you may have to wait for some time.

- Put in those targets and stop losses. These ensure that you are going to get the best results and won't lose too much money.

- If you hear that there is a major news event that is about to happen, you need to leave all of your positions a minimum of two minutes ahead of that. You don't want to trade again until after the news is released, so even cancel all pending orders when you hear of new news or when you plan to be away from the computer. This makes sure that you aren't going to stay in the market and get on the wrong side of consumer sentiment about the news.

- Create a good day trading routine. This keeps you on track and can help you avoid some mistakes in the process.

There are some investors who want to trade in other markets, but usually until you become more accustomed to working in day trading, it is best to stay with the US market. This way, it is easier for you to get the news that you need to make informed decisions.

Day trading with crypto currencies

A newer option you can choose for day trading is crypto currencies. These crypto currencies are taking over the world and many people are starting to notice. There are thousands of these currencies available and they offer security, anonymity, and a great way to make a profit if you use them the right way. And since their volatility is high, you can easily make a lot of profit in a short amount of time.

You have to be careful with this kind of investing though. There are no regulations on the currency and they aren't available on the stock market. They also have a lot of ups and downs with them so it is also easy to lose your money quickly if you aren't careful. You really need to do your due diligence here because with so many options of crypto currencies to work with, many of them are not strong, and many can be fakes. And since these currencies aren't regulated, you won't be able to get anyone to help you out if you pick the wrong type of currency.

Now, if you take the right precautions and are willing to watch the market to protect your money, crypto currencies can be perfect for earning money with day trading. In fact, after seeing the crash of Bit coin in January 2018 after the currency reached almost $20,000 and then crashed to under $10,000 in a few days, investing in these currencies over the long-term isn't the best. But the high volatility in these currencies make them perfect to join into the crypto currency market, stay in for a few hours, and then get out and make a good profit in the process.

If you do decide to invest in crypto currencies, make sure that you take some time to research charts and the history of that currency. There won't be any reports from the SEC for you to read through and make informed decisions. Instead, you need to look online, read the charts, and learn the patterns of the currency on your own. But a smart investor who is willing to take the time and learn can make a big profit in no time.

Some crypto currencies, such as Bit coin, are more established and can be great options to go with. Others are newer and you may need to do your research on as well. You also need to check the amount of variation that comes with the market. If you are only going to make a few dollars on a trade, it may not be worth your time. Just like with your broker, these crypto currency markets are going to charge you to exchange your fiat money with the crypto currency of your choice.

Chapter 4) Strategies and say how to use it in the stocks market, forex and options

Options are unique among all the many types of securities in that each gives its own the opportunity, but not the obligation to either buy or sell the underlying asset it is related to for a fixed price for a set period of time. Each option is essentially a type of contract that is binding in a very limited and specific way. While this might all sound terribly complicated, millions of people around the world apply the same principals each day when they sign the paperwork to purchase a property without having been preapproved for a loan. As long as that paperwork is considered valid, the buyers don't need to worry about having to pay more if the market improves and the sellers don't need to worry about making less profit if the market prices decrease before the keys change hands.

The key takeaway here is that an option is simply a contract that relates to an associated asset which makes it a type of derivative which is any type of security that doesn't have innate value on its own. This includes things like indexes or stocks but not commodities. When employees are offered the opportunity to by company stock at a fixed point that is another type of option. All told, every type of option can be divided into two categories those that are puts and those that are calls.

Call: A call option allows its owner to purchase a specific asset at a set price and is similar to taking a long position on a specific stock. If you purchase a call option, then you are going to want the underlying asset to increase dramatically in the time the option is valid.

Put: A put option allows its owner to sell a given underlying asset at a specific price by a specific deadline which makes them most similar to a short stock. If you purchase a put option, you are going to either be worried that an underlying asset you already own is going to experience a sharp decrease or you are hoping for it.

Types of options traders: Those who actively buy and sell in the options market can typically be divided into 4 different categories. Those who purchase the options are often referred to as holders and those who sell are called writers. Writers and holders then typically tend to focus on either calls or puts, though there are those who go both ways as well. The biggest difference between writers and holders is that holders can either buy or sell depending on the way the market is going while writers are required to go along with what a holder wants, even if it is not in their best interest.

Options Trading Lingo

In order to effective operate in the options market; you will need to be familiar with numerous key phrases.

Strike Price: The strike price is the amount at which the stock underlying the option can ultimately be either sold or purchased for based on the agreement in the option.

Exercised: When the holder determines that the agreement in a specific option is in their best interest and decides to put it into action then that option is said to be exercised.

Trading out: While options can be either exercised or not, they can also be traded out. Also known as closing out, this is when an investor sells an option that could be profitably exercised onto the open market where it is then bought back by the original writer who buys the positions back and closes it. In general, just over 50 percent of all options are traded out while 10 percent are actually exercised, and the rest expire worthlessly.

Listed: Options are traded via official and unofficial channels, those that are traded on a nation exchange for options are said to be listed. They then have a strike price that is fixed as well as a clearly defined date of expiration. Listed options typically count for 100 shares of the underlying stock.

In the money: Call options can be considered in the money if the current share of the underlying stock is above the strike price at the given moment.

Intrinsic value: When an option is in the money, its intrinsic value is the different between its current price and its strike price.

Time value: The amount of time a specific option has left is said to be its remaining time value.

Volatility: The price that an option currently occupies can be either stable or precarious and prone to additional positive or negative movement, an option related to an unstable stock is said to have a higher amount of volatility.

Premium: The complete price of a specific option which is a combination of volatility, time value, strike price and stock price.

Option functions

Speculation: The two most common reasons that traders buy options are to hedge an existing trade or to speculate on future movement. Options are ideal for speculation purposes as traders can bet that an underlying security is going to move in a specific way with confidence as they can always choose not to exercise their option. This does not mean it is not without risk, however, as you still have to choose correctly when it comes to the direction the underlying asset is going to move in as well as the amount of that movement in order to find success. Nevertheless, options trading remain a popular investment choice as it doesn't take much to start seeing a profit.

Hedging: Hedging, on the other hand, can be considered a type of insurance policy that can help traders ensure that an existing investment is covered when they expect that sector of the market to take a significant hit. Alternately, it can make otherwise risky investments far more manageable as traders can purchase their risky proposition, along with an option for the same amount of the underlying asset at the current price, before moving forward confident that they will at least be able to break even.

Types of options

American/European: Generally speaking, the main two classifications of option types are European and American options. While you might expect this classification to come from an obvious source, the truth of the matter is that the difference between the two is how they can be exercised, not where they are located. American options can be exercised at any point before they expire, and European options can only be exercised at the point at which they expire.

Short-term/long-term: All of the options that have been discussed up to this point have been what are known as short-term options. Long-term options tend to have termination periods that are years away which make them more useful for investors than traders. They are known as LEAPS or long-term equity anticipation securities and can be purchased just like any other type of option.

Vanilla and exotic options: Generally speaking, all of the options you are going to come across on a regular basis are going to be vanilla options. An exotic option is any type of option whose rules are above or beyond what you would expect when purchasing an option. This includes things like different methods of return calculation, termination points or terms related to the related assets. There are three primary types of exotic options, chooser options, barrier options and compound options.

A compound option allows its owner to purchase a different option by the expiration date. Compound options can either be put on call, put on put; call on call or call on put and can commonly be found in either the fixed income market or the foreign exchange market.

Barrier options tend to be the type of exotic option that appears to be the most similar to a vanilla option. The only exception is the fact that they can only be exercised if the underlying asset hits a target level. They can be down and in, up and in, down and out or up and out and are often found in both the equity markets and the foreign exchange markets.

Finally, chooser options are those that all the owner to create an option at one point, and then determine if it is going to be a put or a call at a later time. This type of option can only be orchestrated in European markets, primarily with equities as the underlying asset and generally when it comes to indices. They are considered a good choice if the market in question is expecting serious fluctuations in the future though they are quite complicated which means that you are going to want to avoid them until you become more familiar with the options trading process as a whole.

Tips for success

Avoid out of the money options: While many investment markets focus on buying low and selling high, the simple fact of the matter is that this doesn't work when it comes to options trading. In fact, putting any of your trading capital towards a call option that is out of the money is little better than gambling and there are far more effective ways to gamble if that is what you are looking to do. Furthermore, making these types of trades can also make it difficult for you to understand just why the trade failed in the first place, meaning you can't even learn from your mistakes.

To understand just why a call option that is currently out of the money is such a poor choice, the first thing you are going to want to keep in mind is that why you are purchasing an option, what you are really doing is indicating to the world that not only do you know the direction a given underlying asset is going to move in, you also know, generally speaking, when that movement is going to occur. This means that if you make a mistake in either of these two key areas you are going to be out the out the premium you paid on the option along with the cost of the commission as well.

What's worse, your funds will then be tied up until the option expires meaning you may miss out on a preferable alternative in the interim. Remember, in order to see a return on this type of trade the underlying asset of an option that is out of the money needs to not only increase, it needs to reach all the way to the strike price.

Lean when to use varying strategies: When it comes to trading in the options market successfully, there are countless different strategies to choose from which means you have no excuse when it comes to attempting to fit a square peg into a round hole. For example, if you decide to buy on spread, this could be an excellent way of capitalizing on some very profitable market conditions, but only if you know the specifics before you get started. Not only will focusing on a single strategy cost you money regularly, it will also skew your overall results with that strategy as it will include countless false losses that could have been turned around if you had been using the right tool for the job.

Always know the spread: A long spread is made up of a pair of options that are similar in every way except one has a higher strike price than the other. The option with the higher cost is being purchased while the other is being sold. These options can be either puts or calls. Long spreads comprised of calls are bullish and those comprised of puts are bearish.

While the time lapse is going to hurt part of the spread, it will always help the other which means that the spread is typically going to hurt your profit in most cases. This is due to the fact that half of the pair is almost always going to expire assuming the underlying asset isn't overly volatile. Even still, if you are interested in a trade that is guaranteed to turn some type of profit you could certainly do a lot worse.

Have a clear idea for every entry and exit point: In order to ensure you can eventually turn a profit in the options market, it is crucial that you always have a clear idea of both what your entry and exit points are going to be. Failing to do so will make it difficult to mitigate the influence your emotion might otherwise have on your trade. It will also serve to ensure that you remain in the black over the long term. While it can be difficult to exit a trade when there is still the potential of money on the table, it is important to keep in mind that the potential for loss is also ever present. Setting a reasonable exit point and sticking with it is going to generate a larger profit over a prolonged period of time, guaranteed.

Never double up: If you are in the midst of a trade that is going your way, only to have it turn on you at the very last minute, it can only be natural to want to do everything in your power to save it. Unfortunately, the best option practically every single time is going to be to simply cut your losses and move on. Never forget, options are derivatives which mean that the price is likely to change with little notice which means that doubling down is only going to end up ultimately costing you more in the long run.

While it can certainly feel like the right move in the moment, if you take an extra moment to really stop and think about what you are doing, you will find that you are making a mistake. All you need to do is ask yourself if you would make the trade you are about to make if it was the first trade of the day and you had a clear head and you will likely find your answer. Nine times out of 10 the correct decision is going to be just to cut your losses and move on.

Stay away from illiquid options: Illiquidity measures the speed at which a specific option can be either bought or sold without causing the price to shift noticeably. Liquidity, on the other hand, can be thought of as a chance that the second round of trading for a given underlying asset will end up taking place at a price that is close to the same price as the first round.

Don't buy back short options: While, theoretically, it could seem like buying back short options at the last moment is an ideal choice, the fact of the matter it is almost always going to hurt you more than help you in the long run. Additionally, it may be tempting to hold onto profitable options in order to squeeze the maximum return out of each investment, but you need to be aware that the potential for a reversal is always lurking in the shadows. Instead, a good rule of thumb is to buy back options that are currently at 80 percent of your ideal return or higher and let the extra take care of itself. While it may hurt to leave some potential profit on the table, it will improve your overall reliability, netting you a profit in the long run.

Don't forget key dividend and earnings dates: When trading in options it is extremely important to keep an eye on the particulars of the underlying assets you are working with as if you are holding calls you will have to deal with the possibility of assigning early dividends. Due to the fact that owning an option and owning an underlying asset isn't the same thing, if the early dividends are assigned, if this happens to you then you won't be able to collect on your hard-earned money. Early assignment is largely a random occurrence which means that if you don't keep your ear to the ground it can be easy to get caught unaware and be unable to exercise the option before you miss the boat.

Along similar lines, you are going to also always want to be aware of when the earning season is going to take place for any of your underlying assets as it is likely going to increase the price of all of the contracts related to the underlying asset in question. Additionally, you will need to be caught up on current events as even the threat of influential news can be enough to cause a significant spike in volatility and premiums as well. In order to ensure your costs are minimized to the greatest degree possible when trading during these periods, you are going to want to utilize the spread. This will serve to minimize the cost that inflation would otherwise add to your bottom line.

When you do have to sell the options you have purchased, you are going to want to avoid lower-striking the long option in order to generate enough of the required underlying asset. Rather, you are going to want to place the long option onto the open market which will provide you with the chance to profit from the premium caused by the remaining time. You can then use your new funds to purchase the underlying asset that you are on the hook for, netting a profit in the process.

When you find yourself in this situation, it is important to not let it get the better of you. Instead, it is important to remember that early assignment is essentially random which means that there is little point in worrying about it too much. The best you can do is aim to negate the chances of it affecting you to the greatest degree possible by ensuring that you are prepared for it if the market seems to be moving in that direction.

Trade more index options: Index options are a great choice if the market is currently in an extremely volatile state as they are far less likely to experience sudden changes when compared to other options as they are based on an index which, in turn, is based on a variety of stocks so things like news reports and the like are going to cause much less of an uproar. The larger the index the option is based on the more likely it is that it will remain neutral in the face of high volatility.

Alternately if you feel that the market is holding its own, then you are going to want to look at indices with shorter spreads. This means you will want to choose a pair of options with different strikes prices to ensure you remove time decay from the equation while also ensuring that you will make a profit as long as the price doesn't decrease.

Never make a trade you can't afford to lose: When it comes to deciding on how much you are going to spend on your new options adventure, it is important to keep in mind that you should never invest more than you can afford to lose. If you decide to invest money that you need for more pressing matters in a volatile market, then you will never be able to look at your trades rationally and will always be concerned about protecting those funds. It is also important to factor in how long you anticipate holding the options for as the more time you have, the more you will be able to let loose and take risks as you will have plenty of time to correct them if things don't work out.

Avoid discounting volatility: Being aware of the amount of volatility that is currently plaguing a specific market is crucial when to comes to making positive trades that are going to end up paying out in your favor in both the short and the long term. Understanding the current level of volatility in the market of your choice is actually quite simple as all you need to do is consider the stock market as the volatility of all the other markets is likely to reflect the same level of volatility as it does at least 9 times out of 10. The greater the degree of stability that the stock market is experiencing the more confident the majority of traders are going to be across the board which means the overall level of stability is going to more or less remain the same.

Avoid making a mistake when choosing a broker: Perhaps more so than most other types of trading, choosing the right options broker is a key part of being successful at the process in the long-term. Don't forget, your investment capital is going to be in their hands which are why it is so important for you to know what else they have been up to. After all, it doesn't take much to create a website that appears as though it is on the up and up when in reality it functions as a way to bilk ignorant investors out of their hard-earned cash.

Luckily, these sorts of things are very easy to check, as the internet never forgets. First things first, you are going to want to look into what current or previous customers have to say, not just on the company's website, of course, but on forums and subreddits dedicated to options trading as well. One of the things you are going to want to look for is a record of reliable customer service as well as technology to ensure that every trade you make is going to be completed in record time.

You will also want to contact the customer service for the broker you are considering and see how long it takes them to get back to you. If it is more than 24 hours then you are going to want to go elsewhere as if they can't respond to new customers in a reasonable time, then it is extremely unlikely they will respond to existing customers any faster. Finally, it is generally a good idea to choose a broker that is in your home country for a few reasons. First, you are far more likely to find some kind of third-party oversight locally, than you ever are anywhere else; and second, you are far more likely to speak the same language in this scenario which will make the whole process easier for everyone involved.

Don't overcommit: While sticking with a single asset makes sense when you are learning the ropes of option trading, sticking with one underlying asset for too long can severely curtail your potential for profit. As such, once you feel comfortable trading options it is best to start looking into multiple different assets to ensure that if one segment of the market unexpectedly turns sour that you don't lose all of the trading capital in one fell swoop. Remember, there is plenty of uncertainty in even the calmest markets as uncertainty is what leads to profit as far as investment is concerned.

Generally speaking, when it comes to being successful with options trading, a good rule to stick with is the greater the degree of diversification the better. You may even want to go so far as to utilize different financial advisors or brokers depending on the specialty that each provides. While this will likely be more time consuming than simply sticking with what you know, it will be worth it the first time that things go wrong with one asset and you have saved yourself from a potential financial disaster.

Chapter 5) Step-by-step guide for beginners

Now that this guidebook has taken some time to discuss a lot of the great trading strategies that you can use to see success with day trading, we are going to put it all together to help you come up with the steps you need to take to really get your trade off the ground. You will have to do a bit of the work here such as setting up the account and picking out the strategy that you want to work with but this chapter can be your checklist to help you out when you are ready to perform the actual trade. Let's take a look at the steps that you should take in order to do a successful trade in day trading.

Building up Your Watch List

The first step when you are ready to get started in day trading is to do some research. When you first wake up in the morning, look over your notes and your research and then use that information to create a good watch list. This watch list can be important because it can limit you down to just a few options that you plan to use for trading on that day. There are thousands of stocks on the market and making this watch list will make it so much easier for you to pick the right stocks to invest in.

There are different methods you can use to create this watch list. But one of the best options is to use a scanner. These scanners can look for specific criteria that you want out of a stock and can make things faster than trying to look through them all on your own. To make the scanner work, you just need to list out the requirements that you want the stock to meet and then the scanner will alert you as soon as it finds one that meets these.

You do need to take this a step further. When you see a few stocks show up on the scanner, make sure to check them out personally rather than just investing in the first ones that show up. When you look through the results on the scanner, you will quickly see that a few are worth your time and you may invest in them, but there will be plenty that is not worth your time and you can skip over these.

Decide Which of These Stocks Work Best for You

After the scanner has given you a few options for stocks that meet your requirements, you can decide which of these the best stocks are. You may have a specific strategy that you would like to go with and then choose the stock that seems to be following that strategy the best. You can always change strategies from one day to the next, or you can choose to stick with one strategy if it is serving your purpose.

As we discussed in some of our strategies before, make sure that you do not trade in the market for at least the first five minutes after the market opens. Some professionals wait even longer than these five minutes for the market to settle down.

There can be a ton of commotion and crazy ups and downs in the market during those first few minutes and investing at this time can hurt your profits. If you spend time looking at your scanner and then investigating the stocks that you receive, it will probably be at least five or more minutes before you are ready to enter the market anyway, but it is still important to be aware of this volatility and learn how to avoid it.

Put That Entry and Exit Strategy in Place

Now that you have a few stocks that are ready to go, you're probably excited to get into the market and start doing you is trading. Before you make that purchase, you need to finish up your strategies. This isn't just the overall strategy but also the center and the exit strategy so you know how to get into and out of the market at the right times.

The first strategy you should work with here is your entry strategy. This is the place where you are comfortable and will purchase your stock. Your aim is to get this entry point as low as you can so that you don't spend too much money and to increase your profits later on. When you look through the charts for that stock, you should be able to figure out a safe entry point that will provide you with a reasonable price on that stock.

You also need to come up with an exit strategy. It is important to have a stop for losing money and one for earning money. First, let's look at the stop for losing money. There are times when the strategies that you pick or the decisions that you make are not going to turn out how you wanted and the stock may start to lose money. The point of this stop is to ensure that you can control how much money you will lose in the process. Once the stock ends up reaching this number, you will withdraw from the market, no matter what the stock does later on.

Without this stop, you could end up with a little bit of trouble. Many new traders see that the stock is going down, and they keep riding it out. They hope that the market will turn around. Sometimes the market will turn around, but then there are times when the market will stay low or keep going down. And without a stop, you could be without a whole bunch of money. Depending on how far the market goes, you may not be able to cover the losses either. It is much better to have that stop in place and then exit the market at a comfortable loss rather than letting things get out of hand. You can always get back into the market later on if things begin to improve.

After you pick out the stop loss, it is time to get your profit stop in place. This is one that a lot of beginners are going to skip because they assume that it is best to just ride out the market until they stop making profits. But day trading finds that the market is going to do a lot of ups and downs, even in markets that are pretty stable. You want to have a profit stop so that you can get out of the market before the prices go down and you are not able to earn any profits at all. Yes, it's possible that the market will have a big breakout and you are going to miss out on some potential profits, but it's just as possible that the market could tank as well and you would lose your profits.

Purchase the Stocks You Want

After you created your watch list and came up with your enter and exit strategies to keep you safe, it is time to actually go into the market and make your purchase. You will want to have all the criteria in place for that stock before doing this. But if you are working with a strategy, that is going to outline the criteria for you, so just follow that.

If you plan to work with your broker when doing day trading, you would just give them your order to get the trade started. The order is going to include a ton of information that can help the broker do everything that you want. This would include information on which stocks, in particular, you want to purchase, how many shares of each you want to purchase, how much you will spend on these stocks, when you want to enter the market, and when you want to exit the market. The broker is then able to take that information and place the order for you in the system.

There is also the option for you to do all of the work on your own. This is fine to do but most beginner traders are not going to pick this option because they worry about messing things up or doing something wrong. Make sure that if you are doing this choice that you work with a good platform that can get the work done quickly for you. If the platform ends up being really slow, or there are some mistakes done on your side, it could really ruin your trade.

Pay Attention to the Market Until the Trade Is Closed

You will quickly find that day trading has some differences compared to other stock trading options. Many other options are longer-term; you purchase the stock and then ride out the market, hoping that your choice will go up over some time. But with day trading, you are only letting the trade occur in one day. The purchase of the stock, as well as the sale of it, all need to happen sometime between open and close of the same day.

This does make day trading a riskier option to work with compared to some of the other stock trading options. This means that you need to really want the market and make some quick decisions on when to buy and sell your stocks. If you don't watch the market, then how are you going to be able to make these quick changes when needed?

Day trading is unique as it takes advantage of the little ups and downs in the value of a stock during the day. If you look at the long-term charts of a stock, you will notice that it stays pretty steady. There may have been a few news announcements or a few other things that come up on the charts that change the trend, but overall, the stock will probably go upwards. But if you look at a week or even a day of historical value on the stock, you will see a lot of little ups and downs. None of them are that big, but they are there. Day trading is attempting to capitalize on these.

As a day trader, you get to focus on watching these ups and downs that occur during the day. This can make it easier to know when you should purchase a stock in the first place and then it helps you to figure out when you can sell the stocks to make the biggest profits, or to keep your losses to a minimum.

Once you enter into a trade, you need to pay attention to the market and there may be times when the market changes quickly and you will need to make some quick changes to your position, or close it out, to help you earn more profits or keep the losses down as much as possible. Day trading is not one of those methods where you can place the order and then walk away. If you don't have the time to sit and closely watch the market, make sure to not place an order until you have more time.

Sell Your Stocks When They Reach Your Original Exit Points

Remember how we sent some exit strategies earlier? This is when they are going to come into play. These numbers are important to the day trading because they take some of the risks that come with day trading and will limit how much money you will lose if the market doesn't go the way you would like to. Regardless of how the market goes, you want to stick with your exit and entry points. The second you ignore them, you have let the emotions play into the mix, and you are not going to win as much as you think.

It is a good idea to listen to your exit point not only when the market is going down but also when the market is going up. Some people understand why they should follow the exit strategy when the market is going down and they do not want to end up losing too much money in the market. It is a bit harder on them when the market is going up. They may have placed a stop for how much profit they wanted to make, but then they see the market still goes up and they do not want to get out at that time.

While it may be hard, make sure that you are listening to your exit strategy, even when the market is going up. Sure, the market may go past that point, but then it may hit a sharp downturn and you could lose all of that profit. This is another method in place to ensure that your investment stays safe. If the market continues to do well and keeps going up, you will be able to jump back in later on.

Take Some Time to Reflect on That Trade and Write Down Some of the Information as Research Later

As a beginner in the day trading world, there are a lot of things to learn about the market. This is even truer if you have never invested in the past. As a trader, it is your job to learn as you go and make some changes if it is needed. But when you are learning a lot of strategies and keeping track of a large number of trades that are done in day trading, it can be hard to remember everything over time.

Getting a journal and writing down some of your mistakes, your tips, and more after each trade can make a difference. You don't have to write down a lot of information unless you want to. Just have a few lines or a paragraph. This may seem like it wastes your time. But if you ever get stuck on a trade later on, or if you are trying to figure out why you are in a slump and not getting the profits that you want, looking back through this information can make a big difference in how things go in the future.

Startup Your Second (And Third and Fourth and So on) Trade

Day trading moves very fast. It is likely that your first trade can be done in a few minutes, though as a beginner it will probably take a little bit longer to finish. If there is still time left in the day when you finish up that first trade, then go through these steps again and complete the next trade. Day traders earn a big profit simply by doing a bunch of little trades.

The more of these successful trades that you can get into one day, the more profit you will make. Just make sure that you are following the same steps that we talked about above and take the same precautions that you did with your first trade. If there is not enough time during the day, or you worry that you will rush yourself if you try to do another trade, it is fine to take a break and resume the next day.

There are times when you are going to get into the day trading market and you will make a bad trade in the morning. It may not have gone your way, you may have tried to switch your strategy part way through, or maybe you let your emotions get in the way. If the trade was really bad and you feel upset about it, then it is best to just call it good and take a step away from the market for the rest of the day.

As a beginner, this is especially important as you get your bearings. These losses can hurt a professional investor, much less a beginner, and if you stay in, you may resort to revenge trading, which basically leads to a downward spiral that can cost you way more money than just taking a break. Yes, you may want to earn more profit or get more experience in the market. But taking a break can give you time to get your head back in the game and will give you the renewed confidence to do better in the morning.

Getting started with your day trading adventure can be an exciting time. As long as you follow the rules, learn to read the market and you pick out a good strategy, you can make money with this investment choice! It is hard and very fast paced, but it is also a very rewarding form of investing that many people enjoy working with.

Chapter 6) Common mistake with day trading

As a beginner, you have a large learning curve that you need to work with before you are able to profit on a consistent basis with options. It may sound pretty simple from some of the examples that we have provided so far, but you do need to take the time to learn as much about options as possible and to get the most out of your investment.

Learning what mistakes other beginners make and how to avoid them can make all the difference in how successful you can be with options trading. Let's take a look at some of the common mistakes that happen with options and how you can avoid them to earn as much as possible.

Buying Options without Hedging

This is a big mistake that a lot of beginners will make, and it can end up costing you a lot of money. Buying a naked option means that you are purchasing an option without any protective trades in order to cover your investment, in case it goes the wrong way and ends up hurting your profits. It is really hard to predict how the stock is going to move over the short-term, and there are going to be times when you are not accurate. If you keep on purchasing naked options, you are basically hoping to get lucky each time, and you are hoping that you will not lose more than you gain over the long term.

In order to make a good profit after purchasing a naked option, there are a few things that need to happening including:

• The trader needs to be able to predict the direction the stock will move accurately.

• The movement of that stock needs to be fast enough so that the position of the trader can close before its gains get overrun with time-decay.

• The rise of the options premium price needs to compensate for any drops that may happen from the time that the option was purchased.

• The trader needs to be able to exit the trade before the reversal of the stock price happens.

As you can see, there are going to be times when it is a challenge for all of these things to occur and fall into place. This is why it is common for naked-options traders to lose money, even if they were able to correctly guess the way the stock would move. There are still many traders who assume that if they keep following the same steps, they will end up with good results in the long run. The best way to make an income from options is to never purchase a naked option, unless you are doing it to hedge another position, because the risk is too big.

Underestimating Your Time-Decay

Another mistake that you may make as a beginner is that you underestimate your time-decay. This can be one of the worst parts of being an options trade if you are not able to exit the trade fast enough.

As a call options buyer, you may notice that sometimes, even when the price of the stock is increasing on a daily basis, the call option's price is not rising or falling. As a put options buyer, you can sometimes notice that your put options price is not increasing, even if there is a fall in the price of your stock. This can be a bit confusing to someone who is just starting out as an options trader.

These problems are going to occur in the market when the increase or the decrease of the stock's price is just not going at a rate fast enough to outstrip the rate at which the options time-value is eroding each day. This means that with the strategy that you employ for trading, you should have some method of minimizing or at least countering the effect of time-decay. There are even some strategies that will use time-decay in their favor to ensure that the trader gets a profitable trade.

The spread-based strategies that we will discuss later in this book will really take a look at how to do this so you don't end up losing money, even if you made some good predictions along the way.

Buying an Option with High Volatility

Another mistake that you can make is to purchase options in a time of high volatility. During these times, option premiums will often get overpriced, and if you purchase an option, you could still lose. There are times when the stock can move sharply in line with what you are expecting; a large drop in the implied volatility could make the price of the option fall quite a bit, resulting in you losing money.

You want to make sure that you are purchasing options when the price is not so volatile. This will ensure that the price of the option or the stock doesn't go down further than you were expecting and that you will not pay too much for your options premium.

Not Cutting Out On Your Losses When Needed

A good saying that you should stick with when it comes to options trading is to cut your losses short and let the winners run. Even those who have been working in options trading will find that one of their trades has gone badly on occasion. The difference between the novice and a more experienced trader is that the experienced trader knows when they have lost and when they should get out of the market. Many beginners keep holding on to trades that are losing in the hopes that these options will bounce back and they will make money.

The issue with this is that when they hold onto these options, they hold onto them a lot longer and lose a big chunk of their capital. Rather than losing a lot of money, an experienced trader will know when to admit that they were wrong, and they will pull out early when the losses are low. Then they will still have some capital leftover in order to spend on another options contract.

Being able to cut your losses in time is crucial, especially if you are working with a directional strategy and you make the wrong call. The most practical thing that you can do is exit your losing position once you notice that it is moving against your expectations and it erodes over two to three percent of the total capital you want to earn.

If you are someone who likes to use the spread-based strategies, the losses that you have will always be more limited when you have made a wrong call. However, no matter what strategy you are using, once you notice that your trade is not going to profit you well, it is time to cut off the losses and choose to reinvest in a different position that can bring in better profits.

Adding Too Many Eggs into the Same Basket

As mentioned, there are going to be times when you will make a bad trade, no matter how much time you have spent in the options market. An experienced trader knows that they should never place all of their bets on a single trade. If you do this and the trade goes wrong, it means that you are going to lose a lot of your capital all in one place.

Professional traders know that they should spread out their risks across at least a few different trades so they won't lose all their money in one place. It is best to keep no more than five percent of your available capital in one trade in order to keep things safe. So, if you have $10,000 to invest total, it is best to never enter into a trade where you will risk losing over $500 if things go wrong. If you are able to follow this practice, it will ensure that losing on occasion is something that can happen without you eating up all of your cash reserves. If you do not follow this advice, you can easily place too much of your money into one trade, and if it goes wrong, you will lose a lot of your capital.

Using Brokers Who Charge Too Much

When you are investing, it is important to cut down your costs as much as possible. While you do not want to be cheap and cut corners, there are some brokers who will charge way more for their services compared to others. You can choose to go with another option that will save you some money.

You do need to do some research ahead of time. Just because a broker charges less doesn't mean that they are the best ones for you. There are many brokers who will charge you a fair rate, but make sure that you look at some of the features that each one offers and pick one that will provide you with the results that you would like.

As you can see, there are some common mistakes that beginners can make that will cost them a lot of money on options trading. But when you learn about these mistakes and how to avoid them, you have a head start to making money with your options trading.

Chapter 7) Advice for beginners

There are a lot of benefits to working in options trading. You can make a lot of profit and even limit your losses if you know how to make the market work for you. The best thing that you can do is pick out the right strategy to help you no matter how the market is moving. Later in this guidebook, we are going to take an in-depth look at each of these strategies, as well as take a look at a case study of how each one works so you can really get that strategy down. For now, we are going to look at some of the basics of each strategy, so you can get a feel for how they are all different and you can choose which strategy you think will work the best for you.

First is the bull put spread. This is considered a directional and a credit spread. One advantage that you will find is that it is able to work against the time decay issue, so you won't lose money from that. You would choose to work with the bull put spread any time that you expect a stock to either fall, stay stagnant, or fall just a little bit (if at all) during the near future. The risk on this one is pretty low, so it is often a good strategy for beginners to get started with.

You can also choose to work with the bear call spread. This is another strategy that is directional, a credit spread, and gives you the advantage of working against the issue of time decay. You would choose to go with the bear call spread any time that you expect a fall, stagnant, or rise just a bit over the short term. This one is another low-risk strategy that can help you to get used to the market and see some results.

The bull call spread is the next strategy for options trading on our list. This one is a bit different than the other two in that it is a debit spread, and you will have to still work against the issue of time decay with it.

336

It is still a directional choice, though, which is something you may be familiar with if you have used some of the other strategies. You will want to work with the bull call spread any time that you expect your stock is going to rise moderately over the short term. The risk that you will face when working with the bull call spread is considered to be moderate.

The bear put spread is one that is similar to the bull call spread, but it works in the opposite way. This is another debit spread, and it will not help you to fight against the issue of time decay, so you will have to limit the amount of time that you are holding onto the option. It is still considered one of the directional strategies, though. This is the strategy that you will work with any time that you think your chosen stock is going to fall moderately within a short amount of time. The risk that comes with this strategy is considered moderate, so a bit riskier than the first two we talked about, but not too bad for a beginner to work with.

Next on the list is the iron condor strategy. This one is considered a credit spread. You will still get the advantage against the time decay issue, but it is considered a non-directional strategy because you are betting against both directions rather than just one. You would choose to work with this strategy when you have a stock that is either stable or not moving all that much, or you have one that goes up and down, but those movements stay within a specified range and you think the stock will stay there for the short term. The risk on the iron condor strategy is considered low.

And finally, you can also choose to work with the long straddle or strangle. This is a debit spread that is also non-directional, just like the iron condor. It does have the disadvantage of not being able to work against the time decay issue. You would choose this strategy any time that the market, or at least the stock you are working with, is going to be really volatile for a short amount of time. It is used by traders who see a high probability of imminent sharp rise and fall in the stock price. This method can be used to catch both of them if you are not sure which way the market will go. The risk on this one is pretty high; if the market doesn't get as volatile as you predicted, you could lose a lot of money. However, there is the potential for unlimited profits, so if there is going to be a big change in the market soon, this may be the right one to go with.

Remember that when you are picking out the strategy that you want to use, the directional debit strategies are going to help you to get a fast and bigger return. They have a good risk to reward ratio, and they have the issue of time decay that is working with them. This is why most professional traders stay away from the debit spreads in most cases, even though these may look like good options to work with.

For the most part, it is not a good idea to use the long straddle/strangle position, especially as a beginner. There are not that many times when the market is going to behave the way that you want for this strategy to work. In addition, if you are in this kind of strategy and you get the expected directional move to occur, you need to square off your position as quickly as possible because you are working against the time decay. This time decay is accelerated in the long straddle/strangle because it occurs on both ends of the playing field. Getting out of the position as soon as possible after you make a profit can help

As a beginner, you may find that using the credit based strategies (not the selling strategies) will give you the best luck. They will give smaller returns compared to some of the other strategies, but the returns are more consistent than you can find with other choices. This can help you to earn a steady stream of income over the long term without very much risk. This is because time and probability often favor these kinds of strategies over the others. It is at least worth your time to consider starting out with these strategies to learn the market and to stay safe.

If you are looking for the strategy that is going to be the most consistent when it comes to generating income, you will want to work with the Iron Condor. This is because in addition to getting the same benefits as the other credit spreads when it comes to time decay and probability, it is also considered a neutral position. The stock can go up and down with this strategy, and you still have the potential to make a profit, as long as your strike points are in the right place.

As you can see, there are a number of different strategies that you can use when you decide to work in options trading. Each of them is a bit different, and the situations when you use each will vary as well. Knowing how each one works and how they can be used in the market will help you to make smart and informed decisions along the way and will increase the amount of profit that you can make overall.

The other strategies that we have talked about for day trading are great options for a beginner. And many times, there will be one of the strategies that you choose to go with. As long as you use the strategy in the proper manner, and you stick with it for you're the entirety of your trade, you can see success with it. However, you may find that you don't like one option or the market is not doing what you want, so you are ready to change things up a little bit. Let's take some time to look at some of the other strategies that you can consider when you want to get into day trading.

Gap Up, Inside Bar, Breakout Strategy

The first strategy we are going to work on is the gap up, inside the bar, breakout strategy. This trading signal is going to start when you look at some of your charts and you see there is a gap up. Then, if the second or the third ten-minute bar develops and it becomes an inside bar, then this is the perfect setup that you need to make this strategy work for you.

Some traders will do this option but change it up a bit. They will work with some stocks that have a partial gap up, rather than the full gap. But traders only want to do this if they are listed high on the gainer's list. When we are looking for this partial gap, rather than a full gap we are talking about our setup having a gap that is higher than were it ended up at the previous days close. In addition, this gap still needs to come in lower than the previous days' high. This can provide you with some good signals that the stock is the right one but it ensures that you have more options to work with from the beginning compared to working with the full gap.

When you are working with this strategy, you want to keep the charts to a minimum time frame. For example, you may only want to go with one or two of these ten-minute bars before you start with your inside bar. Beware though, if you see that there are more than these two ten-minute bars, it means that the price has had way too much movement at this point and you should avoid this option because it isn't the most effective setup.

As soon as you have the right inside bar, without too much volatility going on in the market, it is time to purchase your stop. Make sure that this stop is right about the high you see in your bar. The trigger is the breakout that is above your inside bar.

At this point, you may have to wait for a little bit. You want to find the right trade signal that will make you go long. Then, if you have already put the right stop in place, it is time for you to think about some logistics such as where and when you want to exit this trade. You need to put the stop in the right place because if it is hit, you will want to cut your losses and get out of the market before trying out some new trade.

Gap Up, Attempt to Fill, Breakout

We can also use the gap up idea to work on the next strategy. This one is pretty simple to work with and it can rely on the common sense of the trader to make it work. As the name sounds, you will look for a stock that has a new gap up, and that is then trying to get this gap filled. Whether the stock is actually able to fill up this gap to the previous day's high or not isn't going to be as important with this strategy. The important thing with this particular strategy is that the market needs to look like it is trying to fill up that gap. Even if it doesn't succeed, it should at least try, or this is not the right stock.

For this process to work, you must look at the chart and see that the price dips down below the first ten-minute bar you set. You do not want to see the first bar being the one that fills in the gap, or you can't use this method and see success. A small and gradual attempt to fill this gap after the first bar can work because it shows that the price will head in the right direction, but it won't do it too quickly.

When you see that after these few steps the stock starts to gap up a bit and then the market continues to try and close that gap, it means that you will be able to find quite a few traders who are trading short. And these traders will look at the market and assume that the stock is going to finish its downward trend. They will either sell off to not lose

341

money, or they will trade with the assumption that the stock goes down.

When the stock does turn around and with the pattern we are looking at, it will go back up and these traders will be in a bad position. They may have lost any gains that they earned in the process and they will need to decide whether the stop they picked out, in the beginning, can actually make them some money or not.

From here, the pattern is going to continue and you will notice the breakout. This breakout is going to be very fast paced and it can occur at a volume that is higher than normal. The traders that went short in this situation will feel squeezed without the stop. Some of these traders will decide that it is best to get back into the market here using the long position instead of the short position.

This helps to increase the breakout even more than before. You can get in on the low part of the trend, when the price of the stocks is lower, and then sell once that breakout occurs and everyone is trying to get back in. If you can read the charts and know that the trend is not going to continue down but will end with a breakout that goes upwards, you can get on at the right time and see some profits in the process.

The Gap Up, Afternoon Breakout (Also Known as the Gainer)

Depending on the market you enter when you are ready to trade, another simple option that you can choose for your trading is known as the gap up, afternoon breakout. Just like with the other few strategies that we have discussed in this guidebook, you are going to use your scanner to help you find the gap. The difference here is that you are not going to do this right when the market opens, like what you would do with the other options. Instead, you are going to search around for these gaps in the late morning or early in the afternoon.

During your scan for this one, you want to search around for some simple patterns. In specific, you want to look for consolidating and basing patterns. You want to look at the charts and see that there is a big and strong rise in the price that occurred throughout the whole morning. Then, you want to look at the later morning, or even in the early afternoon, and see that the price has settled down a bit to be less volatile than before.

Often when you are looking at the stocks that did well in the morning with their performance because they have a higher than average volume are the ones that will often make a high that is a bit more than average. Then these stocks are going to settle down a bit and relax. At the time period when you should trade, these stocks will look pretty steady and like they aren't heading up or down. If you see this, then you know that is the stock you want to trade here. Once you see that stock inching back up to its resistance point, then it is time to put in a buy stop order and then wait for the breakout that will come soon.

While this is a simple method to work with and can be a great way for a beginner to start, there are a few drawbacks with it because there are a few stocks that won't be able to make it to the right starting points. You can always leave the stock and take the loss if it doesn't move. But there are some stocks that will do really well with this and will explode quickly. If you jump on at the right time, you can make a ton of money with this.

The Fibonacci Retracement Pattern

Some of the other strategies that we have discussed in this chapter are a bit shorter in time frame compared to some of the others. This one is going to be used on a thirty-minute chart. On this chart, you want to look for a stock that reached higher highs compared to what it did on the two days before. You want to have a 15 SMA cross above the 35 SMA on that day. The main thing that you want to look for when using this idea is to find a price that can give you a retracement back to both the 28 and the 68 percent the next morning. You will see that this happens when you look through your 30-minute chart and you see that there is either an inverted M or U pattern.

Once you see that this price is moving back over to the retracement level on the following morning, and then you can look to see that the price is forming on a rising bar looking at the MACD histogram. Remember that you do not need to get the numbers at perfect levels but you will need to stay near that 62 and 38 percent as much as possible. The main thing here is that you want to see a good retracement with the movement back to where that first impulse showed up. Once you are able to find this setup on the chart, you will notice that it is time to see a breakout trigger on the ten-minute chart.

Once you see that this happens, you need to switch over and start looking at the ten-minute chart. This chart is going to show you the right information. You will wait for the breakout of the high that was on your thirty-minute bar. When you see this happen, enter into the market and then you can wait for that breakout to occur so you can make a profit.

Gap Down, Fill Gap, Inside Bar, Breakout

There are some traders who feel that it is a bad idea for you to enter the market with a stock that is gapped down. If you look at the stock and see that it meets some other criteria, you can find that a short squeeze action is the best way to help send these stocks up for that day which will result in you earning a profit as well.

This is an easier option that you may think in the beginning. You will need to use some of the ten-minute charts in the beginning. If you are looking at these charts and notice that there is a down gap that is filling up, and then there are some second and third ten-minute bars that form as the inside bar, then you are into e perfect setup to make this strategy work.

When you see this happen, you will need to place the buy stop above the high for this new inside bar. The trigger that will tell you to make a purchase is when you see that a breakout is going to occur above the high for that bar that is on the inside. You can then place the stop order so that it is low of the inside bar. You can also choose to do another area if you find that it is lower than the bar to increase your profits.

Other Methods That Can Help with Day Trading for a Beginner

This guidebook has spent some time talking about the different day trading strategies that you can use when it comes to doing this trading strategy. All of these have provided professional traders with success and some good profits, but you need to know which one to use and work on learning exactly how to do it. If you know how to use the strategy properly and you learn how to keep with it throughout the whole trade, then you can make any of them work for you.

There are also a few other popular trading strategies that you can work with that will make it easier for you to earn money in the stock market with day trading. Some of the best trading strategies that you can use and that work well for a beginner include:

- News trading.

News trading is a great option to go with because you will listen for some big news events and watch out for new trends that can form before others find out about them. If you know that a company is about to release a big announcement soon, you can easily get onto the stock, purchase it when the price is low, and later that day, when the announcement is out, you can sell the stock for a higher price when everyone else jumps on. You need to be able to read hints in the market to make this work. If you jump on after the news is released, you will be too late and won't make much of a profit.

- Range trading.

This is a good strategy to use for those traders who have a lot of time and patience to help them get the right research done. With this trading strategy, you may need to spend some time following a stock, learning the range for lows and highs for that stock throughout time. You can then pick out the best time to trade based on these highs and lows.

- Pairs trading.

For this one to work, you need to make sure that you are trading in pairs. You want to first work on picking a category that you want to trade in and then you will go short on the stock that you see as well. You would do the second trade as well, going long on a trade that you consider strong. When you do these two trades at the same time, it is much easier for you to make some profits in the process.

- Contrarian trading.

We spent some time earlier in this guidebook talking about one of the strategies where you are going to follow the actions that the market is taking. If you see that the overall market is going up, you would make a purchase. But if you see that the market is going down, you would sell the stocks. This strategy is going to work a bit different. You will look at the trends that come with the market and then trade against them. When you see that the market is starting to go up, you sell the stock. And when the market is heading down, you will make a purchase. This can be hard to work with as a day trader because it is the opposite of what they are used to working with. But if you do it properly, it can be a good way to make money.

- Chart patterns.

The chart pattern is a great option to work with when you are trying to earn profits in day trading. It often helps out when finding the right entry and exit points on an investment. If you use these charts and use some technical indicators such as the relative strength index, the rate of change, or the commodity channel index, you will be able to figure out the best times to enter and exit a trade. You can pick out the chart pattern that makes the most sense for you. Just put the right information into your chart and then make decisions from there.

- Technical indicators.
  If you like to have a lot of information before you make your decisions with day trading, then technical indicators will be the best option for you. These technical indicators will be important to the day traders because they can help show trends in the market that may be hard to see on their

347

own. Looking at these indicators and making sure that you can interpret them the proper way will ensure that you can make a profit.

As you can see, there are a lot of different trading strategies. Many traders have worked over the years to create strategies that can help them to earn a profit with their stocks, and with all of the different types of stocks that are available, you are sure to find one that will work with the strategy that you would prefer. As a beginner, it is up to you to learn some more about these strategies and then pick out the one that you would like to use. With the right strategy and the right stock, you will be able to earn a good profit in no time with day trading.

Conclusion

Thank you for making it through to the end of **Day Trading**. Let's hope it was informative and able to provide you with all of the tools you need to achieve your goals whatever they may be.

The next step is to take a look at the market at the time you read this guidebook and decide the best strategy to use. There are a lot of different strategies that you can work with, whether you are a beginner in day trading or not and the one that you choose can often help you pick out which stocks you want to invest in, as well as the enter and exit points of your trade. This guidebook will provide you with the information that you need to start out in day trading and make a profit, even as a beginner.

There are many traders, especially those who are beginners, who worry about getting started in day trading. They think that this is a dangerous or risky method of trading and they may choose to go with something else. But for those who truly know how to read the market, and who are willing to choose the right strategy and stick with it, day trading can be a great way to enter the market and make some good profits in the process. This guidebook will give you the tools and information that you need to be successful as a beginner in day trading.

Whether you are just getting started exploring some of your investment options in the stock market, or you are seriously considering day trading as your chosen investment vehicle, take some time to read through this guidebook to learn more about day trading and how it can work for you.

Stock trading

a guide for beginners for investing in the stock market with proven strategies and learn to understand futures and make technical analysis.

[Henry Hill]

TABLE OF CONTENTS:

Chapter 1: What is Stock Trading?

You may have heard words such as stock market and stock trading before. However, you are not exactly sure what they mean. They are simply words that mean money and investment to you. This chapter, however, demystifies the ideas you may have about stock trading and the stock market. By the end of the chapter, you will have a clear understanding of what the stock market is and how it works. Read on for more.

The stock market is a platform in which investors buy and sell stock and other investments. Stocks are also called equities and are a representation of fractional ownership of a company. For an economy to develop efficiently, there must be a well-functioning stock market that allows organizations quick access to capital from the public. It is, therefore, not uncommon to hear terms such as the S&P 500 and Dow Jones Industrial Average when dealing with the stock market. These are some of the major stock indexes that any fairly experienced trader would know. It is, however, important to note that you cannot keep track of every single stock. The major stock indexes are, therefore, just a section of the entire stock market. When you keep track of these major stock indexes, you have a fairly good representation of the entire stock market.

You may have come across news headlines that say that the stock market has closed p for the day or that it has moved lower and may not know what this means. However, we have some good news for you. You do not have to wonder what exactly that means anymore. The above statements have a simple implication as they mean that the stocks within that specific stock market index have moved either up or down, and as such, gained or lost value. If you are an investor, this movement is crucial for you because when you buy and sell stocks, you hope to return profits. Only through keen monitoring of the stock movements can you be sure you are making the right steps towards earning money from stock trading.

If you are wondering how the stock market works, then read on as I explain.

Understanding how the stock market works is not difficult. Think of it like an auction house, where buyers and sellers negotiate prices and find the best compromise before making a trade. The only aspect that differentiates the stock market from an auction house is the fact that the latter works through a network of exchanges. Take the example of the popular NASDAQ or New York Stock Exchange. A company will list its stocks' shares on an exchange in a process commonly known as IPO- an initial public offering. As an investor, you would purchase the shares, and the company you buy from will get the chance to raise money for their business.

On the other hand, you are free to buy and sell these stocks among other investors like you. The exchange plays a vital role in tracking the demand and supply of the different stocks, so you have all the necessary resources you need to trade. The willingness of the investors and traders to buy and sell-supply and demand- helps determine the price of each of the securities. It gets a bit complex here because computer algorithms are involved in doing the calculations.

The process of buying and selling begins with the buyers offering a bid-the highest amount they can pay, or are willing to pay. Normally, the bid is usually a lower price than that set by the sellers. This difference has a term, the bid-ask spread. For a trade to be successful, one of the two parties involved in the exchange has to budge. That means that the seller has to lower his price or the buyer has to increase his bid or price.

While it is likely that stock trades took place in physical marketplaces before the arrival of the internet, this trade today is done electronically. There are two platforms, online stockbrokers and the internet. The trade happens on a stock by stock basis, but often, you find that the stock prices move simultaneously because they are all affected by similar political events, news, and economic reports.

You may probably be wondering how to best invest in the stock market. However, if you are working and you have a 401(k) plan, there is a chance you have already invested in the stock market. The 401(k) plan usually has mutual funds, which is a composition of stocks from different companies. Alternatively, you can purchase stocks through an individual retirement account or a brokerage account. Opening both accounts can be done through online brokers, and you can as well buy and sell investments. These online brokers act as middlemen between stock exchanges and people who buy stocks like you.

What you need to know as you begin your trading journey is that stock trading is an investment like any other. However, it carries more risk than a standard investment and has the potential to offer you more returns as well in comparison to other securities. There are some smart alternatives that as an individual, you can consider while stock trading to avoid purchasing many different funds. For example, you can invest in an exchange-traded fund or index fund. The exchange-traded and index funds mirror the performance of a specific index by holding all the investments and stocks in the index.

Most importantly, you should remember that stock trading is best done as a long-term investment solution. It cannot be an option for short-term investment because if you consider it a short term investment, there is a likelihood that you may need your money back before the end of the short term period. It is exceedingly difficult to recover your money in case the market suffered losses.

Chapter 2: Main Strategies for Investing in the Stock Market

Now that you understand the basics of the stock market, I am going to take you through the main strategies that you can use to invest in the stock market. This is not simply an explanation of strategies but also an explanation of how you can win with them. these strategies have been tried and tested over time. Therefore, I guarantee you that you will be getting only the best there is in the market when you use these strategies. Just to give you a glimpse of what to expect in this chapter, I will tell you that stock trading is far from taking a step in the dark. However, you must be willing to wait and by this, I mean invest in the long-term, know how to speculate, invest in daytime trading, and understand index-fund marketing. To delve into the finer details, continue reading below.

The best strategies for investing in the stock market include:

- *Investing in the long-term.* As mentioned earlier, if you consider stock trading as a short-term investment, you are likely to want your money back before five years end. Note that when people invest in stocks, they intend to be long-term owners of the companies they purchase these shares from. They expect that as the company grows profits and revenues, so do their shares. These choices are usually made after analyzing the products or services offered by the company, their production and delivery systems, and as such, the investors are usually confident in their choices. Investors choose companies for what these companies will produce in the future and not what others are willing to pay for the stocks. Through the use of a technique known as value analysis, investors can understand how to do value analysis.

Value analysts work by examining assets, dividends, earnings, quality ratios, research, and new products. They make use of tools such as charts to find out market trends and identify price patterns which they can exploit to their advantage. When using charts, the analysts search for price chart patterns, including double top/bottom reversal patterns, and head and shoulders. They also look out for lines of support, flags, pennants, cup and handle patterns, balance days, and moving averages to get an idea of the possible next pattern. To ascertain whether an asset is trending, analysts look at various market indicators including mathematical price transformations such as decline or advance of data and increase or decrease of volume. These analysts will also often study the relationship between indices and their prices and volumes and market indicators to get a deeper understanding of the market at large. There is also the study of put/call ratios, short interest, and bull/bear ratios to come up with the most viable stock on the market. By doing such a detailed analysis, the analysts can know trending assets and the likely directions these assets will take in the future.

When it comes to value analysis, there are different techniques. However, these techniques are most commonly used simultaneously by analysts to help them understand the best the stock market and make the right moves. Other technical analysts may choose to use subjective judgment instead to determine how patterns reflect and how to interpret them. Other analysts still prefer to apply a systematic or mechanical approach to the identification of stock market patterns.

It is almost impossible to talk about value analysis without mentioning fundamental analysis. Fundamental analysis involves studying economic factors that influence financial markets to come up with the potential directions the financial market is likely to take. Technical indicators uncover these trends. Traders use these two types of analysis together while others use only fundamental analysis.

Some of the best stock traders of all time, including Warren Buffet, believe in the power of a long-term investment. In fact, he looks for companies with a competitive advantage as he believes such companies are in a position to make profits annually despite the changing political and economic environments. Investors such as Buffet prefer a long-holding period and recommend that a stock can only be sold if, after three years, it is still under-performing. To reduce their risks, investors should identify and purchase stocks from companies whose stock prices are lower than their intrinsic value. The intrinsic value is determined by the use of fundamental analysis and by comparing the company with the entire market and competitors. To further reduce risks when stock trading, investors can use tactics such as diversifying their holdings into different markets, companies, and industries.
Some people think of the strategy of investing long-term to be outdated. However, the strategy has stood the test of time and proved to be worth the while.

- *Speculation.* Another important strategy when it comes to stock trading is speculation. The speculation involves purchasing or selling commodities or stocks with the expectation that you may profit when prices fluctuate. Combining fundamental analysis with speculation can help you as a trader to effectively identify market trends. The art of speculation is, however, not as easy as it may seem. Some people like to think of it as gambling. There are, however, some stack differences between speculation and gambling. For instance, a seasoned speculation professional usually has the knowledge advantage, which enables them to make profits even when other people involved in stock trading are not. The art of speculation is, therefore, based on a perceived advantage in information.

Some of the most remarkable stock traders in the United States, such as Lauriston Livermore, developed the skill of speculation in the mid-nineties. He would buy and sell stocks in unregulated business, an equivalent of the modern-day betting parlors that are off the track. The playing field was free of securities, and the transactions made did not affect the movement of stock prices. Livermore, however, was able to detect and interpret stock pattern movements, making him a well-known figure in the field. This shows that some people are gifted with the ability to foresee the stock movement even before it happens. He could easily identify levels of resistance and support (pivot points), and this knowledge guided how he bought and sole. He could easily buy stocks when they were rebounding and sell when they were approaching resistance. He, therefore, could change direction depending on the mood of the investors in the stock market.

Other sub-strategies that fall under speculation include buying when stocks rise and selling falling ones and trading when the market is bearish or bullish and then moving in its general direction. Additionally, do not meet marginal calls; it is better to get out and do not average your losses by buying more fallen stock. When stocks reach a new high, see an opportunity therein and go long, and when they reach a new low, you should, of course, sell short. You should, however, note that not even one of these strategies can deliver profits fully all the time. It is, therefore, possible to stay on the sidelines and only get into the market when an opportunity readily presents itself.

Livermore's strategies evolved into what is known as technical analysis. His pivot points were extended into volume and price patterns. Believers in speculation understand that patterns repeat themselves and reviewing past and current prices can be a mirror into the future prices if well done.

- *Day trading.* Trading today can be done with ease because the platforms available provide the best conditions to do so. Technology has quickly advanced, commission rates are low, and online brokerage firms have played a role in giving individuals tools to follow the trends in the stock market. Some artificial programs and algorithms help in the trading of huge stocks in short periods. The difference between traders and speculation experts is that traders often buy and sell stocks within a short period, mostly less than a single trading day. They look for price volatility that will enable them to make quick profits and move to the next opportunity quickly. They, therefore, focus on current trends rather than future trends that speculators rely on. They always make small profits before the trends end.

Algorithmic trading happens when trades are entered when specific criteria are met, and a majority of this kind of trading occurs through financial institutions that program their systems to analyze trends and place orders as described. Interestingly, the returns for this type of trading can sometimes be extraordinarily high. These high returns come as a result of more frequent trading, which may lead them to make better returns than firms that only do few transactions.

There are, however, concerns related to algorithmic trading. For instance, it is believed that this kind of trading has an effect on market liquidity and aggravates market disruptions. Trade marketing is still a popular strategy even though day traders are likely to run out of money and quit. Other people have seen significant loopholes in the day trading industry. The industry remains largely unregulated, and it mostly thrives on selling automated trading software and instruction to its clientele who believe that these material are sophisticated and similar to those of big sophisticated traders such as Goldman Sachs. It is, therefore, important that you realize that this may not be the best option for you, as it makes use of margins and several trades within the day to make small profits that the trader hopes can amount to something. A margin is the money borrowed from these brokerage firms, and they are offered to pattern day traders under special margin rules and an equity balance of mostly $25,000.

- *Index fund Investing*. Some people find it hard to implement the fundamentalist strategies and to keep up with speculations. If you feel that you do not fit into either strategy, then index fund investing may be the right choice for you. Index funding provides you with a chance to get professional portfolio management via mutual funds. This is the option preferred by most people. The only challenge is that not many fund managers can keep up with the market and beat it over an extended period. John Bogle, former chairman of Wellington Management Group and Founder of the Vanguard Group, however, tried to reason otherwise. He noted that it was virtually impossible for investors to outperform what they essentially are-the market and they must underperform because participation costs are deducted from the market's returns.

Index funds are, nonetheless, successful, even today and over time, exchange-traded funds developed. Just like the index mutual funds, exchange-traded funds track commodity and security indexes, but trade like stocks on an exchange. Over time, it has been proven through various studies that just as Bogle speculated, beating the market is indeed an uphill task and beating the market is just but a matter of luck.

 Bogleheads- adherents of index investment reduce risk in their portfolio by buying ETFs or index funds rather than individual securities. They can ensure gains in their portfolios and reduce risk by rebalancing and restoring the initial allocation in their variety of asset classes. Robo advising has also become popular lately, as a new type of professional management that thrives on index fund investment principles, they suggest that portfolio investments should be allocated according to the objectives and age of the clients.

In conclusion, it is important to note that making profits from the stock market can be elusive, and it takes time and patience to learn the art and make returns. To find a way through which you can make the most profit, it is important to understand that this is a type of investment that carries risk and that so far, nobody has one strategy that can assure you of 100% success. Owning these securities can, therefore, cause stress for you as you are not certain of the events of the future and how investors will react to the same. Even though the profits are not fully assured, it is important for you to enjoy them when they come and brace yourself for the day you shall experience disappointment

Chapter 3: The Future of the Stock Market

This chapter builds on what you have learned in chapter 2. Here, we let you understand how you can maintain a top position in the market and how you can negotiate the possibilities of a market crash that can happen at any time. Stock trading will throw many curveballs at you, but with the information, I present below, you shall be better prepared. I also let you know what to expect in the future with regards to stock trading, which also serves to prepare you for any eventualities in the market.

Before going any further, it is important to know that as a retail investor, it is a minimal strategy to try timing the market. Small crashes will occur much more often than major crushes, which is a reassurance. While a crash in the future is a possibility, rather than worrying, there are steps that you can take to ensure that you remain at the top.

- *Diversify your portfolio.* From the discussion above, you must have realized that there is a higher risk in a single stock dropping than the whole market dropping at once. So diversifying your portfolio is a viable idea. Additionally, you can invest in many asset classes. By diversifying your portfolio across industries and asset classes, you are cushioning yourself against risks unique to companies or industries at large.
- *Consider your financial position and goals.* As mentioned above, Robo-advisors advise clients based on their age and objectives. As such, if you are saving for the short-term, for example, to afford a very expensive trip to an island, you are better off putting your money in a savings account that offers high interest than exposing it to the volatility of the stock market. You will also need to make different choices if you are considering saving for

your child's college expenses. If you are nearing retirement or are already retires, it would be wise to consider the volatility of stocks before investing.

- *Consider your feelings towards volatility.* If you would be comfortable rebalancing your portfolio and continuing to invest when there is a significant drop in it, then you can consider a diversified portfolio. If, however, you are not sure of your reaction and you think you may be tempted to retract when there is a dip in market values, then you may consider staying on the conservative side of your portfolio as these fluctuations may end up interfering with your confidence as an investor.
- *Rebalance your portfolio.* This is a strategy that may work, especially when the values of equities drop, and the remaining asset classes take up a huge chunk of the portfolio. Rebalancing will mean that you will have to sell some of the other asset classes and buy more equities. The trick is that when the market recovers from a crash, you will be better because you were able to buy equities when their cost was at the lowest.
- *Do not panic sell.* When the market falls, there is likely to have panic among investors. Many will sell off their investments at this time. However, my advice is that you do not give in to the general mood of the public. Should the market recover after you sell, then you will have sealed your fate. Instead, consider this a buying opportunity. Also, consider that when a crash is happening, you may not know the bottom of it. This information can only be ascertained aftermarket recovery. It is, therefore, not a good idea to try timing the marketing.

For semi and retired persons, it would be wise to hold cash reserves that can sustain you for up to 3 years or for a duration that will not allow you to sell your equities if there is a stock crash.

- *Understand the history of the stock market.* This may seem like a herculean task, but trust me, you can do it, and it will save you so much energy. You see, the past performance of the market is not a guarantee of success in the future. You, however, have to admit that understanding market trends can be of comfort. For instance, the average annual return of the S&P 500 index since 1957 is 8%. It is quite difficult to know whether a year will be good or bad as can be seen from the chart below. Only a long-term investment is the answer because from the trends if you tend to sell out at every low point, you will end up missing out on strong recoveries.

-

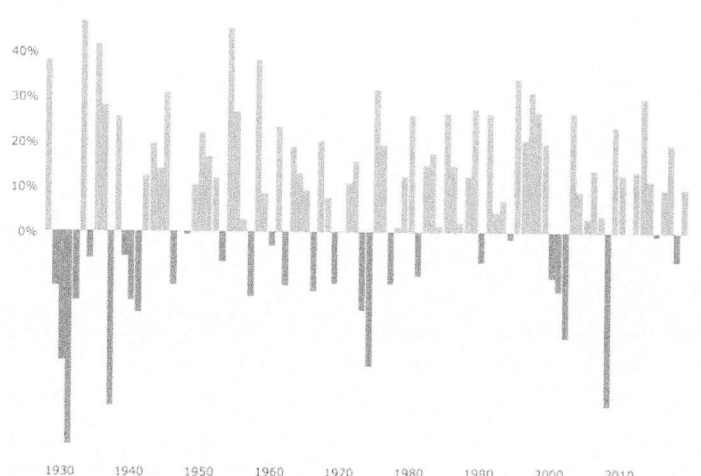

Historical Returns of the S&P 500

Artificial intelligence for data history

There have been advancements in technology that have provided stock market enthusiasts with a platform for making better investment decisions. One trend that is likely to continue into the future is the use of artificial intelligence for predictions. The stock market moves fast, and by all means, investors want

365

to catch up. With large sets of numbers to analyze even before the market opens, machines can help a big deal when dealing with stock markets. Today, investors can readily access market analysis history through artificial intelligence technologies, giving them an edge as they try to gather the information they need to make decisions on future investments. This does not mean that investors can slack because it is the investors who make the final judgment. AI just offers information, interprets and analyzes it in the context of the stock market but cannot yet verify the future of stock markets. As such, speculators still have a role to play as they are the only ones with the unique ability to find insight into the numbers.

There is also a general fear that artificial intelligence will soon be replacing humans. However, with stock markets, the arrival of artificial intelligence will probably mean stricter career planning. Think of it this way:

Who wants to leave hundreds of thousands of dollars fully at the discretion of machines?

Data history is likely the only aspect that financial managers are going to leave to be purely automated. Data specialists, on the other hand, will take more specialized roles and will use the information provided to improve overall business efficiency and to ensure better career planning. This technology is, therefore, an opener to help humans find out how they can delve further into what they can offer as human judgment is still one of the most highly prized possessions humanity can offer when it comes to investments.

Chapter 4: Technical Analysis of Stocks and Tools Used

So far, we have only dealt with the theoretical aspects of stock trading. In this chapter, we take a more technical view of things. Prepare to delve deeper into the mathematical and analytical aspects of stock trading so that you can start doing your own analysis. The tactics explained below will help you as a newbie and even as a professional when you need subtle reminders that can make a difference in how you trade.

Analysts often analyze stocks to understand the probable direction they are likely to take. Take a look at some of the variables that stock analysts rely on and define some important terms that will help you understand further:

A stock's market cap/capitalization is defined as the value of outstanding shares of the stock. The higher it is, the better established a company. Exchange regulatory bodies require that publicly traded companies provide quarterly or annual earnings reports. Market analysts usually use these reports as indicators for how companies are performing. They analyze aspects such as the earnings per share of a company, which often reflects the company's profits divided among stock shares. They also analyze financial ratios that indicate financial profitability, stability, and growth potential. These ratios are described below

1. Debt to Equity Ratio: The debt to equity ratio is the primary metric analysts use to measure a company's financial stability. This ratio shows the percentage of operations funded by debt in a company in comparison to the percentage funded by equity investors. Analysts find that a lower debt: equity ratio is best as an indicator for those looking to invest.
2. Price to earnings ratio: This is the ratio of stock in a company in relation to its earning per share. Higher

ratios denote that investors are willing to pay higher share prices for the stock of the company. They believe that the company is likely to grow and that the stock price is likely to go higher as well.

3. Return on equity ratio: The return on equity ratio is an expression of the company's net income in comparison to the company's equity investment and indicates a company's potential to grow.
4. Profit margin. The profit margin ratios vary, and investors may look at different profit margins to determine which companies are ripe for investment. There are many types, for instance, net profit margins and operating profit margins. Analysts may look at the absolute monetary profits of a company, but they prefer these margins because they are usually an indicator of a company's percentage profitability. An example is when a company shows a large profit, let us say, $5 million. While this may look like a big figure, it may translate to a 4% profit margin. In such a case, even a small revenue decline may prove fatal to the company's profitability.

There are mainly two approaches to investing in the stock market: growth investing and value investing.

Value investing involves investing in well-established companies that have proved to be profitable over time and are likely to offer dividend income regularly. This method of investing is more vested in avoiding risk compared to growth investing, and that is why investors go with already established companies. Still, investors, in this case, prefer to buy when they feel the stock is undervalued.

Growth investment, on the other hand, involves seeking out companies with high growth potential. The ultimate aim here is to realize optimum appreciation in the share prices of these companies. Such investors do not care for dividend incomes and only see the potential to grow. Such investment, therefore, focuses on small companies. Growth investors usually tend to favor technology stocks for this very reason.

Technical analysis

This type of analysis is usable on securities that have trading data from the past, such as currencies, fixed income, and stocks. The technique was originally introduced by Charles Dow in the later years of the 1800s, and other researchers contributed to its refinement including Robert Rhea, John Magee, William P. Hamilton, and Edson Gould. Today, it is used by analysts independent of other analysis techniques or can be used in tandem with other techniques.

To establish the future price movements of a stock, it is critical to look at price changes and past trading activity. Technical analysis makes the assumption that the price of a security reflects the information available publicly and therefore, makes an effort to understand these price patterns and trends instead of analyzing the primary attributes of the security. The original technical analysis bases itself on two assumptions as stated by Charles Dow:

- Values in the market are reflective of the factors that influence the price of a security. Therefore, markets are efficient
- Market prices are not anywhere near random. Some distinguishable patterns and trends are repeated over time.

These assumptions are usually true in light of the theory. However, it is important to realize that announcements and news relating to securities may have a short term effect on these trends. Technical analysts believe that short and long-term market trends can be easily identified and thus traders can make profits if they analyze trends.

The modern-day technical analysis is based on three assumptions:

- There are trends in prices. There is a general belief that there are short, medium, and long-term trends in the security markets. Stock prices are not likely to move erratically and are more likely to be part of a continuing trend.
- There is a tendency for the market to discount everything. Technical analysts believe that market factors and company fundamentals are all priced in the stock. They, therefore, do not need to consider such factors before making investment decisions. They only have to analyze price movements. This assumption has led to a criticism of the technique because it ignores some fundamental factors that need to be put in place for successful calculation of prices.
- History repeats itself. Technical analysts forecast the movement of prices based on tradable instruments that are subject to supply and demand forces. As such, trade analysts track price changes, open interest figures, and trading volume. Today, there are many types of trading systems that can help an individual forecast price movements. Technical analysis makes use of trading rules and models including the relative strength index, regression, intra and inter-market price correlations, relative strength index, business cycles, moving averages and stock market cycles

Chapter 5: Tips for Success When Trading Stocks

There are some important tips that you must have at your fingertips when trading forex. These tips do not guarantee absolute success, but they will be vital in helping you understand how the world of trading works in simpler terms. Additionally, they will help you stay ahead of the game so that nothing catches you unexpectedly. The bottom-line when trading is that you should understand yourself as much as you understand the market. Read on for more.

Perhaps the biggest tip when it comes to stock market training is that you should invest long-term. So far, this has been a key point. Notice that analysis is done over the long term and that many stock trade pros advise that you trade only if you do not need investment returns in a few years. The stock market is volatile, and therefore, there is no assurance that your capital will be available when you need it. By knowing the amount of capital you will need at a certain time in the future, you can have an idea of how much you need to invest to get a particular result. Today, there are many tools, including financial calculators that you can find on the internet that can help you track the necessary investments. They range from simple to complex calculators and can help determine the future of your capital if invested today.

Another valuable tip when it comes to trading is to understand how risk-tolerant you are. This phenomenon is described as how much a person is willing to risk experiencing negative outcomes to pursue a more favorable outcome in the future. Risk tolerance is genetically based. However, education, wealth, and income influence risk tolerance positively. As such, the more of those above you have, the more likely you are to be risk-tolerant. Risk tolerance, however, goes down with age, but it is important to remember that everyone has a varying degree of risk tolerance, and there is no right amount of it. Risk tolerance can also be affected by an individual's risk perception. Think of it this way, in the early 20th century, riding on a plane would have been perceived as risky, even dangerous in some cases. Today, however, it is a common and reliable means of transport. So one person may view a potential stock crash, for example, as a risk that they cannot take, but another person will see it as an opportunity to buy at low prices and wait for better outcomes. The advantage of understanding your risk tolerance is that it can be a crucial step in helping you make decisions that do not leave you anxious. The effects of anxiety are dire, and sometimes, it can lead to negative health outcomes. It is important to care for your health before anything else and to understand your risk tolerance is the first way to ensure that the stock market is not going to be detrimental to your health and well-being.

The stock market can easily interfere with an investor's ability to make logical decisions and control their emotions. When investors worry about stock, the prices are likely to go down, but when they feel positive towards a stock, the prices are likely to go up. Those who tend to feel negative are referred to as bears, while the more positive investors are referred to as bulls. A trading day is composed of constant battles between the bears and bulls as is reflected in the ever-changing stock prices. The long-term prices are driven by logical analysis, while short term prices are usually a result of speculations and emotions. When the prices of a stock move contrary to expectation, you may be tempted to take drastic steps such as selling, or you may be confused, wondering whether the stock is worth keeping. When the stock performs better than expected, you can also begin to wonder if the best step to take would be to take your profits when the mood is still good. The good news is that no you know that heeding to your emotions could be the cause of your downfall in the stock market. Be sure of when you want to liquidate your holdings. An exit strategy is key to avoid being swayed by emotions.

Understand the basics as you set out on your stock market journey. The stock market is not only complicated but delicate as well, and it will pay to know your way around before you start making investments. Familiarize yourself with different areas before making your first purchase. Understand definitions and financial metrics, stock market order types, methods of stock timing and selection, and different types of investment accounts. This is a step that can help improve your risk tolerance, which can help you make better stock market investment decisions.

Lastly, avoid leverage, especially when you are new to the field. Leverage is making use of borrowed money to achieve your stock market strategy. Brokerage firms and even banks offer clients loans to buy stocks. For instance, take the case where you want to buy 200 shares of a stock that goes for $200. You will need a total of $40,000. Your bank or brokerage firm can offer you up to half of this amount, so you complete the transaction. Note that if you had used your money for the initial purchase, your returns would be yours, 100%. If you borrowed money for the initial purchase, the returns would be lower because you would need to repay the loan and interest to the bank or broker. The implications would be worse if the stock fell as you risk losing a big chunk of your initial investment plus interest costs to the broker or bank. Leverage should only be used after you gain experience, and you are fully confident of your decision-making abilities.

Forex trading

advanced strategies to start investing with forex trading and also forex scalping strategies for a beginner who wants to make big money

[Henry Hill]

TABLE OF CONTENTS:

Chapter 1: What is Forex?

In this chapter, I highlight the basics of forex trading to help you understand how to navigate the forex market at the most basic level. By reading through this chapter, you will be enlightened with an understanding of the forex market and how it operates. This is a chapter that works to provide a strong foundation for your understanding of more complex aspects of the trade discussed in later chapters.

Forex trading is also called FX or foreign exchange trading. As such, it is the art of converting one currency to another. Today, this one of the most actively traded markets with a daily trade volume of an astounding $5 trillion. Forex trading involves a network of sellers and buyers who transfer currencies to each other at agreed prices. Banks, companies, and individuals all convert currencies from one to another through this channel. Initially, foreign exchange was done mainly when people needed to travel to another country. Travelers would exchange some of their country's local currency for the foreign currency at a bank or foreign exchange broker. Today, the market has evolved, and foreign exchange is done almost purely for profit. The current type of foreign exchange is a type of investment trading. Foreign exchange trading is just like trading stocks as the traders usually speculate on the values of currencies between two currencies. Most learners usually think that forex trading is an easy venture. Contrary to popular belief, there is a high rate of failure among beginner traders of foreign exchange, and this is not as a result of any fault of their own but because there is a steep learning curve. Also, these traders may have false motives, inappropriate haste, and may be moved by unrealistic goals. It is, therefore, not surprising to find that new traders walk out empty-handed after making significant investments in the forex market

Exchange rates usually go up and down several times a minute, which means that in a day, there is a lot of action going on in the day and a business week. The currency exchange rate reflects the health of an economy. If therefore, the US economy is doing better than the Eurozone, then the dollar will go up compared to the dollar. There are some basic concepts that you have to understand if you intend to get into foreign exchange trade. They include:

- *Spread*. Spread is the difference between the ask and bid price. The ask price is the price at which you can buy, and the bid price is the price at which you can sell. Usually, these prices are stated as forex quotes on the platforms used for trading, and they occur on each currency pair.
- *Leverage*. Leverage is the amount a forex account broker offers you for trade. For instance, if your broker offers you a 200:1 leverage, then it means that they are allowing you to trade with 200 times more money than you have deposited. Just as is the case with stocks, with leverage you can buy 200 more times than what you have, but you have to be prepared for any eventualities, which are 200 times bigger profits or 200 times losses. Before placing a trade, it is important to understand and evaluate whether you need leverage.

To understand better how the foreign exchange market works, it would be useful to look at the diagram below:

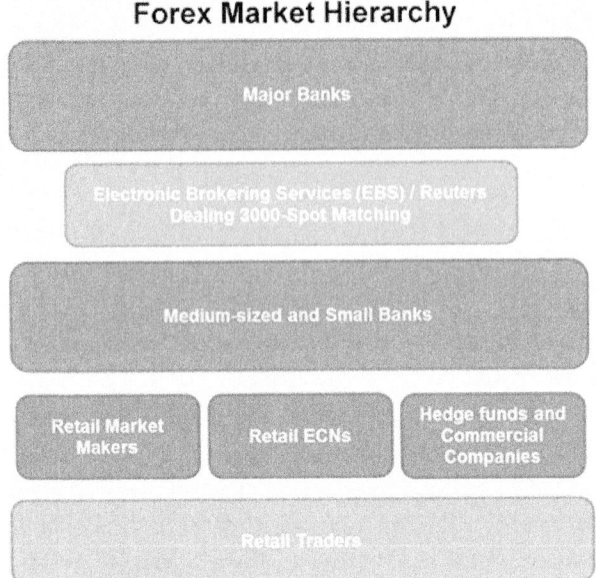

Forex Market Hierarchy

Major banks top the system, and they put in big orders compared to the rest, that is why they stay on top. Major banks also move or influence the market. Banks communicate among themselves through the electronic brokering services. Next on the ladder is the retail market makers and ECNs and brokers. Lastly, there are retail traders at the bottom and who do not have any influence on the market.

Advantages of foreign exchange trading

- *Low entry barriers*. Getting started as a foreign exchange trader is relatively easy. First, it is not a costly venture when compared to trading stocks. There are a lot of options available in the market and offering micro, and mini trading accounts do not require exorbitant minimum amounts to get you started on your journey. While it may not be the best option to open an account using the bare minimum, this is an advantage that means that a person who does not have much capital still has a chance at forex trading.

- *High liquidity.* The forex market is big and liquid as well. The implications are that under normal circumstances, and market conditions, there is always someone willing to buy and sell no matter the conditions. Just a simple click of the mouse and you can make a trade. You, therefore, do not risk getting stuck in a trade. With the advent of online platforms, you can even close your position once you hit your targets or when a trade begins to go against you.

- *Better risk management through hedging.* Hedging allows the trader to reduce risk in the forex market because it provides several strategic positions. The market is highly volatile, but the fact that risks can be reduced is a plus as you can simply limit the losses to a certain amount. One of the best strategies for hedging us by hedging using multiple currency pairs. You can do this by simply taking forex pairs that are correlated positively. For instance, you can choose to use the British pound and the US dollar and take the opposite direction. In this way, you reduce the downside risk largely. Forex hedge can also be used against loss in other markets as well. The US dollar and Canadian dollar, for example, tends to have an inverse relationship with oil. As such, traders use it as a hedge against oil prices when they begin to fall.

- *Ability to trade at any time.* You can trade any time as the market is open from Sunday to Friday. The long hours are because of the direct nature of the forex market where people complete transactions directly and over-the-counter rather than through a central party. A trick to trading is that you can take advantage of the active sessions of different places. Timing is, however, affected by daylight savings in March, April, October, and November.

- *Low Transaction Costs.* The transaction costs when trading forex are low because they are already built into the forex price as a spread. Spread has been defined above as the difference between buying and selling prices.
- *It is possible to use leverage.* Leverage allows traders to trade even without the amount they are using in their deposit account. If for example, you are trading at a 50:1 leverage, you can control the trading of up to $5,000 with only $100 in your account. However, leverage can be a double-edged sword. The chances of incurring losses are still existent.
- *Potential profit from rising and falling prices.* The forex market does not restrict directional trading. You can, therefore, buy currency or go long when you feel that a currency pair is going to experience value increment. If you suspect a decrease, you have the choice to go short or sell all together.

Scalping

Forex scalping involves buying or selling a currency then withholding it for a while hoping to make a profit. Usually, traders who utilize this strategy make many trades while taking advantage of the small price movements seen throughout a forex trading day. This strategy looks to capture 5 to 20 pips per trade. And the profits are then magnified when position size increases. While holding trades may seem like a time-consuming process, traders often only hold trades for seconds or minutes and will open and close many positions within a day. Another fact that you need to understand about scalping is that most scalpers usually utilize leverage, which allows larger position sizes. It, therefore, follows that when a small change happens in price, the result will be a reasonable profit.

Scalping is usually either automated or manual. In the manual system, the trader sits at the computer screen looking for signals that will tell him whether to buy or sell. Automated scalping, on the other hand, makes use of an automated trading system to instruct software on when to buy or sell according to the parameters that were inputted.

Most forex traders turn to scalping when important data that shows the nature of the market is released. It is not uncommon to find traders turning to this strategy after the announcement of interest rates or the release of employment reports. Such changes usually happen because news such as those mentioned are usually high-impact and cause significant price movements in short spans of time. Such scalpers are usually well timed and like to get in and out of trades quickly. Usually, traders make about ten pips, but when major news announcements are made, the scalper is likely to make over 20 pips. There are both advantages and disadvantages of scalping as discussed below:

Pros

- Scalping may be the right option for you if you do not appreciate waiting for a trade to close
- Scalpers do not wait for long for the closing of trades. This is a good thing because it reduces the chances for reversals, which may be deleterious for a trading position.
- It is a tactic that can be successfully used by newbies in the market who do not yet know trading theories.

Cons

- One loss can make all other profits obsolete.
- The profits on each trade are small
- Playing in a long position may be beneficial for traders than scalping.

From the explanation about scalping, you may have realized that not every strategy will fit every trader. To know whether scalping is the right one for you, consider whether you are a calm person and if you can make snap decisions correctly. Scalping will usually require that you think quicker than a bullet takes to hit its target. Thinking for a long time can cause you to lose many valuable opportunities. To eliminate excessive thinking, you may consider developing an appropriate trading plan. Note that even with a plan, you will still need to make decisions to ensure successful scalping. You must ensure you adhere to your trading plan because a slight deviation may cause a loss that will wipe out all your savings. Also, if you can create quality time to trade by scalping, then it may be a worthy venture.

Automated scalping systems

Scalping can be a time-consuming venture, and yet, many people look to it to add additional income. This means that they may not have enough time to sit and walk through a scalping session a few hours every day. Some people will try to circumvent this shortcoming by using automated trading systems. Still, there is no guarantee when it comes to forex trading as you will majorly be relying on your knowledge and gut feeling. This is why, even in the case of automated products, you will have to be on the lookout. A lot of products promise the best in terms of profitability, but at the end of the day, they are just but sham products, sold by people looking to make quick gains.

On the other hand, if you get a good automated trading tool, it can work to your advantage. Additionally, you need to understand how they are used; it can be a major plus. Consider this; you can set the automated trading system such that it understands when to take profit and stop loss. While the system handles these simple tasks, you could concentrate more on the bulk work that comes with trading. As a scalper, you need to learn the ar, so you know which actions are best to take and why.

Chapter 2: Budgeting for Profit, Risk Management, Leverage, and Time Frame

This chapter focuses on how to budget for profit when trading forex and expounds on how you can manage risk and use leverage to your advantage. The chapter also addresses how the timeframe affects operations in forex. The risk management strategies in this chapter especially, are essential for your success as a trader.

Budgeting for profit

Budgeting for profit means that you have to understand how the forex market works. You will have to understand risk and other basic concepts and how to manage your account. In this chapter is an explanation of how to budget for profit, how to manage risk, an in-depth look at leverage and time frame as it relates to forex.

If you want to make profits when forex trading, there are a few tips you can use. For instance, ensure that you start small. This advice applies mainly to those who are new to forex trading; you can only be successful at trading millions when you have learned how to handle a few dollars as you can be successful in trading dollars when you have learned how to trade pennies. If you are lucky enough to buy many small stocks, there is a probability that they could tremendously increase in value, earning you profits. Luckily, there are traders today who can allow you to open an account with just a few dollars. If you constantly use the account, over time, your profits will begin to grow, and you will begin to experience success.

Additionally, if you want to succeed, you should be a regular investor. This does not mean you have to put in huge chunks of money for trading each time. It simply means that you could add manageable amounts to your investment every week — for instance, $10 or $20 per week. Being a regular investor not only refines your craft but also grows a sizeable account when the profits are compounded over time. When you invest small amounts, you will not feel the pinch, but the rewards will be great regardless.

Another tip when budgeting for profit is to be patient. As has been highlighted above, starting small is a good move. However, many people get frustrated because of the slow process. To enhance your tolerance, trade small, but do not view these small amounts as dollars. Instead, view them as percentages. If you get a profit of, let us say $1 when you have a $10 dollar account, then you have made a 10% profit.

On the other hand, if you lose a dollar, then you have lost 10%. You will then have learned a valuable lesson about forex trading at a low cost of just a dollar. Also, when you trade in bits, you learn to deal with the hurdles associated with learning how to trade forex.

Risk management

Risk management involves reducing the size of potential losses while getting the most benefit out of a single trade. Risk management is highly-debated as a topic in forex trading and, yet, it remains important as an aspect of trading because of the volatile nature of the forex market. To understand risk management in detail, read on.

One of the fundamental rules of managing risk when trading forex is to ensure that you only risk what you can afford to lose. Interestingly, many traders make the mistake of investing more than they can afford to lose, especially when they are learning the trade. As a forex trader, however, you can avoid some of the fundamental mistakes made by traders and become an outstanding trader yourself. You should know when to cut your losses. Cutting of losses can be done in two ways. The first is when you impose a mental stop and decide that the right thing to do would be to limit the drawdown, you can take on a trade. Another way through which you can control losses is by using a trading platform that has technology that allows you to lock in stops when your losses reach a particular level.

To control risks, you can also use the correct lot sizes. When accounts are advertised by brokers, they make it seem like a good idea to open an account with, let us say, $300 and use leverage to enhance mini-lot trades. They make it look like this technique will help double your money in just a single trade. This kind of thinking can sometimes deviate so far from the reality. When starting as a new trader, it is important to start small so that you have many options for managing the trade.

You should also be able to track your overall exposure. Reducing lot size is a good step to take. However, other steps, such as opening many lots with currency pairs, could have serious implications. For instance, when you go long on USD/CHF and short on EUR/USD, you are exposed twice to the realities of the dollar movement. Should the dollar tumble, you will suffer double losses which can be a painful eventuality. If, however, you keep your exposure limited, you have better chances at reducing risk and increasing your chances at success in the future.

Trading with a plan is also essential. This is because when you have a plan, you can easily avoid emotional responses, which are a natural part of trading forex. Having a trading plan will help you know what steps to take from the beginning to the end of your trading session before you open a position. An additional pro of trading with a plan is that it will keep you from speculations and possible overtrading as a result of there being an open position. Understand that in forex, you have to have strong will power. Your trading plan is not going to work magically. You must have a plan and follow it to the latter for this risk management strategy to be effective.

Another risk management strategy that you can employ in your trading is to understand the nature of the currency pairs you have decided to trade. Understand the events scheduled to take place in the day and even week ahead and how the data looks. Look at your trade plan's time horizon and consider liquidity conditions. Have a clear view of what the market has priced in and out because anticipating market events can alert you of the possible disruptive circumstances even if it is not a complete indicator of how you can win a trade. By understanding that risk varies across currency pairs, based on different factors such as liquidity, data sensitivity, and volatility, you will be better placed at understanding the analytical tools and strategies that are best for you. Different currency pairs also carry with them higher or lower pip values and margin utilization. When you understand the nature of the currency pair you are trading, you can factor the currency pair selections when making your trading plan.

Also, you can trade with an edge. This means that you do not have to be in the market all the time despite the fact that the currency market operates round the clock. Block the noise and do not let it pull you in. You can do this, for instance, by picking a spot and timing yourself. Also, look for setups in which there is a clear risk/reward scenario to avoid an unnecessary headache. Being an opportunist in the real world can be a problem, but that does not mean this strategy cannot work in the digital world of forex trading. You can take your time looking at the coming trade opportunities and use these chances instead of getting caught up in the market moves of a single moment.

Look forward to future opportunities because there will be more opportunities and it pays to be ready.

Sometimes in life, it is good to take a step back from situations because it provides an individual with moments of clarity. This is why it is advisable to take a step back from forex trading as a whole sometimes. Yes, this means that you need to take time off the markets completely for a while and no, you will not miss out on important trades. On the contrary, when you take this break, you may find that it was much needed and that you are more objective when you trade and you have a clearer perspective that does not allow you to emotionally invest in a market position. Also, you can use this downtime to develop other skills, such as your understanding of fundamental analysis and to prepare yourself for fresh trading opportunities.

It is also important that as a trader, you take your profits regularly. When you take your profits, you are, in essence, reducing your exposure to risks in the market. You may find that your trade plan has an aggressive profit target, but imagine what would happen if events do not play in your favor. It is, therefore, a better idea to protect what you have already worked for instead. You can do this by taking part in your profit or by adjusting your stop-loss orders so that you lock in some of the profits you have made. After all, nobody has ever gone broke while taking profit.

Another piece of advice that is usually mostly off the books is that you should regularly take money out of your trading account, especially if you make profits. This is a tactic that can be referred to as taking money off the table. If you keep your profits in your margin account, you are likely to be subject to future trading decisions and are susceptible to unknown risks. Taking money out of your account keeps you in a position where you can trade in comfortable sizes. As you trade, remember that trading is not purely a game of profits, you can as well use the profits you make to do other things. You can invest the profits into another venture once you withdraw them.

Additionally, you should ensure accuracy by double-checking. By now, you must have understood that currency trading takes place in a fairly fast-paced environment. It is even faster, thanks to electronic trading. There is, therefore, a risk in human error when inputting orders and trades, and this may have serious implications for you as a trader. For instance, what would be the benefit of putting in place a stop-loss order if it not entered for the right amount of currency? As a result, it would pay to make it a part of your routine to double-check your order and trade entries to avoid unnecessary mistakes that may prove costly to your forex trading venture. Ideally, it would be good to double-check figures immediately you input them and just before submission. Mistakes happen, but this does not mean you let minor errors become the source of your downfall.

Leverage

By now, you must have an idea of what leverage is and what it can do for you in forex trading. In this section, however, we discuss leverage in detail.

In forex, leverage can be described as the ratio of the trader's funds that you are allowed to use to the size of the broker's available funds. In essence, leverage is whatever capital you borrow to increase your returns potentially. In reality, the leverage size usually exceeds invested capital to a large extent. Leverage is not fixed in all companies and may largely depend on the trading conditions provided by the forex brokers. Using leverage can sometimes be a risky affair because just like a double-edged sword, it may work to your favor or not. Below, we highlight how leverage works and how it can affect your bottom-line.

How leverage works

When you take leverage, it essentially means that you have borrowed from a broker. To calculate the margin-based average, you should divide your total transaction value by the amount of margin required.

The formula is thus:

Margin-Based Leverage = Total Value of Transaction / Margin Required

If therefore, you are required to top up 2% of the transaction's total value as margin, and you intend to trade a standard lot of USD/CHF equivalent to $200,000, the required margin would be 4,000 dollars. The margin-based leverage, in this case, would be 200,000/4,000, which equates to 50:1.

Interestingly, margin-based leverage does not affect risk. Whether a trader is required to top up a percentage of the transaction, therefore, does not influence the profits and losses they make. An investor always has the chance to attribute more than the required margin when trading. Real leverages rather than margin-based leverages have a stronger influence on profit and loss.

Calculating the real average would require you to divide the total face value of open positions by the capital you have for trading. As such:

Real Leverage = Total Value of Transaction / Total Trading Capital

For instance, let us say you have $20,000 in your our account and the position you open is worth $200,000 (one lot). Your leverage will be 200,000/20,000. If you traded two lots with the same amount in your account, then the leverage on your account would be 400,000/20,000, which is 20 times.

The margin-based leverage is, therefore, equal to the real leverage you can use to trade. Most traders, however, do not make use of their entire accounts as margin, and this is why their real and margin-based leverages tend to differ. It is generally advised that you do not use all your available margin.

You should only use your leverage if you clearly have an advantage on your side.

You should first establish the extent of risk in terms of pips numbers so that you determine the potential capital loss you are likely to incur. The general rule states that the loss should be less than 3% of your capital, if you leverage a position and the potential loss comes to approximately 30% of the capital, then you should reduce your leverage by an equal 30%. As an experienced trader, you may deviate from the standard 3%.

You may also calculate the margin level that you should use, to determine the level of risk a trade poses. Let us say you have $ 10,000 in your account and you decide that you are trading ten mini USD/JPY lots. A move in one pip in a mini account is around a dollar, but when trading minis, the amount rises to approximately $10 each. If you trade 100 minis, then a pip move will be worth approximately $100. If therefore, you take a stop-loss of 30 pips, you have a representation of a potential $30 in a mini lot and $3,000 for 100 mini lots. With $10,000, you should leverage 30 mini lots at most, even when you can possibly trade more.

Chapter 3: Forex Scalping Strategies

Forex scalping is important if at all you want to make the best of your experience forex trading. I this chapter, we help you understand this concept in detail by providing an overview of the primary scalping strategies you can use to ensure you succeed in this field. Combine these strategies with the others you will learn for the utmost profit.

To be able to scalp correctly, there are major scalping strategies that you have to understand.

An example is the *1-Minute Scalping Strategy.* We explain below:

The 1-minute scalping strategy is a good one for beginners to use. However, this strategy will demand a lot of attention and time from you. You should, therefore, be able to dedicate a few hours of your days to this strategy. If you do not have enough time to dedicate to the course, then this may not be the strategy for you.

The strategy essentially involves opening a position, gaining several pips then closing it afterward. While a basic strategy, it is one of the most resourceful that you can use to profit. The major focus of this strategy is the quantity. A trader can even place over a hundred trades a day. You should, therefore, choose a broker with small spreads and whose commissions are small as well. There are other aspects of the strategy that are important, including:

- The validity of each currency pair
- A one minute time frame
- Indicators: Stochastic 5, 3, 3, and 50 EMA
- Preferred sessions

EMA is the exponential moving average, which is a type of moving average. This moving average is popular, only seconding the simple moving average. There are risk-free demo accounts offered by brokers that allow you to explore entry points and stop levels, so do not be afraid to try them out.

There are two approaches to this strategy:

1-minute Scalping Strategy Purchase (Long) Entry point

In this strategy, the first EMA should be positioned below the second. You will have to wait until the price returns to the EMAs and utilize the Stochastic Oscillator to cross over level 20 from below. When all the items are in place, you can open a long order non-hesitantly. You can stay safe here by using stop-losses which are arranged to come around 2-3 pips below the last point of a swing. You can gain 8 to 12 pips within a trade. Therefore, you must remain within this number from the entry price.

1-Minute Scalping strategy Sell short Entry Point

The first EMA goes below the second. Just like has been explained above, you will have to wait for the price to return to the EMAs and utilize the stochastic oscillator to cross over level80from above. When the items are set in place, you can sell order or sell short minus hesitations. You position stop-losses 2-3 pips above the last high point and swing accordingly. Take profits are typically within 8-12 pips from the entry price.

There are advantages and disadvantages of 1-minute scalping

Pros include:

- Fewer exposure risks. Slight exposure to the market, such as the one done in this one-minute strategy makes it difficult to run into events that can alter the market.

- Small movements are easy to come into achievement. Thus, a large supply and demand imbalance may be needed to realize big price changes.
- You take advantage of the smaller moves that occur more frequently.
- You can take advantage of comparatively quiet times to make small moves.

Cons include:

- Large deposits
- dealers and bankers understand the market better, so they have an advantage over amateur scalpers
- A scalper should have good mathematical skills, quick reflexes, and good instincts. Not all traders have these qualities.
- Maintaining a good risk/reward ratio while scalping can be difficult
- Scalping may be stressful and time-consuming.

The second strategy that you can use also involves using the stochastic indicator and 200 EMA.

To enhance the understanding of this concept, there is a graph that shows all the elements being discussed.

The timeframe to conduct the trade can be 5 minutes. Currency pairs suitable include EUR/USD, GBP/USD, USD/JPY, USD/CHF, AUD/USD. The forex indicators, as outlined above, are the 200 EMA and stochastic indicator when at default.

To trade well, you have to find a trend with the 200 EMA. If prices fall above 200 EMA, then the trends are upward, and you have no option but to look for good buying opportunities. If the price falls below, you should look for selling opportunities. The stochastic indicator, on the other hand, oscillates to let you know whether the market has been overbought or oversold. Hence it is a sort of signal that makes you know when it is right to execute your move. You sell when the trend goes down, and the lines produced by the stochastic indicator are well above the 80 marks. On the other hand, you buy when there is an upward trend, and stochastic lines are way below the 20-line.

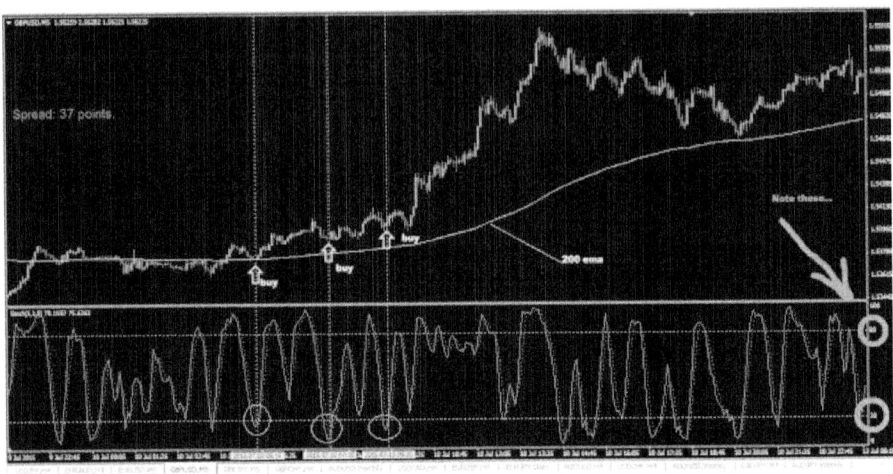

Below, we explain the above image illustration,

The take setup

1. Price travels below 200 EMA
2. Stochastic lines must go above the 80 lines and must point downwards
3. Activate your sell market order
4. Place the stop loss 15 to 20 pips away
5. Set the take profit target 20 to 30 pips away.

The buy setup

1. The line travels over 200 EMA
2. Stochastic lines go below 20 and are pointing upwards
3. Activate buy market order
4. Place stop-loss 15-20 pips away
5. Set the target for take-profit at approximately 20-3-pips.

Also, you can attach a stop-loss for every position you opened. This is a strategy that eliminates the risks of generating losses in short order and can also have a positive effect if you are trading multiple currency pairs. While this strategy is effective, it can be problematic when there is a ranging market. The problem may occur when several false trading signals make the trader get stopped a lot of times. To successfully avoid an eventuality of the sort, it is advised that you should be keen on the angle of the 200 EMA. If the line falls flat, it is not advisable to trade, if it does not look flat, it is safe to trade. Additionally, avoid the Asian trading session and trade mostly in New York and London.

Other strategies include:

1. *The Bladerunner Trade Strategy.* This is a unique strategy that utilizes all currency pairings and is suitable no matter the timeframe. The strategy gets its interesting name from the fact that the 20 EMA pierces through the price like a blade would cut twice. The Bladerunner trade strategy uses the 20-periods EMA as the technical indicator. The example used below is for the USD/SEK pairing. If the price falls above the EMA and retests it, there is a high probability that there is a likely upward trend that will continue. When the price falls below and retests it, the market is likely to continue with the same trend.

   A trader's bias tends to be long when the price goes above the EMA. The trader will, therefore, be looking to see a price drop before hitting the EMA, bouncing from it and then moving on the upside. If the price, for any reason, moves through the EMA and closes below, the trader may suspect that the polarity has changed and their bias changes to short When the price is below the EMA, a trader tends to have a short bias. As such, they are likely to look for an advance price and then they will hit up, bounce from it then move to the downside. If, however, prices close above the EMA, the trader will consider that polarity may have changed and therefore, the reaction will be to change to a long bias.

To make an entry into the market, therefore, you should take into account the fact that price must break out from the trading range before your entry and the price must successfully retest the EMA. Should the price be below the EMA, it needs to bounce from that position and remain below it, and the same applies if the price is above the EMA. The concept of the signal candle comes up here, as the first candle that came into contact with the EMA must close on the same side of the moving average as it emanated. Once this is achieved, it guides as the signal candle, and the next move has to be confirmed by the next candle. If indeed, the trend continues and the second candle distances from the EMA, then it is a confirmation. Some traders like to have additional confirmation, for example, a candlestick formation, for them to be sure of taking a trade.

A trader may also feel that it is safe to enter a position when they have two or more reasons to trade and not want to only rely on EMA. In such a case, it is better if the signal occurs at a pivot point or support or resistance level.

In the case where a trader you go long, you may place two stop orders to buy, and entries are 2-3 pips below the signal candle. The targeted profit on the first stop order has to be set at a distance that equals the risk in pips. If therefore, the position risks 25 pips, the profit target should as well be 25 pips. The profit target on the second stop order should also be set at a distance that is equal to double the risk in pips if the profit target should, therefore, be 50 for a 25 pips risk.

When you as a trader is going short, you may place 2 stop orders to sell. Entries should be 2-3 pips below the signal. The profit target on the first order ought to be set in a way that the distance equals the risk in pips. The profit target on the second-order needs to set such that the distance equals to double the risk in pips.

2. *Daily Fibonacci Pivot Trade Strategy.* This strategy makes use of the Fibonacci retracements together with daily pivot levels to get trade entries. To effectively use this strategy, you will need to understand the illustrations looking next page:

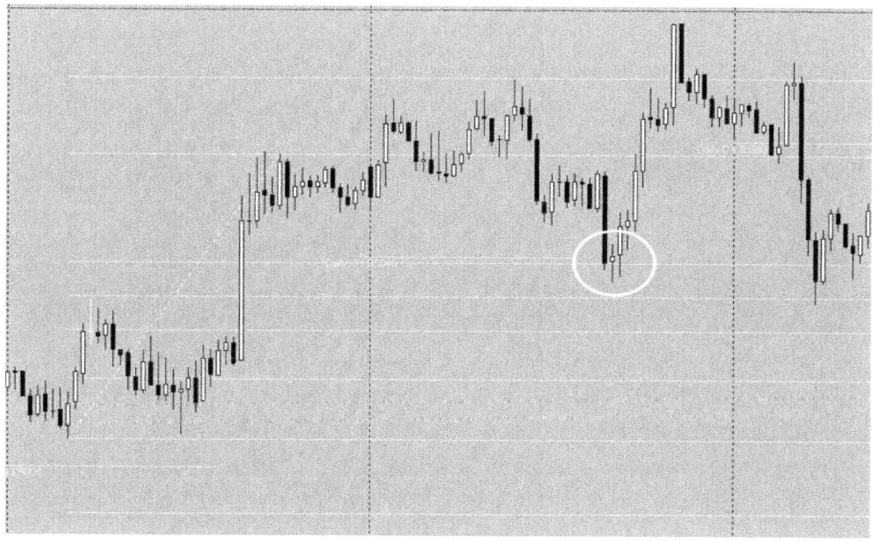

The preferred parameters here would be 38% Fibonacci levels in confluence with the daily central pivot point. The above illustration shows 38% Fibonacci retracement levels in confluence with the daily central pivot. This forex strategy, like every other strategy, can be interpreted in different ways and with variations. The one I use takes the following path of reason:

Find an entry for any currency pair where the average true range for the past five day period exceeds the one for the trading session the previous day.

Draw fibs at the start of the current trading session for the following:

- ✓ Previous day-high to low, if the current price stands below the day's central pivot.
- ✓ Previous day-low to high, if the current price stands above the day's central pivot.

Search for a confluence of the daily central pivot with the Fibonacci retracement

If there is a retracement of the price to the confluence, identified at either entry into the market or by waiting for the confirmatory candle to happen at the confluence prior to entry, then understand that it is riskier to enter the market before getting a signal to confirm. It also yields a greater possible ratio for risk to reward.

In the chart above, the depiction is that of a long entry at the confluence of the daily central pivot and 38% of the Fibonacci retracement. It is possible to enter by buying at the first level touch or by waiting for a possible morning star candle formation. From either angle, a trader would have gotten the 127% Fibonacci extension level. If the trader takes a stop loss for the trades a level away from where they take the trade behind the Fibonacci level, it results in the 50% retracement level and daily central pivot.

3. *The pop and stop trade strategy.* If you are a trader, then you probably have been in a situation where you are watching price trading in a tight range. You have waited

with tightly clenched fists for the trade to break out from this arrange and for logical reasons. Normally, breakouts happen in a different direction from that which trade was heading and usually abruptly and you hope that by getting onto that move ahead of time, you would make a fortune. Unfortunately, things never go according to plan and most times; the prices do not come to you and either they go up or down, disapproving all your speculations and crashing any dreams of future prosperity. You think you have missed a great move and begin to think that you should change directions and chase the price. The results are usually as disastrous because once you jump into the trade, it begins to stall and reverses and a loss follows. It is natural to want to trade a breakout, but for most traders, this is not an easy task. The pop n stop strategy is a savior that could help anyone who wants trade breakouts. It works by combining the rejection bar candlestick pattern with the price action to make trade safer. The picture below is an illustration:

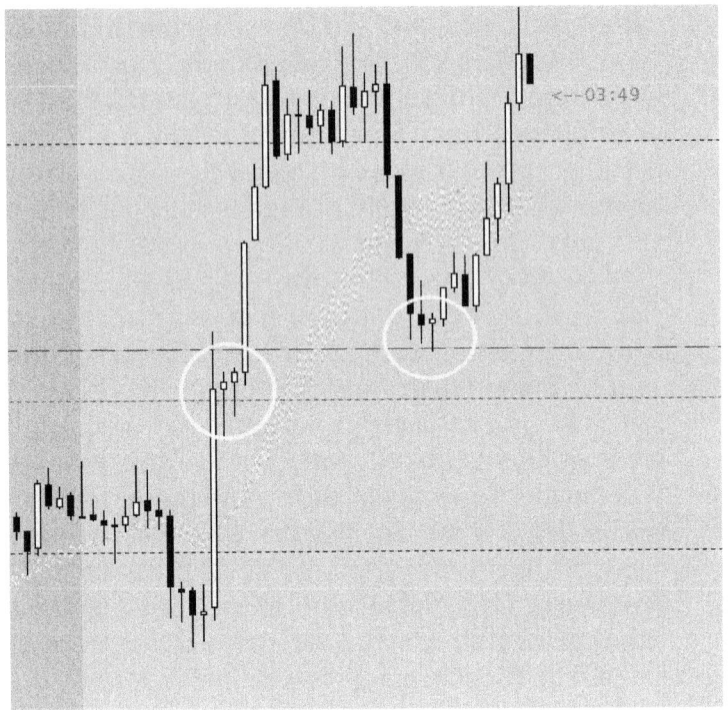

The price breaks out of range just as trade begins. This is what is known as popping out of the range. Temporarily, it also stopped before resuming an upward trend. This makes up a pop n stop trade as indicated by the white circle on the left. The second circled area on the right shows another possible trade entry set up. Upon the formation of a more bullish rejection bar from a significant level, the confluence at the pop and stop and the monthly pivot moves leftwards.

This strategy may work in your favor if you want to trade breakouts. However, always remember that the strategy is risky as you count on a gap left by a sharp move not to be filled. Use rejection candlesticks to confirm the move so that you counter risk. Also, this strategy involves trading of sentiment in the direction of sentiment after news causes a breakout from a trading range that seemed tight. You should, additionally, take advantage of highly liquid sessions so that there is enough support for the continuation of the movement. Stay cautious of any news announcements that may cause a reversal of the sentiment and possibly fill the gap. Breakouts that allow the use of such a strategy often happen at the open of forex market sessions, for instance, the London and New York ones. Lastly, remember that this is a scalping technique, so it is in your favor to set tight stops and to quickly make the decision of taking your profits. Prices are unlikely to fly higher after popping, so avoid being driven by greed in any way. The white circle that was highlighted above shows that you can trade this strategy in conjunction with countermove strategies if there is an outrageous reversal of price that fills the gap.

To understand which scalping strategy is right for you, you ought to weigh the pros and cons of each and see what could work in your favor depending on your abilities and finances. Together with the technological resources offered by brokers, you can have an enjoyable experience using the strategies discussed above.

Chapter 4: Guide on How to Create a Plan and Managing Multiple Accounts

It is commonly said that the devil is in the details. When it comes to forex trading, you may have all the necessary skills, but without a proper detailed plan, you cannot succeed as you will always wallow in confusion. Below, we provide a detailed guide on how to create a forex trading plan and manage many accounts.

With forex, you may find it difficult to create a plan because of the multitude of information that is now becoming available at your disposal. If you have a lot of information to work with, there is a chance that it makes you insecure and creates doubt, and soon, other negative emotions begin to kick in. At the same time, as traders, we have to be objective with where we are going and how we will get there. You have to set up a plan that you will follow and develop proper strategies to get you there and to enable you to measure how successful you have become. If you have a proper plan, you have a fairly clearer vision of where you are going, and this makes it easier not to lose your money, and you will be profitable, which is a key goal of trading.

How to create a trading plan

Building a plan will require you to do thorough research and build something that will suit your needs. You have to choose a strategy or strategies that you will use and the tools that you will need for your strategy. Test your plan so that you know you are moving in the right direction and continue to check yourself regularly once you start trading so that you ensure you are on the right path. As you progress, figure out what works for you and what will not work. Adjust your plan according to what works and what does not and see how your progress is contributing to your overall goals. Some of the elements that will be fundamental for your journey as you seek to establish a plan include:

✓ The reason why you are trading

Most people come to forex trading as a way to make money. While this motive is not explicitly wrong, there is more to Forex trading than just making money. If therefore, you are in this trade thinking of it as a quick fix to your financial situation, you are heading the wrong way. First, you will never get enough from the market, and secondly, you should concentrate more on loss management so that you can effectively make profits.

✓ Primary motivations

Consider why you are coming into forex trading. Do you want to have it as part of your retirement plan? Is it a new career that you intend to get into? Do you intend to make it a side hustle? Are you taking it up so that you spend more time with your friends and family? Whatever your motivations, ensure that you can find the right balance between other activities and forex trading.

✓ Strengths and weaknesses

What are your major strengths and weaknesses, and how can they work to the advantage of your new-found path? How do you maximize the strengths and minimize the weaknesses for best results?

✓ Your finances

As I have mentioned above, leverage is a double-edged sword that cuts both ways. It can, therefore, either lead to your failure or success. Look at your finances in percentages and decide the kind of trader you need to be based on your characteristics and behavior and financial position. Remember managing your money and the risks you may run into is key to your success.

Having said all the above, it is worth noting that matching yourself to a style of trading is not easy. You still have to match your goals to a trading style. Once you have decided the type of trader you are, it may yay to go into research and education. Continuously strive to learn about that trading style but understand that you cannot replicate a person's strategy and methodology and so you will have to develop your own unique style as you are the only one who fully understands your needs.

Evaluate these needs as sometimes; your monetary investment can end up making big differences in the long-term. Ensure that you keep up with global events and keep up with the available technological tools that can help you with data analysis so that you always stay ahead of the competition. Decide whether you use a fundamentalist approach to forex trading or whether you rely more on technical analysis to achieve your goals. Choosing a school of thought is key to prosperity in the sector. Fundamentalists tend to rely more on events such as the environmental, political, and economic news while technical analysts tend to rely more on technical analysis of mathematical probabilities. Other traders usually combine elements of both to come up with a solid strategy. A good trading plan should include:

- Your trading goals
- Types of tools to be used for analysis
- Broker partnership
- Trading journal entries
- Trade entry and exit criteria
- Money management
- Timeframe within which you will use the tools
- Sequence of analysis
- What to look for in high probability trade and. '
- Types of orders to be utilized

What many people do not know is that many experienced traders keep a journal detailing their trades and their rationale for trading how they did. This is a tool that can be adopted by new entrants into the market since having a journal can help you to quickly identify trading errors and subsequently, improve your trading skills.

Additionally, your journal can act as the base for revising your trade plan whenever necessary. Normally, people go back to their journals to look over their activities and reflect on how these activities affected them. The same goes for forex trading. When a trader goes over their trading activities, they can identify patterns and see what played in their favor and what did not and adjust accordingly. They then make resolutions to do better in areas where they did not excel, resulting in success. Some traders go the extra mile to ensure that their plans are feasible.

Conclusion

I hope you loved the content of your copy of *Stock market investing for beginners*. We also hope that it's been informative and that we have disseminated vital information regarding all the trading tools you need in order to acquire your objectives in the business. Perhaps, the next step is to vividly recall the trading strategies that have been appended to these chapters and delve into the trading business as soon as you can. You should also pay attention to various seasons while preparing yourself to take over the trading world. Pay attention to the policies of the business and consider implementing these strategies to guide you in becoming successful in the trading business. You can save time by using the demo account to take up new challenges related to the trading investment. You may also prepare to get out of your comfort zone by using these strategies.

In the long run, the idea is to assist you in taking up new roles in the industry while implementing revolutionary trading ideas to assist you in decision-making. Recall all steps involved in becoming a successful trader and put them into action. Use some of the handy ideas to dive into the challenging stock trading industry as soon as possible. Finally, if this book has been constructive in any way, you may leave an opinion on Amazon. This will always be appreciated not only by novice traders but professionals too!

Trading psychology

develop a growth mindset and control your emotion. become a trader 2.0 with the best winning psychology attitude, overcome your dark fear and make money!

[Henry Hill]

TABLE OF CONTENTS:

Chapter 1: Trader's Isolation

Traders experience emotions differently from those of regular people and this is why we dedicate this chapter to addressing isolation among traders.

You may have been attracted to trading mainly because of the circulation of money, fast movement, and excitement that is associated with the sector. What you may not know, however, is that forex trading can have you using a considerable amount of time figuring out the market. As a result, you may have been finding yourself stuck in a web where you are spending large chunks of your time in isolation. However, isolation usually spreads its cold tentacles, and you begin to feel lonely. Now imagine if you left your workplace with the trading mentality. Speaking to people would still not produce the same quality of conversation because you and the rest of the world are not on a similar wavelength. If you are one of these people, then the good news is that you are not alone. Many other forex traders are just like you, and who are looking for solutions to their problems that relate to isolation. Further, to make everything easier for you, I am going to discuss the trader's isolation and tell what the advantages if any, and the disadvantages of the trader's isolation are.

So, what exactly causes loneliness and feelings of isolation among traders?

Many factors can contribute to the feeling of loneliness and isolation among traders.

As a trader, you probably understand that you will have to face a series of losses over time. What you may not know is that these losses have an effect on you, negative ones. For example, when traders face losses, their confidence wanes. The effect becomes worse when the loss lasts beyond the maximum drawdown period. Imagine being a top trader. Everybody looks up to you. You are the master of winning until you are not. As you continue to lose, you begin to feel alone. You feel as if nobody understands and you are convinced that they see you differently now. This is why they say it is lonely at the top.

Beginners, on the other hand, can feel isolated for different reasons. The trading marketplace is vast, and trying to understand what is going on can be difficult. You are trying to trade, but you do not understand whether the approach you take is the best. You can start to question your methods as you come across more information and may start questioning your past successes. Maybe you are considering a change of careers, and you are not sure whether it is the right step to take and yet, there is nobody you can readily turn to and discuss your fears.

Basically, anything that causes doubt in your financial life can create feelings of isolation for traders.

Additionally, there is a general rule in trading that requires the trader to learn how to repress emotions so that they are not deeply affected by wins and losses. While this is a good strategy when trading, traders tend to carry this philosophy outside of the trade room. They hide what they truly feel so well that it does not easily creep to the surface and show. Just as they can push a button and not worry about how much they are losing or gaining, they can also go through life without fully expressing their feelings, which eventually leads to them feeling isolated. For instance, it may be difficult for them to explain to their spouses that they had a bad trade day. When these feelings are not expressed, they lead to bigger problems as they create a situation where these professionals are ticking bombs waiting to explode.

Advantages and disadvantages of isolation for a trader

The only big advantage of being in isolation may be the concentration that isolation can offer you. Let us face it; you will not be impressed by the noisy nature of your workmates, Tom and Elizabeth when you are trying to understand the rigorous process of trading. You may also not appreciate your little daughter or your nieces and nephews coming around every so often to see how you are doing when you are trying to trade. You, therefore, lock yourself in your study where you know that you will not have any disturbance. True to your word, you have a successful session, and soon, you are doing the same thing daily. You are making the right moves, and you develop some strong ideas that you believe could be crucial in the future of your trading.

Everything is going great, and then suddenly, it is not. You are not used to the new feeling of isolation anymore, and then it dawns on you that trading can have a downside as well. I discuss some of the disadvantages of a trader's isolation below:

- *No socialization.* When you get involved in trading, something changes. Often, you have to adjust your hours to meet some targets. You have to spend some extra time out of your home and office in an effort to learn and stay ahead of the rest or to at least understand the basics for newcomers. Over time, you realize that you are distanced from the rest of society. You find that you no longer talk so much at work. You spend your breaks bent over your desk, trying to understand these new concepts. When you go back home, you take supper and dedicate any further minute you have towards your understanding of the new trade. You suddenly want to stay on top of the news, and you find yourself repeating this cycle over and over again. Over time, this becomes your life, and you do not know how to stop. This has become a reality for many people who are learning to trade forex. They find that they are isolated from society, and this isolation interferes with their lives and the quality of their relationships, which will, in turn, end up deteriorating over time. There is, therefore, a general lack of connection associated with trading.

- *Getting stuck in a rut.* You find that when a trader begins to concentrate on the market and isolates themselves, they find themselves in a fix. They always want to be alone because they feel that this is the best platform for them to learn. Sadly, over time, they learn that they are stuck with the same figures, every day and that if they are not careful, they could potentially be stuck at their screens for a while, this creates feelings of loneliness, which can be deleterious for their work quality and the general quality of life. What started as an enjoyable phase of life soon becomes a cycle of worry and stress, with the trader wondering if they can be able to recover from the loneliness they feel and if the rest of the world understands how they feel.

- *Lack of new challenges.* Over time, a trader gets used to isolation, a cycle in which they come from work, for example, and spend the two hours they should spend with their families in the study trying to grasp the intricacies of trading concepts. They experience nothing out of the mundane as they do not experience anything new and do not get the chance to collaborate with others on projects the way they are used to doing in their workplaces.

- *Physical repercussions.* In other cases, traders may find themselves staying up late for one or two reasons connected to trading. While this is a show of your dedication and willingness to learn, you may find yourself in a situation where you are constantly tired. The worst part is that sometimes, nobody else will understand why you are so tired. Over time, you become lethargic.

Trading alone is, therefore, not beneficial to an individual over time. A trader needs to understand that these feelings are normal, but that they do not have to stay that way when they realize that they could be suffering from the trader's isolation. When isolation becomes an issue, you can deal with it in the following ways:

- *Stop and take a break.* When you think that you are alone or feel lonely as a result of spending too much time learning about trading, take a break from the activity. During this time, make a point to spend some time alone from the books and screen and feel once again, what it is like to be alive. Take part in activities that you like, such as taking walks, playing with your pet, or spending time with your family. A little deviation from your trader routine can help to make things easier on you mentally and make subsequent sessions more successful. Also, coming out of your isolation can be an important way to help you get new perspectives that would have been impossible to get when stuck in the same position for hours.

- *Get out of your home or the office.* Isolation can become so serious that an individual simply forgets they have friends and family who need them as well. If you are in this case, forget about forex for just a short time, take some time to make a difference even if you still want to learn about the trade. Take your laptop and head out of the usual area in which you take part in the trading activities. For example, you can go to a coffee shop, a new area in your town or to a place that you usually do not visit. Getting out of your comfort zone will break the monotony and isolation while still giving you a chance to continue being productive with your trading activities. This step will also help to reduce mind clutter, and you will find yourself feeling different and better.

- *Interact with other traders.* Sometimes, you may feel like nobody can understand your situation as a trader. However, who else can do better at understanding your trade more than a fellow trader? Interact with other traders within your network as they will not only provide you with relief but are in the best position to understand the circumstances. Besides, you will enjoy discussions centered around trading that can help build on your knowledge and enhance your understanding of trade concepts. Interacting with other traders is like killing two birds with one stone as you will get insights from other traders and get a boost of confidence from your own methods.

- *Be deliberate about new connections.* It is easy to become comfortable and complacent in our isolation despite knowledge of the effects of such isolation. This is why, as a trader, it is important that you start making efforts to meet new people. Today, numerous avenues can help spur conversations. You can plan for face-to-face meetings and even join like-minded people in a club. You can also choose to go and learn your trading in a shared working space instead of isolating yourself. Best of all, you can scour online trading forums to find like-minded individuals. Who knows, you may be able to pick the brains of the experts you meet there. This move can be helpful, especially for those who are trying to learn trading so that they can change to doing it full-time. Not only will this work to erase the guesswork from the process, but you will meet new friends and keep isolation at bay.

- *Journaling.* Earlier, I explained journaling could be a good way for traders to understand their moves and make better ones next time. The benefits of journaling, however, cannot be underestimated. For people who are taught by trade to repress their emotions, it may provide the best platform to share their feelings and get the clarity that they crave for but cannot find in normal conversations.

- *Take a break and locate a mentor.* Sometimes, it would be beneficial to give yourself a much-needed break by withdrawing completely from the trading scene for a part of your day. For example, you can decide that between 1 and 4 pm, every day, unless something urgent comes up, you will spend time with your family. Additionally, find a mentor because, with one, you have the highest chances of learning how to trade in a short time.

Chapter 2: Why a Routine is Important

There is power in the routine. Find out why and how below.

Habits are the secret to success or failure in every endeavor. From childhood to adulthood, we are products of many different factors, including habits. As traders, we can only develop the right habits by establishing routines. Just like good behavior, we have to model proper trading habits which over time, become part of us. Forming habits can be hard work because sometimes, they can even take years. To develop these habits, it is essential to remain positive and consciously make these choices deliberately. Routine is the secret of most creative and gifted people as normally, they follow these routines like clockwork. Eventually, what happens is that routine soon becomes a habit and afterward bears fruits of consistency and success.

Is there power in a routine?

In trading, you can only make it with a routine. This routine should include, among other things, a trading plan. Routines vary widely, but there are some general aspects that transverse borders and professions. Below is an example of the elements that are likely to be found in the routine of a serious trader:

- Ideally, the trader gets 8 hours of sleep a day.
- Eat a healthy breakfast.
- Identify the daily chart trend. This step is not as easy as the first two, and this is where the discipline starts. The daily chart trends are checked for the markets that are traded.
- Identify key resistance and horizontal support levels at the start of the week.
- Checking charts to scan for price action signals that have confluence with the resistance or chart trends.

- Scanning for price action signals that may have formed in favorite markets after the New York Close
- Setting up trades that have met the trading criteria and walking away until the next day
- Checking open trades in the morning and taking note of what happened without taking any extra actions. It takes discipline to observe only.

This routine is short and simple. However, it is vital to realize that it does not say anything about consistently entering trades and analyzing the market. Instead, the trader approaches the market from a certain angle and at almost the same time daily. The mid is, therefore, inclined to turn this simplistic routine into a positive routine. You should customize your routine so that it fits within the confines of your life.

Why routines are powerful

While it is quite evident that routines work to your benefit, it does not hurt to get a scientific perspective on the same.

Routine is a game-changer because it affects creativity positively. Routine projects and gets through to the subconscious mind. Knowing how essential the subconscious mind can be in helping achieve better decisions, you can understand why routine is essential. Additionally, as you continue to do something every day and as part of your routine, you become better at it, and you start achieving better results than you would with active thought. The magic of success is in daily practice. A routine will keep you connected to the most important things in your day and helps you do things naturally, and that keeps you sane as a trader. Routines also help give you the best chance at synchronizing with the market, understanding its rules and synchronizing with it when you finally put a trading plan in place.

The end-of-day trading routine

The end-of-day trading routine involves trading based on a daily chart-time frame. As such, the focus is on daily chart candles that are closed out rather than still open. The daily close happens at 5 pm New York time. Not every broker will provide a chart that shows the New York close. You will need to ensure that you see the daily close by choosing a broker that offers 5 daily bars weekly that close at the time stated above.

This method of trade works to your advantage in many ways. For example, it simplifies what is commonly a great and complex process of trading and also improves your trading results. These improvements in process efficiency and trade results happen in multiple ways:

- By reducing the number of variables and amount of time needed to trade. This naturally corrects the trading mindset as you are not watching charts all day.
- When you do not watch charts all day, you do not overthink or overanalyze situations, which is how most traders lose money. Over-analysis and overthinking leads to more trades and eventually losses
- This type of trading helps to improve your time management and money management because of the set-and-forget approach that comes with it.

If you utilize, this strategy, you will avoid most of the mistakes that traders are prone to make just by virtue of being human beings. As humans, we want to trade always because it makes us feel in control and excites us, but this can prove to be fatal as the results may not always be what we want. The strategy essentially allows you to circumnavigate your faulty natural trading wiring to become a winning trader.

Most importantly, this trading method will allow you to enjoy the results of your hard work and improve your trading. Some successful traders employ this routine and find it easy to implement because it allows you to fully make use of your day, and as such, you have enough time away from the charts. Most traders prefer this routine because it means that they get away from the 9 to 5 job mentality that they found boring in the first place.

When trading at the end of the day, you can use maybe an hour or two to analyze the market and charts and the rest of your time can be used in other productive matters. Trading at the end of the day needs the internet, a laptop, and it also needs you to set and forget as part of your routine (discussed above). You can trade from anywhere because you really do not need to take ages in front of your computer.

Chapter 3: The Right Mentality: How to React When You Lose Money and You Earn Money

There are many skills and abilities that traders possess and that they need to experience market success when trading. They have to understand how the company works, and they must be able to determine the general direction of the trend of a stock. These are just but technical skills that are needed to survive in the sometimes harsh terrain that is trading. Many a time, the soft skills associated with the trade are ignored, and yet they are as important to the trader's success as much as the technical skills are. Some of these include:

- Ability to remain calm and contain emotion
- Ability to think quickly
- Discipline

These skills may look ordinary, but they hold deep importance for traders, and that is why they are commonly referred to as trading psychology. Trading psychology is important because to trade successfully; traders need aspects of it to think fast, make equally fast decisions and dart in and out of stocks on a short leash. They need a presence of mind to accomplish these goals. They also need this kind of discipline because of the reasons discussed above. When a trader has a trading plan, they need to use trading psychology to stick to their goals. They also need trading psychology to know when to book losses and profits without letting emotions get in their way.

Some of the emotions experienced by traders include:

- ✓ *Fear*. Traders feel fearful when they receive negative news related to the market in general or about a certain stock. Mostly, their direct reaction is an overreaction in which they feel forced to liquidate their holdings and refrain from taking any further risks. They feel that by taking these actions, they are avoiding losses. However, most time, as a trader, you will realize that while avoiding loss, you will also miss out on bargains. Sometimes, just after you have liquidated, you may find that the scales start tilting in your favor, and that is how you miss out on something with great potential. Traders tend to experience fear during bear markets and can have devastating effects when it goes a notch higher and turns into a panic, causing investors to make selloffs as a result of panic selling.

Thankfully, fear is a natural reaction that we have as humans. We react this way to what we feel are threats. In this case, you feel that your money-making and profit-making potential is under threat. However, this does not mean that you should let the mention override your objectives in the market; you should find ways to go around it. For example, you can quantify the fear by considering how much fear you experience and what scares you the most. By having these thoughts well in advance of the occurrences, there is a likelihood that you will be mentally prepared for any eventuality and should a situation that scares you come by, you may know how to react non-instinctively in your favor. When you think about unpleasant situations, it gives you the ability to isolate yourself when they happen during the trade session and identify them. This is not something that you will understand how to do right off the bat. Normally, you will have to learn it over time, like an art. You will have to work on your skills over time so that you can be sure that you will be keeping your portfolio healthy instead of making decisions that can cause ill financial health in the end.

✓ *Greed.* It is not uncommon to hear the saying "pigs get eaten" on Wall Street. Wall Street is the holy ground of traders and where the biggest players on the stock exchange play. Hearing such simple yet profound words from such a highly regarded place should tell you something. In reality, they do not mean literal pigs get slaughtered. Instead, they refer to greedy investors, like pigs. Usually, when you win, you may get the urge to hang onto positions you feel are winning, hoping to get every last tick. This can be tricky because you run a much bigger risk of being blown out of a position or getting whipsawed.

Greed is a big temptation, especially when things are going your way, so it has to take a great amount of will-power to overcome it. Just like fear, greed is a natural instinct that pushes you as a trader towards doing better by giving just a little more. As such, investors may take actions such as making high-risk trades hoping for profits, buying shares of an untested technology because of an upward price trend, or buying shares prior to doing their groundwork. You can also find yourself staying in a trade for longer than is advisable simply because you feel that you may squeeze out a few extra bucks from it and thus, this emotion is most prominent in the final phase of bull markets where investors usually like to take their guard down. You should learn to recognize when your greed button is almost getting turned on and switch it off effectively. Much like every other emotion, you will encounter on this list; you will need to exercise patience when trying to deal with greed. You will learn over time how and when it is best to best count your profits and take leave.

✓ *Hope and regret.* Hope and regret are like two sides of a coin. While fear and greed are the primary drivers of most traders, fear and regret take a close position behind them because they also influence the decisions of investors in a significant amount of cases. For instance, when a trader feels fearful, and they liquidate their holdings, they may feel that they are missing out when things start looking up again. A trader may also regret and get into a trade after missing out initially as a result of stock moving too fast, sadly, this is a violation of trading discipline, something that all traders strive for and the results are always not favorable as they result in direct losses when security prices begin to fall from those peak highs. Hope and regret may work hand in hand because after regretting missing out, traders get back into the market with the hope of gaining on what they missed.

How to build a successful trading mentality and eliminate poor habits

Building a successful trading mentality does not come easy. However, it is not impossible. There are habits that you can eliminate from your routine and those you can add to successfully adjust and become a psychologically fit trader.

✓ *Check your posture.* Before starting to trade and throughout the day, ensure that you take a moment to consider your physical posture if you find yourself slouching with your neck bending forward or backward, correct the sitting position by sitting up upright and straightening your spine. Your posture affects how you breathe and how you think. When you slouch, energy does not flow smoothly through your body from up to down, and it impairs blood flow from the head to heart. You, therefore, do not think clearly. Also, when your head bends either backward or forwards, it cuts down energy flow to the spine, which can make you stuck in your head, literally. Keeping your head up and rectifying your posture can help you have a clear head that will enable you to trade better.

✓ *Find ways to increase your focus.* As you read this book, find ways to increase your focus and concentration. You could take simple steps such as turning off the television, turning off the internet browser, turning off your cell phone, stopping email checks or you could take advanced actions such as meditating before you start your day. Meditating improves concentration and thus, can be beneficial for your trading. Then after meditation, you should focus on the markets that you want to trade for the day. Once you have tried this habit for a few days, check how your focus was impacted, and if it has changed your trading experience in any way. If you like the results of the new habit, you can as well make it a permanent part of your routine.

✓ *Check your energy levels as you trade throughout the day.* If you are not using the end-of-day trading routine, this tip can work well for you. Before you sit down to trade and at several points during the day, you should ask yourself if your overall energy level is high when you start trading or if it is low. It may help to place it on a scale of 1 to 10 with 10 expressing optimal energy and 1 expressing minimal energy. If your energy is weak, figure out whether it is physical or mental. If it is physical, check on things such as posture, whether you have eaten and drank enough water and feel your body generally to get an idea of what is going on. If it is mental, then it would be a good time to task yourself by tapping into your mind to find out if you are engaging in any negative thought patterns, and once you become aware of what is happening, you should take a moment to clear your head, for example, through meditation, before resuming work.

This strategy is a powerful one and can be done at several key points in your day, or you could schedule it as part of your trade routine. If your energy levels fall below your standards of what should be ideal and you are having a difficult time rectifying it, it is better to take some time off before resuming trade as these low energy levels may interfere with your ability to make the right decisions. If you feel that your body is just fine, on the other hand, then do not waste this opportunity on anything else. Use it to trade as there is a likelihood that you will make the best decisions in this way.

✓ *Inculcate positive thoughts.* Now that you understand the kind of bearing negative thoughts may have on your success as a trader, you must find a remedy. While it may go contrary to your feelings and emotions, deliberately choosing positive actions will help build your confidence and experience. Positive thoughts do more than we can imagine. Your vision becomes more panoramic, you become a stable trader, your determination is enhanced, and you have a renewed, deep understanding of the market. Over time, you will be able to trade confidently over days, months, and years. You will no longer have excuses for what you have not done, cut down on procrastination, and not subscribe to your emotions, which are dangerous for a trader.

Take the trading market as a platform on which you can challenge yourself and prove through your actions that your positive attitude is paying off. Choose a time every day where you will say positive affirmations to yourself as this will be a crucial step in determining how your day. Talk to yourself confidently, getting yourself out of mental laziness, emotionality, and hesitation. This self-talk is important as your subconscious mind rewires itself to help you achieve the positive goals you have. This can be one of the first steps you take towards financial wealth and stability. If you make this a part of your routine for a week or two, you can take time to review your progress. If

425

you like the results, you can choose to make this a part of your routine.

- ✓ *The 5% rule.* Resolve that for the next trading week; you will give just 5% more of your energy to trading. To make use of this rule, identify the areas where you perceive yourself to be poor, and need development. The extra 5% of your time should be dedicated to strengthening your weaknesses in these areas. Over a few weeks, you will notice that this method has yielded results as there will be a difference in your trading, mindset, or the results of your trading. You can then decide to take it a notch higher by putting in an extra 10% of your time, or you can decide to make the 5% final and part of your routine.

The tips and tactics above will help you develop positive trade ethics. The secret to knowing what works for you is through evaluating results. That is why, at every step, I ensured that I asked that you review how you trade after a few days or weeks of the tactics. Note how your trade experience changes and see what you have accomplished and if you can use the experience to continue developing your forex trading skills. When this happens, you will have a self-reinforcing process that eliminates the need for a mentor. In short, you will become a self-taught master trader.

To control your emotions, two main strategies can help you:

- ✓ *Setting rules well in advance.* As a trader, you should learn to get your head in the right place before you get psychological crunches. As such, it would be wise to lay out guidelines for any trade based on your risk tolerance and have a plan for when you will enter and exit the trade. You will need to know whether a stop loss or profit target will be the exit signal and take all emotion out of the trading process. You can also decide that in the wake of some events such as macroeconomic news and positive or negative earnings.

You can also consider setting limits to the amount of money you are willing to lose or win in a day. If you hit your profit target, take your earnings, and stop for the day. If the loss hits the limit, it is also time to pack up and go as leaving will prevent you from further losses

✓ *Doing research and reviews.* As a trader, it is upon you to learn as much as you can about your area of interest. Educate yourself through reading and go for seminars and conferences that relate to your interests. As directed above, ensure that you dedicate a certain amount of time to research. Take part in activities that help build your knowledge base, such as studying charts, reading trade journals, and studying the analysis methods of the trade so that you are up to speed even before you start trading. Remember to remain flexible and consider experimenting with different techniques and instruments time and again. For instance, you can set stop losses at different places. To ensure that you are learning well, do your experiments within reason.

Chapter 4: How to Learn from Your Mistakes and Your Mental Crisis

Once in a while, any trader is likely to face a big loss in their career. For instance, there may be a technological breakdown, discipline lapse, and running out of capital that hut you unexpectedly. When this happens, most people do not have any idea of how they should bounce back. However, bouncing back is not rocket science. What usually is difficult is repairing the mental damage that results from such losses. To get back on the saddle, you can take a series of steps as outlined below:

What to do on the day you loose

Even though it is hard to accept, on the day, you lose, you will have to understand that every trader has had a bad trading day and that it may continue happening. If therefore, you are tempted to win back trades that have been lost, remember how much you have won. If you earn an average of $1,000 on the days you win, do not be tempted to try to win your trading losses because you will end up losing more. Even though it may go against what you naturally feel, control the downside by not engaging further.

You also have to accept that you will get conflicting feelings when you lose-confusion, anger, frustration-but you must keep your focus because, at this point, you will be unable to trade with a clear head. The day you lose is, therefore, not the day in which you need to gain back what you lost. With over 250 trading days in a year, you have more than enough time to get back what you lost. Take a step back and breathe out on this day as you get ready to fight another day.

Accept responsibility for what just happened

You have lost the biggest trade of your life, or you owe a big amount to your broker because you took a large sum in leverage. You are devastated by this loss, and you do not know what to do. On some days, the best step you can take is to do nothing. The best favor you can do for yourself is to restrain from trading until the issue is resolved. It would be irresponsible to trade, especially with a big debt to your broker over your head. You may want to trade because you think that trading may help you clear your debts. It may not be the case because you may end up losing more, and there is nothing worse for a trader than trading under a lot of pressure. To avoid a further escalation of matters, wait to trade only when you have cleared your debt.

For a trader that has suffered a losing streak, drawn down on his/her account or suffered a big loss. There is still a chance for you. You can be in the game and continue trading. Your ego, on the other hand, may have suffered a little bruising, especially if you were still building your confidence. Remember that all losing trades have a root cause, be it a sudden news announcement that interfered with your stop loss. Your own carelessness, or a technological breakdown that resulted in the loss of your connection with the market and moves against you, you have to pick up yourself and forge ahead with fortitude. Accept that it happened and accept to take responsibility for all the losses incurred and that you are responsible for the losses. If you live in denial, there is a probability that the same thing will happen to you again.

To reduce the chances of the same thing happening again, accept responsibility, and figure out what could have been done differently. This step of action is positive because it is better than bottling up your feelings or blaming others for what happened. When you blame others, it is equivalent to an admission that you are not in control of your trade. After figuring out what caused the loss, figure out what you could do to minimize it, or what changes you need to make to ensure that it does not happen again.

Steps you can take depend on what happened and may include changing markets, having automatic stop losses that are sent out automatically in case of breakdowns, having data backup feeds and connections and setting up of the broker platform to liquidate if you hit a stop loss. One way or another, you can look at the situation critically and come up with a viable solution.

Even after fixing the issue, you have to understand that your ego must have also been hard hit. As such, you may lose your confidence as a trader. To start rebuilding your confidence, realign your focus on how you became successful in the first place. The methods you used to develop confidence in your first days should be used to rebuild it. Adjust your trading plan accordingly and run with it. Trade with small position sizes once more to avoid losing on full position sizes. If you jump right back to the same position size as you were, you risk losing again.

The bottom line is to give yourself time to recover, and all shall go well.

Chapter 5: Decision and Doubt: Why you are Paralyzed when You Buy

When trading binary options, you must have a good decision-making process. You must be able to gauge your options accordingly. The choices you make are about how to trade when to trade, and also what to trade. It is possible to also carry out some research to learn more about the most suitable periods when you should not trade. As a trader, you must be responsible for your actions on a daily basis. The decisions that you make daily determine your financial future and that is why there are many people who are excited by trading. Your success is determined by your ability to make sober decisions since there are high levels of uncertainty when trading. If you can perfect your decision-making process, you can become a better forex trader and you will able in a better position to make suitable life choices.

Some of the challenges that traders face include being tasked with making some serious financial decisions within a limited time frame. When you are trading, and the broker gives you access to tools such as rollover, double up, and early close, it means you should make a hasty decision on the most suitable tool to use in this case. If you are unable to make a decision within the limited time frame, the broker will make the decision for you, and it might not work in your favor.

Some other instances where you have to make a fast decision include the short term binary options. The time frame ranges from 30 to 60 seconds. You should be able to make some suitable decisions that will allow you to gain access to different opportunities. If an opportunity does not seem suitable, you can also bypass it. Most of the traders are not suited to trading using short term options since they are unable to think rapidly; nevertheless, it is possible to gain such skills eventually.

In forex trading, some terms such as analysis paralysis exist. Some of the traders tend to overthink, and they also tend to have lower forms of confidence, and they cannot take any course of action. When a person freezes while trading, they may incur huge losses. You should first gauge whether you can make decisions fast or whether you usually struggle during the decision-making process. Some of the techniques that can help you to improve your decision making process include;

1. Less is more.
2. Always learn from past experiences.
3. Recover from past mistakes.
4. Utilize your intuition accordingly.
5. Play learning games.

We will now expound on each of the stated ideas above. When it comes to trading, you cannot also get rid of instances of uncertainty since such tasks involve making well-calculated risks.

1. Less is more.

As a student, you may have sat for exams that had multiple choices. Some of the questions may have been complicated, and you may have had to reread the questions over and over again while also referring to the answers present. Afterward, you may have realized that only one aspect of the question made sense and it may lead you directly to the answer. The excess information present was meant to bring about some confusion. While referencing the area where a question possesses lots of information yet only a small part of the question would lead you to the answer, you will realize the importance of the concept "less is more." When using such a principle, you can make a trading decision quickly. As you refer to your charts, you should refer to the indicators present. As a newbie trader, you may make different assumptions including assuming that the more the signals, the more the setups. In this case, there will be a set of conflicting signals that may affect the trader in different ways.

If the trader refuses to make a decision accordingly, they will lose a significant amount of money.

Always ensure that your charts are not congested and you can continue trading in every way possible. Also, keep it simple at all times. If you are looking for ideas on how to simplify your trading life, you should try and look into the trading systems that some of the trading communities utilize. For starters, you will notice that every trader has very few indicators. According to the experts, always use one or two indicators, and you will be in a better position to make focused and easy choices.

2. *Learn From Experience*

The experience that you possess when it comes to trading is important. As a result, you should have a trading journal. When you refer to your past experiences, you can make smart choices, and you will have improved your decision-making skills. If your notes are well-organized, you will realize that some of your trading scenarios are familiar, and you will use your knowledge to make smarter choices. As a trader, you will also have the ability to recognize situations faster, and the decisions that you make will also be profitable.

After getting used to the trading process, you will feel like trading has become a part of you. You will also be making the right choices depending on your intuitiveness, among other things. The main aspect here is ensuring that you have an in-depth understanding of trading.

3. *Recover from your Mistakes*

Some of the main reasons why people are affected by analysis paralysis include the lack of confidence, and such an issue affects many traders at the onset of their career. After incurring some losses, some traders may be affected by self-doubt, and they may also be indecisive. You may fail to execute a certain trade although you should. As a result, your account will not showcase any form of progress since you will not be utilizing the necessary opportunities.

Always analyze your past failures so that you may recover from your mistakes. For starters, the main mistake is having a poor decision-making process which will result in huge losses on your account. Such issues will lower your confidence, and you may also be a victim of a financial crisis. Always take a break from the trading activities and try to look into the areas where you went wrong before resuming with trading. Always look for articles that talk more about recovering from trade losses. If you take some proper steps to learn from your mistakes, you can recover and also regain your confidence. You will also feel encouraged by what you have learned. Also, you will be in a better position to believe in your trading abilities. Always learn about how to put some distance between your past and present and do not associate yourself with failure. Although you are the same person who made mistakes in the past, you are still the same [person who will have owned up to their mistakes when it comes to trading.

4. *Utilize Your Intuition Accordingly*
Your intuition is important when it comes to trading and making some critical decisions. When your intuition is not used properly, you may fail. Always trust your gut since it may be in the form of a signal from your brain, and it will allow you to make some smart decisions.

Also, develop some smart goals. With time, you will also learn more about the different types of intuition that you possess. Always take time and try to learn more about expert intuition since it comes about with some of the experienced that you have while trading. In most cases, your brain will have a hyperdrive, and it will tell you about the right choices that you should make without any explanation whatsoever.

Some people have also developed long-term strategic intuitions. Such intuition is not brought about by experience, and it is not based on your understanding of trading. Your brain usually performs different tasks in the background and it always solves some problems accordingly; this is strategic intuition, and it can assist you when making some critical trading decisions.

Ordinary intuition is often termed as wishful thinking. A smart intuition can come in handy when making fast and smart decisions. However, the wrong type of intuition can render your account bankrupt.

5. *Play Learning Games*

There are many ways to train your brain to think fast while also making better decisions. The main agenda is to learn more about how to earn more money while also minimizing the losses. Also, the learning games are meant to make sure that you are able to manage high levels of pressure while also making sure that your thinking process is fast. Many games are meant to improve your thinking speed, and they will also help you to improve your trading skills.

It is not easy to overcome analysis paralysis. The analysis paralysis has also led to the failure of many people who were interested in forex trading since they would freeze and they would give up on the trading practice eventually. When you continue gathering some experience as a trader, you will also be in a better position to engage in binary trading options successfully.

How to react when there are good signals

For starters, there are different ways to find signals, and they include:

- Time zone- before you start trading, always check the broker's time zone since you want the signals to kick in

435

while you are still awake. The signals are not of much use if you are unavailable.

- Track record- ensure that your preferred broker has a good track record.

Always compare the forex signal providers. Also, learn more about how to use different types of trading signals. The way that you react in front of the signals is the main factor that will determine your profit margins. Always make sure that you have taken the profit while avoiding the loss. In some instances, you should remove the take profit and never assume that the signal service provider is liable for the losses.

Chapter 6: Out of the Comfort Zone

Trading binary options aren't for the decision-averse individuals. You are constantly making viable decisions that are supposed to help you in winning your game. You make choices based on how to trade appropriately, including what to trade in the long run. Many traders are often faced with the challenge of making valid decisions based on their requirements. It's important always to remain updated with the needed requirements in order for a trader to make viable decisions based on the trade. Besides, it also means taking consistent responsibility for a person's actions as well as their outcomes. It also implies that the financial future hinges on the existing choices a person makes daily. That is one of the main reasons why trading is exciting to many people. It is not only a test of their ability to make decisions but also their capability to delve into new business ideas. As such, your ability to make the right decision will also be tested in different instances. You'll be a better trader if you watch out for different market shifts that have been affecting the industry. You'll also be in a position to make better decisions in life. This implies that you should always take responsibility for your actions as well as their outcomes. It also implies that your financial future is directly appended on the choices as well as decisions that you make daily. That is one of the main reasons why trading is not only exciting to many people but also a life-changing business. It is a test of a person's ability to delve into better decision-making.

In the long run, a trader will be required to make a smart judgment in various situations where they are meant to deal with. If the trader can become an excellent decision-maker, not only will they make a better trader but also be able to make decisions based on their winning capabilities. Another challenge that most traders are faced with is the ability to make good choices in the long run. There is always a question of how useful this is. Since it's vital for these people to make better trading decisions within a short period, it becomes important to train yourself to understand the implications of poor decision making. When you are in the trading industry, and then the broker allows you to utilize various tools such as double up, early close, as well as rollover, you have a clock running on the ability to make valid decisions. You should be in a position to make a valid decision based on your ability to utilize those tools. If you are not in a position to make such decisions, by the time the trading platform notes successful movements, you'll have to work with a trade expert to help you in decision making so that you don't lose money. The clock is always running out for most traders. Therefore, it's important for them to become acquainted with the major decision making processes as well as how to get out of their comfort zones.

Another different situation where the trader has to make fast decisions is when there's a short term binary option such as 30 or 60 in a few seconds. Such types of trades will flash in the next minute. You need to be able to make the right decision in order to trade quickly. This is immediately you spot an opportunity along the way. Also, alternatively, if some type of trade is not as easy or prime as you may have thought, you'll have to decide to let it go and focus on other businesses. The majority of stock and binary traders aren't cut out to trade the existing trade short-term options. This is because they don't know how to delve into quick decision-making. In many instances, such people are way too comfortable for the business. However, this is just a skill in part. You are always at liberty to take training and delve into creative, better decision making.

Trading Psychology and Getting Out of the Comfort Zone

There are plenty of skills required for traders in order to be successful in the financial market. One needs to have the ability to comprehend a company's significant fundamentals, including how to trade online using the essential tools provided. They also need to be able to determine the direction of a stock's trend. However, neither of the two technical skills is as vital as the mindset of the trader. This is the person's ability to contain their emotions and think quickly while exercising discipline in critical decision making. This is what is fondly referred to as trading psychology. The psychology of online trading is important for all business professionals in the industry. As such, traders often need to think fast in order to make quick decisions based on various timelines of the business. The decisions are based on darting out of stocks within a short time. To accomplish this, they require some presence in mind. They also need the discipline to make viable decisions for themselves and their success. They also, through a certain extension, need the discipline, to stick with the initial established trading plans. They also need to understand when to book losses as well as profits. Emotions cannot get in a person's way during such moments.

Understanding fear

When a trader gets some bad news, regarding stock in the market, it's very common for them to become worried and scared. They may also overreact in such cases. Others may feel the need to relinquish their shares in the market and delve into cash-generating businesses or better yet just refrain from taking any risks in the future. Some traders may become disappointed to the extent of abandoning their holdings. Traders should understand that fear is a completely natural reaction based on what is being perceived at the moment. In this instance, it's the fear of losing business. It is also the fear of potentially not making any profits in the long run. But this also happens to the best of traders who have been comfortable in the business. That's why it's important to get out of the comfort zone. To avoid such cases, one needs to understand the long term implications of succumbing to fear. Quantifying this fear is going to be useful in helping you to overcome the challenges that affect their performance in the industry. One needs to ponder over what could be affecting their performance. They also need to know why they are afraid of facing certain challenges. By thinking of the issues, including how to navigate ahead of time, an individual will be better placed to highlight their fear and address the impending problems affecting them. As such, a trader can only hope to isolate themselves and identify these challenges affecting their performance. The issue can also be thought of ahead of time so that no additional elements are affecting the business. Through a trading session, one can try and focus on moving past the impending trading issues. They may also know to react to anything that will come along the way in the long run. It becomes easy to when an individual is used to practicing. But, it becomes necessary to take practice because this is one of the healthiest ways to create an excellent investor portfolio.

Overcoming greed

According to the Swiss proverb, a greedy person, as well as a pauper, are the same. This couldn't be further than the truth, especially for forex traders. As one may be fully aware already, many traders, as well as their accounts, have been suffering because of the vice, greed. That explains how the saying bulls, as well as bears, make money while hogs get slaughtered came about. No other animal really embodies greed compared to the hog. In the trading business, therefore, the markets have not been showing mercy to these hogs.

This explains why greed has always been considered one of the most precarious vices in the industry of trading. Fear can as well paralyze you while keeping you away from your trading business. However, your capital is often preserved for as long as you may keep your hands in the pockets. On the other side of everything, greed will push you away from everything in ways that you should not be part of. Traders have always been forced to act in ways that they should not in the long run just because of greed. This implies that a person is often determined to take greedy actions towards others in the quest to win. That is why greed is a dangerous vice. Greed prompts a person to act irrationally. They are also pushed to take sides regardless of their stand in certain matters. For most traders, this usually pops up in the form of overleveraging and overtrading. They are also forced to conform to issues such as chasing the markets as well as holding on to the forex traders. When thinking about it, greed isn't really any different from alcoholism as it pushes a person to act foolishly. When it comes to the point in which a person decides to act foolishly in the trading business, their ability to make the right decision is clouded. Like many other worthy causes, overcoming greed in the trading business is a psychological decision that requires an individual to understand the impending challenges and take a look at their impacts on their chances of becoming successful. It is not an easy cause. But, one has to tame their ego. This is also one of the main strategies of getting out of the comfort zone. You will admit that the concept here works for individuals who aspire to take up roles in different trading dockets. That's just how easy it is to overcome some challenges in the business. There will be certain instances when you will not want to catch the full move of the market. There will also be times when you will miss a chance or an opportunity to set up at some point. That is, however, how the trading business goes. In cases where you accept that the market is often bigger than you are and that you are likely to make mistakes in the long run, then you are on the path to success and recovery of any impending loss. Therefore, you'll find it easy to get out of your comfort zone.

Many successful individuals in the trading business have admitted that they would rather be lucky than good. For such people, it's often better to append their success to luck and not their skills. This might not be a great attribute for their ego. However, it's good for their trading psyche. That's perhaps one of the best secrets of becoming a successful trader in the industry. Other than that, it's vital to remember not to be a hog in the sector. Otherwise, you'll be slaughtered. To successfully trade outside your comfort zone, you need to take deliberate practice. Repetition enables traders to work on their trading flaws. This will also determine what works well for the business. In the long run, this can help you in determining what works and what will not work for your business. It will also determine the chances of becoming successful in your trades. But, once you have decided to take a comfortable turn in the business, you may find it important to consider taking new steps and measures that will help you to delve into new markets where you can explore other businesses. When you have exhausted all the other trading options in the business, you will find it important to take up new trading strategies as well as positions and measures that should be out of your comfort zone in order to make more profits. Here, you now need to get rid of the old trading plan that you have been holding onto. You also need to trade in your outside world in order for you to be successful.

Trading outside the comfort zone is going to be simple if you have been in the business for quite some time. It can be simple. As simple as taking the next step in the trading business. It can also be as simple as opening a new chapter after succumbing to losses despite being careful with how you've been trading in the past. Just like in the case of an Olympic swimmer who is often acknowledged in different types of strokes, as a trader in the forex business, you need to be familiar with the different kinds of methods involved in trading. The point of the matter is to consider taking risks and measures in order to start practicing new trading methods for success. It's also important to start exerting your knowledge in these new trading platforms. If done well, the exercise may play a role in boosting your confidence as well as emotional resilience. However, you need to be careful. Stepping out of the comfort zone which has been familiar definitely exposes you to various emotional stresses. This, in turn, increases your chances of failure. You may end up making silly mistakes that can affect your overall revenue. You may even quit because of the challenges you shall be facing. But, you don't need to worry because there is a list we've compiled to assist you in managing your stresses. Rather than breaking out of your comfort zone ease your new trading strategies to assist you in delving into the new platform. Changes don't have to be grand. They can be as simple as increasing the average position sizes one at a time. Better yet, you may also take a new currency pair if the area is small as well as insignificant.

Using a demo account to get out of your comfort zone

As the name suggests, a demo account refers to a platform that traders give to new candidates to use for a pilot test. This is usually done before the trader delves into the business. It enables a novice investor to master some of the trading skills before putting their resources in the business. That way, an individual has zero risks. The only investment they would have is to ensure they create time to learn. If time is an issue on their side, then they can use the help of an expert advisor to become professionals. A backtest mechanical system may also come in handy. You may also use a YouTube channel to upgrade your trading skills and get out of the comfort zone within a few days. Naïve practice is one of the most useful trading strategies that can also get you out of your trading comfort zone. As such, it involves several repetitions based on the same subject. This is pretty mindless. It is also not as challenging in the long run. For instance, if you have grasped lessons regarding how to handle certain situations in the trading world, you will probably implement such strategies into your practice sessions.

Conduct a pilot test

This is like being in some auto-pilot mode, which is not useful. But, by using a demo, you'll be learning how to take risks without actually spending money in some forms of investments.

The next phase in learning how to trade outside your comfort zone is to consider implementing practices that are purposeful. Focused practice away from any form of distraction will help you to take up new trading lessons. Being in a position to maintain motivation and push outside the familiar zone in order to achieve new things in the business is also a major strategy that needs to be considered by many novice traders who want to start taking lessons to help them in getting out of their comfort zones. To fit into the world of trading and the existing models, we would like you as a trader to know how to break down the trading strategies into something specific that can support your growth as well as development. You also need to be able to monitor progress since this will play a key role in determining how far you are with the lessons and what else you should learn. A trading demo also helps you to receive instant feedback based on the questions you have. Perhaps it's vital to note that the first step towards learning how to get out of your comfort zone is to have a certain goal and objective and define your needs.

Have a practice plan

Create a practice plan that can support your new project. You also need to cover all the lessons you need before investing in the next phase of trading. This is important than going through all the basics of trading altogether. Next, you will find it necessary to ensure that you are focused even without distraction. This implies that you can lock yourself away from a certain area in order to focus fully without any distractions. You may also find it necessary to use some music in order to have a viable environment where you can easily grasp the details of the new trading docket. Other than that, it becomes important to delve into some form of entertainment in order to harvest internal stimuli. A demo will play a role in helping you to maintain motivation while learning more about how to leave the comfort zone. Motivation is a key factor in this process. However, it should come from you. In most activities related to trading, you may work with a tutor who can also be termed as a coach who will help you in maintaining motivation throughout the transition process. Next, you will be required to follow a valid plan that can support your cause and dream of becoming an excellent trader. For instance, you can begin by drawing a chart based on the different trends affecting the business. Draw lines based on these factors and then use the lines to help in determining your sole objective and purpose in the business. You may also work in different exercises, including finding a reversal based on the chart as well as aiming to locate any possible trend lines that may be involved in the process.

Chalk it up with the experience you have garnered in the past

Most experienced traders go outside their usual comfort zones in search of better, greener pastures. They also have test accounts where they can experiment with their new trading strategies as well as methods. There are times when the business is profitable. Then there are times when it's not profitable. But, in many cases, such traders are not concerned about profitability. It's not really an issue for them. They are more focused on becoming successful by using new trading strategies. This implies that they are learning in the whole process of taking up new lessons. As such, being a trader who is interested in taking up a new course of direction, you should find a different method of analyzing the trading market. The truth is, trading outside your usual comfort zone is not simple. It is also not easy. To be successful, you need to be observant. You also need to take your time in learning various processes.

Why is it Important to Change?

- When you start trading outside your comfort zone, you will be in a position to stop procrastinating. Successful individuals will not push their projects to the following day since this will limit their chances of becoming successful.

- Immediately you take up trading lessons to trade outside your comfort zone, you'll delve into a lot of practice lessons that will support your growth in the sector.
- You will also take up new challenges regardless of their complexities.

Chapter 7: Motivation: How an Expert Trader Thinks

Difference between A Successful Trader and A Loser Trader

Many traders are experienced when it comes to forex. Although they may have undergone a series of challenges as newbie traders, they learned more about how to stay motivated despite the presence of uncertainty when trading. The major differences between a successful trader and a loser are:

- *A Successful Trader Is Patient*

As a trader, you must outline your expectations first. You must also be patient since the profit margins that you are targeting might take some time to achieve; as a result, patience is paramount. Furthermore, the markets fluctuate from time to time, and it is advisable to keep track of the market trends. Also, an experienced trader is always scouting for new opportunities. In such an instance, patience is important.

On the other hand, a loser trader lacks patience. For starters, it takes time to learn the basics of forex trading. Since some of the loser traders may just be looking for a get-rich-quick scheme, they may fail miserably since they do not want to heed to the learning curve.

- *Experienced Traders Are Disciplined*

Being disciplined goes hand in hand with being patient. You must always be observant while waiting for an opportune moment to trade in the system. At times, you may fail to achieve your targets; however, you should ensure that you are disciplined, and you should also believe in the system. Discipline entails pulling the trigger depending on how the system behaves.

As compared to an experienced trader, the loser traders lack discipline. The main reason why discipline is important is that it influences a person's decision-making process. For example, when a trader makes a loss, they should first carry out an evaluation before proceeding with the trade. On the other hand, the loser traders will always initiate another trade with the sole aim of recovering their initial losses, and that is a wrong strategy. Such a strategy will lead to more losses since the trader will make financial decisions while in an emotional state. Although people do not enjoy making losses, it is good to avoid losses at all costs.

- *Experienced Traders Have Objectivity*

Experienced individuals are never emotionally attached to the system since they understand the significance of objectivity. The objectivity of the trader is mainly determined by the reliability of each system. Also, the trader should also choose wisely between the exit and entry levels. Never allow emotions to affect your judgment. Always focus on ensuring that the system is reliable.

A loser trader may not understand the meaning of objectivity. If a person fails to understand the system, they are bound to fail. To succeed, a trader must first assess the reliability of each system. As for the loser traders, they always fail since they never carry out such assessments.

- *Experienced Traders Have Realistic Expectations*

Although the market is big, you must ensure that each of your goals is realistic, and that means you should anticipate a profit margin that equals the amount of money that you have invested. For instance, you cannot invest $250 and expect profit margins worth $1000. When it comes to forex trading, it is all about the risks involved. Traders who have short-term goals will always have smaller risks. The trader should also exercise some discipline when trading. So, it is good to learn more about the correlation between risks and rewards.

Everyone wants to get rich in one way or another. When a person opts for forex trading, they must ensure that they have set some realistic goals. For example, the amount of starting capitals should always align with your target profit margins. You cannot invest $1000 and expect $10,000 at the end of the month. In some instances, most of the loser traders will invest in a haphazard manner, and they will lose at the end of it all. They may try out binary trading options, although they lack an overview of what it entails. At the end of it all, they will always fail since their expectations were not realistic. Instead, their expectations should have aligned with the capital they were investing and the knowledge base that they possess.

- *Experienced Traders Perform an Analysis Weekly*

During the weekends, the markets are usually closed; as a result, the traders have a chance to come up with a weekly chart that will enlighten them about the market patterns. The analysis performed will enlighten the trader about the changing markets, and they can make informed decisions when trading.

As for the loser traders, they will continue trading without performing any analysis. Eventually, they will make huge losses. The analysis comes in handy since a trader can learn more about the market and they will also learn about the wrong moves that they made within the week; however, a loser trader will bot focus on their mistakes, they will continue to trade blindly.

- *Experienced Traders Keep Printed Records*

Printed records are very good learning tools. Some of these printed records may be in the form of charts after you have carried out some analysis regarding your weekly trades. Always march each chart with an entry and exit points. Also, make sure that you have come up with different comments regarding the chart, including the reasons why you traded in some of the pairs and stocks. The records will allow you to realize your weaknesses and how they affected you during the trading sessions. For example, you may have been greedy; you may have panicked, you may have been too anxious, among other reasons. The analysis through the printed records allows experienced traders to learn more about their strengths and weaknesses. With time, they always gain some mental control and discipline, and they acquire objectivity to execute each trade depending on the system they are utilizing during the trade.

A loser trade will fail to understand the importance of printed records. Without such records, they will fail to understand their weaknesses and how they can overcome them. For instance, an experienced trader understands their emotional limits, and coupled up with objectivity; they can reap huge profit margins. On the other hand, the loser trader will trade while not being in control of their emotions. They will try to recuperate the losses they incur instantly, whereas a successful trader will go back to the drawing board to look into the areas where they had gone wrong.

There are different ways through which forex traders stay motivated. For starters, they have the necessary knowledge and experience to trade in large volumes without relying much on intuitions. Other ways through which the traders stay motivated include:

Alignment

Since forex trading involves trading between two types of currency, commodities, and stocks, the experienced individuals usually form a chart, and they also use a specific time frame. They also use certain methodologies when trading; the traders usually understand the importance of alignment, and they always repeat thus exercise regularly while also keeping track of the market conditions since they change regularly.

The experienced traders are stay motivated by ensuring that they have implemented different forex trading strategies. For starters, they know that profitable trades do not exist since uncertainty exists when trading. Even when a system seems profitable, they always ensure that they understand the profit-to-loss ratio.

Experienced traders also exercise risk control. It is one of the key aspects when carrying out forex trading. For starters, they always evaluate the trading system, and they also try out different attempts before becoming successful. As a result, they are always disciplined and patient, unlike some of the newbie traders. There are also many differences between the experienced traders and the loser trader, and we will now initiate a discussion about the loser traders.

Download the Audio Book Version of This Book for FREE

If you love listening to audio books on-the-go, I have great news for you. You can download the audio book version of this book for **FREE** just by signing up for a **FREE** 30-day audible trial! See below for more details!

Audible Trial Benefits

As an audible customer, you will receive the below benefits with your 30-day free trial:

- FREE audible book copy of this book
- After the trial, you will get 1 credit each month to use on any audiobook
- Your credits automatically roll over to the next month if you don't use them
- Choose from Audible's 200,000 + titles
- Listen anywhere with the Audible app across multiple devices
- Make easy, no-hassle exchanges of any audiobook you don't love
- Keep your audiobooks FOREVER, even if you cancel your membership
- And much more

Copy and paste the links below to get started!

For Audible US: https://www.audible.com/pd/B07ZF82RXK/

For Audible UK: https://www.audible.co.uk/pd/B07ZF57RNS/

For Audible FR: https://www.audible.fr/pd/B07ZF5ZLPX/

For Audible DE: https://www.audible.de/pd/B07ZFBGXR8/

Printed in Great
Britain
by Amazon